$\mathcal{E}_{\nu}$

# Table of Contents

# Preface

## WILDERNESS CONTEMPLATIONS

Welcome to the Weminuche Wilderness. As a wilderness manager, I have visited and worked in many wonderful areas, but the Weminuche is truly one of the special places here on earth. This book gives you an insider's look at the best the Weminuche has to offer and tips on how you can do your part to preserve it. It contains great advice and information.

One of my heroes, Bob Marshall, an early Forest Service crusader for wilderness, said, "The wilderness provides the ultimate delight because it combines the thrills of jeopardy and beauty. It is the last stand for that glorious adventure into the physically unknown that was commonplace in the lives of our ancestors, and has always constituted a major factor in the happiness of many exploratory souls."

I hope that as you travel through the Weminuche, you can experience firsthand the thrills that Bob Marshall wrote about. I know that I have had the thrill of unexpectedly sliding down a steep snowfield toward a deep abyss and lived to tell about it. Although I wouldn't recommend that aspect of snowfield sliding, I believe the exhilaration of risk and challenge is a human need that is an important part of our character. Beauty can be found in every corner of the Weminuche, from the towering peaks to the broad glaciated valleys.

We as wilderness managers face many challenges in trying to maintain a balance that protects the wilderness resource and experience while encouraging public use and enjoyment of that same resource. We spend time encouraging and educating wilderness users on the necessity of packing out what they brought in and how to Leave No Trace, but there are larger and potentially more challenging issues on the horizon.

I anticipate that as our population increases and we become more urbanized, the foresight of those that fought to preserve areas like the Weminuche will become more apparent. Wilderness provides a contrast to the ordinary and to our civilized environment. It is and will continue to be a refuge for those seeking solitude and life enrichment. The challenge will be to keep those experiences available for an ever-expanding population.

As we advance in our technological triumphs, we increase the potential to diminish the very characteristics that make wilderness wild. Our stunning advances in communication threaten the thrill of jeopardy. A cellular phone is a common item carried on many backcountry trips. We now have the ability to locate ourselves instantaneously by homing in on satellites in earth orbit with a handheld GPS unit. We hear of increasing need for products and equipment that allow our aging population to better experience the out-of-doors. While each of these may have a place in bettering our lives, what cost will they extract from wildness?

Some have argued that the rugged American character was wrought through hardships and challenges faced by our ancestors as they settled the vast American wilderness that existed throughout the continent. If our lives become too technologically dependent, if opportunities to face life without fear or challenge is removed, if wilderness becomes less wild, how will our future character be shaped?

These are some of the challenges we as caretakers of wilderness face. We debate them and try to make sense of what is best for the resource and the people who visit the wilderness. Answers will not come easy, but one thing is for certain. If we each do our part to care for and protect this incredible place called the Weminuche Wilderness, there will always be wild places.

Jim Upchurch
Wilderness Coordinator
San Juan/Rio Grande National Forests

# Acknowledgements

So many people have helped me during the two years spent researching and writing this book. I first would like to acknowledge Laurie Gruel and the San Juan Mountains Association for having the vision to believe that a new book about the Weminuche Wilderness is needed. Board president Lois Bartig-Small lent her encouragement, and front office workers Marie Folk and Alan Peterson cheerfully answered questions and helped with research.

Numerous employees of the San Juan/Rio Grande National Forests gave me advice, spent time helping me collect material and offered their professional expertise through interviews and conversations. Wilderness Coordinator Jim Upchurch, a friend and wilderness lover, took time from a busy schedule to consult with me. Wilderness specialists Nancy Berry, Phyllis Decker and Jody Fairchild not only shared their ideas and reviewed trail descriptions, but also gave me the opportunity to travel the backcountry as a wilderness ranger on their districts. I walked the trails with four dedicated summer rangers--Jennifer Zahratka, Miles Newby, Matt Morrissey and Ted Balchunas. Though they are younger than me, they patiently waited as I slowly ascended steep trails, and we shared special treats while out on ten-day trips together. Wilderness ranger Lois MacKenzie willingly taught me how to pack a horse, and I learned about stock travel in the Weminuche Wilderness through her eyes. Ranger Lee Neal turned me on to the history of Stony Pass as we bumped along the rugged four-wheel road toward Beartown to check out conditions on the Continental Divide Trail. Archeologists Sharon Hatch and Vince Spero opened their archives and told me their stories of research on the San Juan/Rio Grande Forests. Retired USFS archeologist Gary Matlock spent a morning listening to my questions and exploring the mystery of ancient dwellers in the Weminuche. The San Juan/Rio Grande Forests have a corp of dedicated employees that include Chris Schultz, Ron Klatt, Brad Morrison, Randy Houtz, Biff Stransky, Kathy Peckham, Dave Gerhardt, Ron Decker, Mark Franklin and others too numerous to mention who assisted me and encouraged me in this process. Regional Forest Service Wilderness Coordinator Ralph Swain whose passion for wilderness has inspired many, guided the San Juan Mountains Association with enthusiasm while I served on the board.

Professional guide Tom VanSoelen gained my respect as he explained the ethics of stock travel. My husband, Bob Boucher, who managed the home front while I was in the field and picked up his backpack to hike numerous trails with me receives special thanks. Historian Allen Nossaman whose marvelous history books detail the mining days in Silverton helped me with place names and fun stories of early visitors in the Weminuche Wilderness. A dear friend, Judith Sumner, read and edited the manuscript despite a busy schedule. Charles Foster and Tina Ochlan's skills with the Macintosh computer gave vision to the book's layout and design. I also wish to thank Walt Walker, Duane Smith and Rob Blair of Fort Lewis College. There are many people who supported me in this project. Thanks to all of them for their belief that the Weminuche Wilderness is a sacred place which must be preserved even as it must be understood.

# Introduction

I first began visiting the Weminuche Wilderness 25 years ago. As a new resident in Southwestern Colorado, I heard brief rumblings about a proposed wilderness in the Durango Herald stories, but I didn't understand the significance. My childhood was spent in Louisiana where public land holdings are few and the concept of designated wilderness nonexistent. In 1964 when the Wilderness Act was passed, I was living in Switzerland hiking, skiing, and mountaineering. I hardly registered the fact that President Lyndon B. Johnson had signed a significant bill which would later become integral to my personal philosophy. I wanted to experience the world, not the forests of Colorado. I was ignorant of the true meaning of wilderness though I was seeking those wild places even then.

I moved to Durango in 1970 and began to visit the San Juan National Forest on week-end outings. In 1973, when my son was eight years old, my family decided to visit a place called Chicago Basin which we had heard about. We bought topo maps and set out on a July morning, riding the narrow gauge train to Needleton and embarking up the Needle Creek Trail. We reached the lower edge of the basin just as a huge thunderstorm began dumping rain and hail. We scurried to set up our tarp, pull out the stove and create warmth in the wetness.

That trip taught me about point to point travel as we hiked out Vallecito Creek Trail rather than return the way we entered. I discovered that wild places existed at my back door, and I knew nothing about them. I didn't recognize the flowers I saw. I could not name a single peak in the Needles. Encountering wildlife was frightening, particularly the possibility that bears walked in the same woods. I could not identify the mushrooms beginning to appear along the trail. I understood nothing about ecosystems or the changes in vegetation at different altitudes. I only knew that this was a land of mystery, and I wanted to know more.

Perhaps because of my busy life caring for two small children while teaching school and certainly because of so little understanding of public land issues, I hardly registered the struggles occurring over the creation of the Weminuche Wilderness. The year 1975 doesn't stir any highlights for me, even though that is when the Weminuche was officially designated. I was busy being a Mom. Family outings were mostly car trips during the mid-seventies--jeeping on four-wheel drive roads or car camping up Hermosa Park beyond Purgatory. These simple excursions around the perimeters of the Weminuche kept my curiosity alive when I had no time to challenge the trails.

In 1977 I again entered the Weminuche, this time by way of Silverton up the Highland Mary Trail, then along the Continental Divide Trail and out by Cunningham Gulch Trail. During that same year my family ventured over Endlich Mesa Trail to City Reservoir. I wondered where the name *Endlich* came from, and I questioned a *city* reservoir located in the middle of wild country, but I found no answers. We also enjoyed day hiking up the Pine River Trail, and we visited Four Mile Lake near Pagosa Springs where we fished for the elusive trout. Through these trips I whetted my appetite to spend more time in the Weminuche Wilderness.

In 1988 when I heard about a group called the San Juan National Forest Association (now the San Juan Mountains Association) which sponsored a wilderness information program for visitors, I wanted to help. Dry summers and heavy visitation to Chicago Basin forced the U.S. Forest Service to enact a fire ban in the Needle Creek drainage that year. Volunteers were needed to explain the ban to backcountry travelers.

Changing people's habits of building fires was quite a challenge. Even so, we "WIS's" (Wilderness Information Specialists) met people at the railbus departure point in Rockwood and told them about Chicago Basin before the train left. (The Durango and Silverton Railroad is owned privately, and management at that time wanted all backpackers to ride the railbus from Rockwood rather than board the train in Durango. This lasted only a couple of years, before it became obvious to railroad management that the expense did not merit the extra service.) I practiced my story detailing the fire ban, Weminuche history, weather conditions and the challenges of camping near marmots and other animals habituated to human activity in the basin. My concern for the wilderness grew.

Perhaps this was the beginning of my belief that visitors to the Weminuche Wilderness needed much more information than was available to help them learn about this wild country. Dennis Gebhardt's book *A Backpacking Guide to the Weminuche Wilderness* published in 1976, had been available for ten years, and though it gave accurate information about trails, it did not tell the history of the area. Nor was it current regarding fire and Leave No Trace ethics.

In 1989 I joined the board of the San Juan Mountains Association (SJMA). The Weminuche Wilderness information program grew. With the cooperation of the Durango and Silverton Narrow Gauge Railroad, volunteers began traveling to the Needle and Elk Creek Trailheads. SJMA established base camps for overnight stays, and volunteers were scheduled to work the trails throughout the summer. For the next several years, I spent at least a week each summer hiking these trails and talking Leave No Trace ethics, safety issues and wilderness requirements. I also watched SJMA grow from a fledgling organization which fostered community involvement in forest issues to an educational organization which today offers numerous programs and opportunities for visitors to the San Juan/Rio Grande National Forests and the Weminuche Wilderness. (See the appendix for further information about the San Juan Mountains Association.)

Another major jump in wilderness awareness for me came when I worked with the Weminuche Wilderness study group for the San Juan National Forest. Our task was to help develop proposed management strategies for the area. Through this two-year process I learned more about the growing pressures on wilderness areas and the impacts on streams, trails, campsites, wildlife and alpine terrain.

I became convinced that the general public needed something which helped them understand this priceless treasure and the importance of preserving it. Surprisingly, I had never read the 1964 Wilderness Act in its entirety until I began working with the study group. I knew this was probably true of most people who traveled in the wilderness. After reading it and learning the history of its passage, I finally understood the challenge surrounding wilderness preservation. I decided to write a new guide book that shared more than trail information. Why not offer a history lesson in wilderness while giving a full explanation of Leave No Trace ethics? The book needed to include the story of the wilderness movement, the efforts of Southwest Colorado residents who fought for wilderness designation, explanations of grazing allotments and inholdings of private land in designated wilderness, insights into the geology and archeology of the San Juan Mountains, the responsibilities of various users who visit the wilderness and much more. I had discovered the "attitudes" held by different groups toward other users -- stock travelers for backpackers, backpackers for hunters, hunters for hikers, hikers for horse travelers, professional outfitters for private horse users, etc. I knew that all deserved the opportunity to enjoy the Weminuche Wilderness. The 1964 Wilderness Act guarantees that right. I also knew that each had its own special needs and code of ethics which, if practiced, would win the respect of other users. So I chose to offer Leave No Trace suggestions for each group.

# VIII Walking in Wildness

With the support of the San Juan Mountains Association, I began planning this book in 1996. Two years later it came together. In partnership with the publishing company affiliated with the Durango Herald, we created a book that hopefully answers many questions even as it provides current trail information. Much of what I have come to know and value about the Weminuche Wilderness in the last 20 years I now offer you. A hundred years from now I expect its wildness to be even more mysterious for all who choose to visit it.

# Part I

# Early Days of the
# San Juan Mountains

"Ability to see the cultural value of wilderness boils down, in the last analysis, to a question of intellectual humility. The shallow-minded modern who has lost his rootage in the land assumes that he has already discovered what is important; it is such who prate of empires, political or economic, that will last a thousand years. It is only the scholar who appreciates that all history consists of successive excursions from a single starting-point, to which man returns again and again to organize yet another search for a durable scale of values. It is only the scholar who understands why the raw wilderness gives definition and meaning to the human enterprise." Aldo Leopold, *A Sand County Almanac*, Oxford University Press, 1966.

# In Search of Stories in the Weminuche

The San Juan Mountains extend south from Ouray, Colorado, into New Mexico. At the heart of these mountains is the Weminuche Wilderness, split in the middle by the Continental Divide that takes a southeastern jog just below Silverton, before bending south again at Wolf Creek Pass some 90 miles away as the crow flies. This 500,000 acre designated wilderness was set aside by an Act of Congress in 1975 after local residents spent seven years hashing out disputes over its boundaries and uses. Today its high alpine meadows, jagged peaks and rushing mountain streams lure backpackers, mountain climbers, stock travelers, anglers, hunters and ardent lovers of nature to its trails summer after summer. Cross country skiers follow the snowy routes during the winter months. No motorized or mechanized vehicles can enter this sanctuary according to the Wilderness Act of 1964. Its seclusion and beauty make it a refuge for every nature lover.

The San Juan Mountains and their heart, the Weminuche Wilderness, have stories to tell--stories of indigenous people who, before European contact, traveled the well worn trails still used today, following the rivers and streams to find game and other food sources. There are stories of French, Spanish and American adventurers struck by wanderlust and gold fever who introduced horses, cattle and sheep to the indigenous people and climbed some of its highest peaks. There is the story of how these two groups met, and the consequent loss of homelands by native tribes. There are stories of fur traders and miners who came to seek their fortune and settled permanently, establishing the communities that are now present-day Silverton, Durango, Pagosa Springs, South Fork, Del Norte and Creede. Their children's children are the movers and shakers in these towns today, and the mountains are still integral to their lives. They cleared the valleys to raise crops and graze cattle. They built schools, churches, hospitals and businesses to serve the growing population. Smelters that processed raw ores taken from the mountains came and went with the cycles of boom and bust in the mines. Railroads were constructed, one of which still carries tourists from Durango to Silverton and back. What were initially toll roads built for mule trains and wagons used by early entrepreneurs became public highways. Settlers who

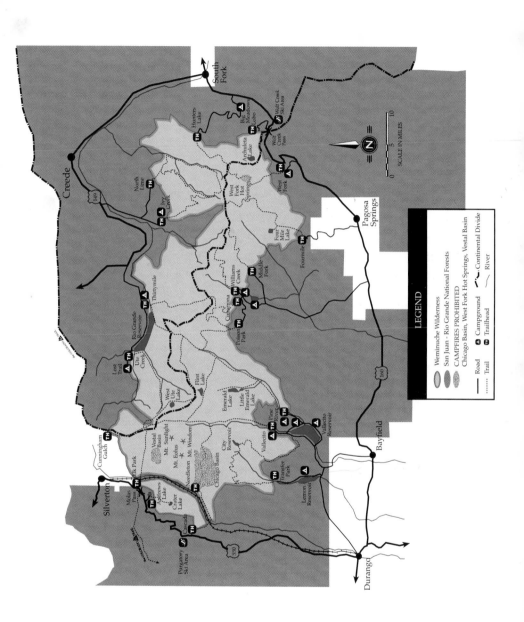

remained came to know well that cliched truth, "if you build it they will come." People have come to the country surrounding the Weminuche Wilderness for the last hundred years, drawn by the beauty of the mountains and the dreams of business success. The combined populations of communities surrounding the San Juan Mountains now probably exceeds 300,000 residents.

A tour of the perimeter of the Weminuche Wilderness will take you through some of the most spectacular mountain scenery and picturesque towns in the west. Driving into San Juan County by way of U.S. 550 from the north to Silverton, you are only a dozen miles from the Weminuche Wilderness. To the east is Kendall Mountain, where each summer a group of diehard locals spends a day running to its top. Mount Kendall is not in the Weminuche, but beyond its southeastern ridges lie the green skirts of Sugarloaf Mountain, whose hemline includes the wilderness boundary and the Highland Mary Lakes.

Kendall Mountain - Silverton, Colorado
*Courtesy of S. Hoffman ©*

Pause in Silverton, first known as Baker's Park, for a day and breathe deeply of its nineteenth century mining town air. Stroll along wide streets bordered by historic buildings that now house curio shops and restaurants frequented by passengers on the Durango and Silverton Narrow Gauge Railroad. The train pulls in four times daily during the summer months, its passengers having just had an experience few lovers of wilderness can comprehend--a ride along a wilderness border for more than 20 miles. Passengers experience high peaks and the Animas River valley from a comfortable seat, no struggle or toil involved.

Heading south out of Silverton on U.S. 550 you follow a route that was formerly a toll road for pack trains of mules bringing supplies to Silverton. Those mule trains climbed up steep Molas Pass just as you do, and the drivers looked east across Molas Lake to the Animas River valley below, where today the Weminuche Wilderness boundary reaches. In the foreground is the West Needle Range, an impressive group of peaks added to the wilderness in 1993, that catch the eye of many a mountain climber seeking a challenge. The highway will skirt within a mile or so of the Weminuche as it continues south. Following the historic Lime Creek burn of 1879 caused by careless miners, it twists and bends and folds back upon itself on its descent down Molas Pass, then climbs up Coalbank Pass before passing Purgatory Ski Area on the hills to the west.

The wilderness boundary traces along the eastern slopes, following Cascade Creek down to the Animas River. In the distance are the Needle Mountains, whose jagged spires reach over 14,000 feet. Nestled under them is beautiful Chicago Basin, now a site where backpackers and mountaineers who expect to escape crowds find they must vie for camping spots in the surrounding alpine meadow. Just over a hundred years ago miners crowded into that alpine valley with their pack animals, sending deer and native Ute hunters to other areas for refuge.

Early picture of Lime Creek burn
*Courtesy of the San Juan County Historical Society*

From Purgatory south, you begin traveling through the urbanized outskirts of the Durango community, and the wilderness is a distant sight. The highway leaves the San Juan National Forest and descends into the Animas River Valley where fertile farmlands scoured by ancient glaciers have been turned into subdivisions surrounding golf courses. This valley is now the winter habitat for elk herds that seek food in peoples' yards. The pinnacles of the Needle Range are hidden by Missionary Ridge to the east of the Animas River, which still courses downhill near the highway. By the time you reach the lower Animas River valley you are miles from the wilderness and traveling beneath glacier sculpted red and purple hillsides.

As you enter the bustling city of Durango from the north, you pass through an older settlement known as Animas City. The nineteenth century residents of Animas City were a bit miffed when in 1880 Durango's founders enticed the railroad builders to construct their station two miles south of Animas City, allowing it to be swallowed by Durango. Now a business center in the San Juan Basin, Durango has a unique story of its own. Its settlers supported the mining industry as suppliers. The smelter was located here, and ore was brought in from surrounding mining communities by train. Boarding houses and saloons, banks and a grist mill, all the necessities of a commercial center--these were Durango's aces in the game that determined the economic hub of the region. The pristine wilderness in the nearby forests spoke to the souls of its settlers, and their

Aerial view of Durango
*Courtesy of Jim Bommarito © (DACRA)*

descendants remain today. Durango is still the hub of Southwestern Colorado and a favorite tourist center for visitors from around the world.

To continue your travel around the circumference of the Weminuche Wilderness, you must turn east on U.S. 160 and drive toward Bayfield, an agricultural and cattle center in the San Juan Basin. Here, the Florida and Los Pinos Rivers, two of the most important drainages in the Weminuche Wilderness, empty into wide alluvial meadows. Ranchers have been driving their cattle and sheep up these river valleys into the mountains to summer grazing spots since the 1870's. In years past, thousands of animals were grazed indiscriminately in the Weminuche Wilderness and surrounding forest country before the U.S. Forest Service was established in 1891 and placed in charge of managing and protecting public lands. But that's another story--how the forest reserves were set aside, and the fights between early ranchers over the high country grazing.

Pagosa Hot Springs,
Pagosa Springs, Colorado
*Courtesy of Suellen Loher ©*

While Bayfield's lush valleys may tempt you to linger, you have to continue on to Pagosa Springs, the military and lumbering center of the area if you want to travel around the entire Weminuche. Pagosa Springs was named after a hot springs (Pagosa means "healing waters" in Ute) considered sacred by both the Ute and Navajo tribes. Story has it that a fight over ownership of the mineral springs occurred between the two tribes in the early nineteenth century, and the Utes won.

When American miners entered the San Juan Mountains, they were trespassing on Ute land. The U.S. government established a military post to protect the land hungry settlers, and the town of Pagosa Springs now sits on that site. After treaties were made with the Utes opening their land for settlement, the military post was moved to its Fort Lewis site just south of Hesperus on

Pagosa Lumber Company Sawmill, ~ Pagosa Springs, Co. ca. 1908
*Courtesy of the La Plata County Historical Society*

the La Plata River. Pagosa Springs became a logging center, the rich forests of Engelman spruce and ponderosa pine cut for use in mining and railroad construction. The timber was also used for homes and for charcoal to fuel the early smelters. The logging industry cleared the forests surrounding the lower slopes of the Weminuche Wilderness, but large sections of its old growth trees remained because of inaccessibility. Pagosa Springs is now a center for summer homes and sports enthusiasts. U.S. 160 follows its winding main street as it curves around the hot springs considered sacred by the Ute Indians, then cuts east to ascend the steep Wolf Creek Pass.

You travel near the Weminuche Wilderness boundary again as you drive east from Pagosa Springs. To the south is another designated wilderness --the South San Juan--with its own stories. A steep uphill grade takes you to Wolf Creek Pass, named after an old trapper, Jim Wolf, who claimed squatter's rights near the mouth of the Rio Grande River. Some of the earliest U.S. Forest Service campgrounds on the San Juan National Forest were constructed west of Wolf Creek Pass by Civilian Conservation Corps (CCC) workers operating out of the Blanco Center south of Pagosa Springs. Their popularity as jumping off points into the San Juan Mountains grew after the public highway across the pass was completed in the 1930's.

At the top of the pass your route takes you across the Continental Divide. You could stop your car travel here and hike the meandering Continental Divide Trail that follows this water dividing ridge northwestward, returning to Silverton through the center of the Weminuche Wilderness. Its wild lands span the Divide and fall into two forests, the San Juan and the Rio Grande National Forests. That's a story, too, since the two forests are now consolidated under single management, their boundaries having changed several times before finally becoming fixed in 1947. In 1995 the two forests were consolidated again. Today, the Weminuche Wilderness is managed as a whole entity rather than having two strategies overseeing its future.

When you reach the community of South Fork on the east side of Wolf Creek Pass, you'll have to turn north on Colorado Highway 149 if you wish to follow your route around the Weminuche's boundaries. You'll now be traveling by the Rio Grande del Norte, the huge river that became a route to the San Juan Mountains from Tierra Amarilla and Taos, New Mexico, for adventurous Spanish and Mexican explorers in the seventeenth and eighteenth centuries. The Rio Grande cuts through a wide valley that is populated with fishing camps and lodges. A hundred years ago, a stage route and railroad followed its meanderings, bringing settlers to the mining camp of Creede. Stage stops where horse teams could be changed were located every ten miles along the route. Twenty-five miles

Creede, Colorado,
*Courtesy of Big Sky Photography ©*

north of South Fork is the historic mining center of Creede whose early stories are replete with barroom brawls, numerous silver strikes and tenacious settlers who refused to leave when the mining industry collapsed. Nicholas Creede struck pay dirt there in 1889, and by 1892 the town had 10,000 residents. At one time Creede was the second largest silver producer in the country. Today the population has dwindled to 400, plus a few thousand "summer settlers" whose cabins and corrals fill the green valleys of the grand river.

From Creede, turn west on Colorado 149 to follow the open valley of the Rio Grande River and the distant Weminuche boundaries. Beautiful fishing waters roll through the wide valley and keep the summer settlers happy. If you continue on Highway149, you'll end up in Lake City, but the more exciting route is to follow the Rio Grande's descent from its head waters. To do this, turn on Forest Service Road 520 and following it for 10 miles to the dam that holds back the Rio Grande Reservoir, a lengthy manmade lake that captures the many tributaries which flow from the Weminuche Wilderness into the Rio Grande River. The wilderness boundary is formed by the reservoir's southwestern shoreline. Water diversion projects built in the early twentieth century took western slope waters and channeled them across the Divide into the Rio Grande drainage to San Luis Valley ranchers and cattlemen. The reservoir itself was constructed by an ambitious group of people who knew the value of water to arid southwestern valleys where farming became important.

After passing along the reservoir's eastern shore, which may be drained in August because of agriculture's thirst, and beyond the Lost Trail Ranch, an old stage stop, it's "four-wheeling" time. You'll ascend a rugged route up steep rocky slopes first traveled by pack trains headed to Silverton via Stony Pass during the mining days. This was the premier road to Silverton until the railroad connected Durango to Silverton. For half a dozen years supply trains bumped their way over its rugged path bringing everything from mining equipment to furnishings for fancy bars. Near Stony Pass is Beartown where old mining cabins still stand, attesting to a thriving community that housed over 400 miners in the 1890's. Continue north on the four-wheel road along the Rio Grande head waters to a gravel road, Colorado 110, which turns west and returns to Silverton. Back in Silverton you will have completed your circle of the Weminuche Wilderness, this wild and scenic place that has many stories to tell. Those stories are the subject of this book.

# 2

# The Geology of the Weminuche

The San Juan Mountains are a magnificent geological specimen. They are the classroom for scientists from all over the world because geologic history is laid bare in their canyon walls and high peaks. Seven different ranges compose the greater San Juans, with several of those ranges -- the Grenadiers, West Needles and Needles -- located almost entirely in the Weminuche Wilderness. Surrounding ranges include the La Plata, La Garita, Sneffels, Silverton and Sawatch Mountains. Beginning in valleys at 6,000 feet in elevation, several peaks in the mountains spire to heights above 14,000 feet. The mountains in the Weminuche Wilderness, once the floor material of seas, have been uplifted into rugged peaks that challenge mountaineers from all over the world.

The Needle Mountains
*Courtesy of B. J. Boucher*

The vast scale of geological time compressed into the San Juan Mountains boggles the human mind. Try to understand a story of earth building that covers four billion years! Imagine millions and millions of years of tumultuous flooding, shifting, bulging, collapsing, freezing, thawing, heating and volcanic spewing on the earth's surface. What was it like during those days of geological uproar and climactic change? What creatures lived for centuries after adapting to their environment, only to be wiped out by rising sea waters or volcanic action or droughts or glaciers? What migration patterns, adaptations and extinctions resulted? All the ages of geologic time compressed into a mountainside is overwhelming to the frail human creature who may, with good health, experience 80 or 90 years of life and hardly notice any shifting of a nearby hillside.

The San Juan Mountains are phenomenal weather makers today, and they have been sculpted by millions of years of changing weather. The high ranges trap moisture laden clouds from the Pacific Ocean, summer and winter. Rain, sleet or snow accumulate quickly in even the hottest month and inundate narrow streambeds with roiling, muddy, bank-scouring currents. Winter snowfall can exceed 200 inches in some areas, and when the spring temperatures rise, unstable snow on steep hillsides slides down the aspen covered slopes, wiping out whole forests.

This water then cascades in streams and rivers that run down from the Continental Divide, the imaginary line dividing eastern and western drainage. The waters wash away rocks and debris. They scour hillsides and remove vegetation. They pocket in bogs and low places, creating lakes and riparian regions. The many mountain streams originating in the Weminuche Wilderness come together into the Rio Grande River on the eastern slope of the San Juan Mountains and the San Juan and Colorado Rivers on the western slope. These huge rivers have shaped the landscape from southern Colorado to the Gulf of Mexico and the Gulf of California, coursing through the valleys and plains, depositing rich soils and providing water to residents of semi-arid and desert lands for thousands of years. Only during the twentieth century have they been conquered by dams and irrigation projects.

GEOLOGICAL ERAS

Changes caused by weather and precipitation are comprehensible to us on a small scale like a season or year or even twenty-five years. But what about the changes over a billion years? Geologists have devised a Geologic Time Scale[1] to help sort out all the periods of rock formation and surface change on Planet Earth. The numerous geologic periods are grouped into four eras. The oldest, the

| Millions of Years | | | | | |
|---|---|---|---|---|---|
| | | | **Present Day** | | |
| San Juan Mountains → | 2 | | Quaternary | Pleistocene Pliocene | Time of Ice |
| Great Volcanic Activity | 25 | Cenozoic | Tertiary | Pleistocene Pliocene | Extinction of Dinosaurs |
| Rocky Mountains → | 135 | Mesozoic | | Cretaceous Jurassic Triassic | First Birds First Mammals First Dinosaurs |
| Ancestral Mountains → Time of Extensive Oceans | 270 | Paleozoic | | Permian Carboniferous Devonian Silurian Ordovician Cambrian | Early Life on Land and Sea |
| | 600 | **Precambrian** | | | Beginnings of Life |

*Courtesy of Steve Wilson*

Precambrian Era, covers the first four billion years of the earth's history and the beginning of life. Next is the Paleozoic Era or the time of early life on land and sea ranging from 570 to 245 million years ago. During this era the earth experienced rising and retreating seas. This is followed by the "middle life" or Mesozoic Era when subtropical climates and seas gave rise to numerous terrestrial life forms, from 245 to 66 million years ago. The first birds and mammals including dinosaurs lived on the earth. Geologic time from 65 million years ago up to the present is known as the Cenozoic Era, a time of repeated glaciation combined with earth shattering volcanic eruptions that caused the extinction of dinosaurs. The Weminuche Wilderness bears testimony to all of these geologic eras.

"Basement" rocks from the Precambrian Era have been exposed in the West Needle Mountains, and specifically on Twilight Peak, after which the granite rock called Twilight Gneiss is named. The Grenadiers are upturned faulted layers of rock that may have been wrenched into their present position from a distant place eons after their billion-year-old formation. Centuries of folding, faulting, erosion and uplifting created the rugged Needle Mountains, which include granite peaks older than a billion years.

Tectonic activity, the shifting of the earth's rigid plates, caused earthquakes and volcanic eruptions along faults or fractures in the earth's crust.

Twilight Peak
*Courtesy of Bill Hayes*

eposited and intruded rock formations were created, scarring huge chunks of
e Weminuche into mountain ranges. These formations eroded away as seas
se. When the water receded, shale, sandstone and limestone deposits were left
hind. Then the sea-deposited sedimentary rocks were swept away and
posited elsewhere by glaciers and more seas. Widespread volcanic action
ewed ash and rock on top of everything from Silverton to the La Garita Range
rth of Creede to Wolf Creek Pass east of Pagosa Springs. What a mixed up
orld of materials remained!

Over millions of years the San Juan Mountains became the rugged peaks
e enjoy visiting today. The joints and fractures in rocks that developed as a
sult of mountain building permitted mineral-rich solutions to move upward
om hot magma deep in the earth. The 50 mile-wide Colorado Mineral Belt
rmed by this process became the focus for European settlement in the valleys
rrounding the San Juan Mountains.

EOLOGIC FACTORS THAT SHAPED THE WEMINUCHE

According to Fort Lewis College Professor Rob Blair,[2] the landscape and
atures we see in the Weminuche Wilderness are the results of seven geologic
ctors occurring during the four-billion-year history of the earth. The sharp
ointed peaks like Mount Eoulus, Mount Windom and Sunlight Peak in the

Pine River Valley carved by glacier
*Courtesy of B. J. Boucher*

Lime deposits above 11,000 feet
*Courtesy of B. J. Boucher*

Needle Mountains, are composed of hard igneous plutonic rocks. The distinctly layered mountain faces composed of different colors and rock types visible throughout the western part of the Weminuche resulted from successive episodes of deposition and layering of rock. Harder layers formed cliffs, and softer layers broke down to form slopes beneath the cliffs.

Uplift and deformation combined with weather, wind and water which eroded surfaces and left different strata of rock exposed to form another group of features. Later volcanic activity deposited magma on or in sedimentary rock, producing what are known as dikes, sills, and laccoliths, particularly in the Eastern Weminuche. Dikes are sheetlike bodies of igneous rock that intruded into fissures in older rock formations while in a molten state. Sills are igneous rock injected between layers of earlier rock formations, like a window sill separating a glass window from the wall. Laccoliths are mushroom shapes of igneous rock that forced existing rock strata upward as the molten rock spewed to the earth's surface.

Volcanoes that collapsed on themselves after spewing out ash and magma over millions of years formed what are known as calderas, cylindrical pits which stretch for miles and miles across the landscape. Numerous calderas are exposed in the Weminuche Wilderness near Silverton, Creede and within the eastern section of the wilderness. The largest volcanic eruption documented on

# Geologic Map of the Weminuche Wilderness

**Quaternary**

- Glacial drift - Glacial debris deposited by the glaciers of the Pleistocene Epoch.
- Landslide deposits - Rock fragments detached from bedrock or loose sediment cascading downslope.
- Volcanic deposits - Complex assemblage of lava and pyroclastic material derived from many different centers.

**Paleozoic & Mesozoic**

- Sedimentary rocks - Paleozoic and Mesozoic rocks forming the southward dipping flank of the Needle Mountains.

**Precambrian**

- Precambrian granites - Consists of the Trimble, Eolus, and Tenmile granites.
- Precambrian metamorphics - Consists of the Uncompahgre Formation, Twilight Gneiss, Irving Formation and the Vallecito Conglomerate.

**Tertiary**

Windom Peak

La Plata County
Hindsdale County

N

Miles

0        10

*Courtesy of Steve Wilson*

the face of the earth, according to USGS studies, occurred on the eastern slopes of the San Juan Mountains. Estimated to have been 8,000 times the magnitude of the Mount St. Helens eruption of 1980, it spewed out ash and tuff, then spread the deposits over great distances.[3] Volcanic action completely covered the older rocks of the eastern San Juan Mountains, capped mountains like Kendall and the Grand Turk near Silverton and spread volcanic rubble still visible today near Wolf Creek Pass.

Multiple glacial periods also left their mark on the Weminuche by gouging out deep, U-shaped valleys and cirques like Chicago Basin. Many of these cirques or bowl-shaped hollows became high alpine lakes or *tarns*. As they moved, glaciers sheared off the sides of mountains, leaving steep rugged walls of exposed rock. Chipping away loose rock, glaciers sculpted mountains like Pigeon and Turret peaks in the Needle Mountains. Most of the river valleys that finger out of the Weminuche Wilderness were shaped by the movement of glaciers. As recently as 15,000 years ago glaciers scraped across the surface of the earth from Silverton to Durango, forming the Animas River Valley. The wide Pine or Los Piños River Valley which stretches westward from the Continental Divide in the Weminuche Wilderness is a good example of glacial action. As the glaciers carved out valleys, they shoved huge boulders along the floor and deposited them in wide boulder fields and rock piles called *moraines*. Moraines finger around present-day Durango and extend south in the Animas River Valley for miles. Geologist Blair says the San Juan Mountains may have experienced fifteen or more glacial advances during the last two million years, though only six are documented by existing glacial deposits.

Postglacial years have added their touch to the Weminuche landscape as rivers cut deep canyons and built terraces of sedimentary deposits. Changes in climate caused freezing and thawing of the deposits, with resulting landslides, avalanches and soil creep that modified and relocated the deposits of rock and soil. All these landscape changes can be seen throughout the Weminuche Wilderness.

ROCK FORMATIONS

The San Juan Mountains contain numerous rock formations. These are dated through radioactive dating, a process that studies radioactive elements such as uranium and their decay or loss of nuclear particles. Geologists studied, named and standardized these rock formations around the world. We can best understand them, however, by the source of their origin. There are three classifications of rock formations which all deposits fit into: *igneous, sedimentary* and *metamorphic* rocks.

*Igneous* rocks result from the crystallization of hot, molten magma from deep in the earth. There are two broad categories of igneous rocks--intrusive and extrusive. The names imply whether they were formed below or above the earth's surface. Explosive ejections (extrusions) create lava flows, ash fall and the resulting extrusive rock forms. Intrusions force their way up through other rock formations to form veins or bulges of granite. Volcanic activity occurring between eighteen and forty million years ago, produced debris that covers the eastern slopes of the Weminuche, from Creede south to the area of Wolf Creek Pass.

*Sedimentary* rocks result when deposits consolidate together, either in water or on land, as a result of temperature or pressure. Pebbles, sand, mud, limestone from sea life and pieces of weathered rock compress into a hardened material. Wind and rain also deposit and consolidate sediments of sand and shale. When a sea recedes the deposits or sediments left behind crystallize as the water evaporates. Limestone deposits of calcium carbonate containing many fossils and left from receding seas can be found at altitudes above 11,000 feet. Take a stroll on Lime Mesa east of Missionary Ridge or above Andrews Lake in the West Needles, to see long ridges of limestone.

*Metamorphic* rocks are created from the crystallization of pre-existing igneous and sedimentary rocks beneath the earth's surface. Heat and intense pressure cause the materials to compress together. These rocks are much harder than sedimentary layers. Metamorphic rocks are strewn throughout the Weminuche, but particularly in the eastern section. Rocks in streambeds and rivers are small samples.

The only way to deeply understand the geology of the Weminuche Wilderness is to carry a detailed source book with you. The Geology Department at Fort Lewis College in Durango has a faculty of geologists who have published several excellent books about the San Juan Mountains. Even with their first-rate information, the geologic puzzle will mystify you. Simply know that when you walk these lands you are seeing a mysterious story that will continue to be unraveled as time passes.

# 3

# The Wilderness Primeval

Archeologists are our major source for information about early visitors or human inhabitants of the primeval Weminuche Wilderness. Unfortunately, archeological research on the San Juan/Rio Grande Forests, and specifically in the high mountains of the wilderness has been minimal because of funding limitations. Even so, thousands of sites have been documented across the greater San Juan/Rio Grande National Forests, and hundreds which represent prehistoric presence in the high country probably exist in areas we travel through today.

PREHISTORIC VISITORS

Archeologist Philip Duke of Fort Lewis College[4] divides early human occupation in Southwestern Colorado into three periods:

- Paleo-Indian from 11,500 B.C. to 5500 B.C.
- Archaic from 5500 B.C. to A.D. 1
- Late Prehistoric, including the Ancestral Puebloan (formerly called Anasazi) and Ute periods from A.D. 1 to European settlement

Paleo-Indian people lived throughout the western part of the American continent hunting the mammoth mastodon during the Pleistocene period. This means earliest human visitation to the Weminuche Wilderness may have occurred over 10,000 years ago, and perhaps even before that. During Pleistocene times, glaciers covered the Weminuche Wilderness, extending from Silverton to Durango. They carved out valleys and meadows where present-day streams and rivers such as the Los Piños, Animas, Vallecito and Rio Grande now flow. As the glaciers melted and retreated from the wide alluvial valleys, prehistoric game followed them. The Paleo-Indian culture followed the game north.

Climatologists now know that droughts overtook the western part of the North American Continent from 7,500 to 4,500 years ago. The dry weather probably forced native hunter/gatherers to live in the high mountains. Excavations in the area of Piedra Pass in the Weminuche Wilderness have

Self Heal collected by native tribes
*Courtesy of the SJMA*

unearthed artifacts characteristic of the Archaic period. By the middle Archaic period the climate had stabilized to what we presently know, and hunting groups ranged from low valleys in the winter to alpine meadows in the summer.

Fires were a natural occurrence in the Weminuche ecosystems during prehistoric times. U. S. Forest Service research through the dating of tree rings reveals frequent fires until 1905, when modern intervention practices changed that pattern. This means that early inhabitants during dry years probably experienced blankets of heavy smoke in the river valleys when summer fires burned, contrary to our expectations of pristine air and countryside during prehistoric times.

From 5,000 B.C. to A.D. 500 Archaic peoples traveled throughout the Weminuche Wilderness gathering the seeds of rice grass, amaranth and other native plants or hunting animals similar to those we know today. Excavations at the Piedra site, according to forest records,[5] reveal a subsistence lifestyle, with pollen samples showing the use of tansy mustard, huckleberry, wild onion, blackbrush, currants, ground berries and other vegetative food and medicinal sources.

Retired Forest Service Archeologist Gary Matlock[6] imagines the Archaic peoples as multi-generational groups who followed spring into the mountains each year. "Each small band probably had their own territory, since there was lots of room for food gathering. Because of their symbiotic relationship with nature, they might spend as little as two hours a day gathering food. The rest of their time could be devoted to storytelling, pursuing crafts and preparing food. That's the lifestyle I like to imagine," Matlock speculated. "Archaic people were skilled in living off the land."

Some of those Archaic bands may have been the ancestors of the agricultural Ancestral Puebloans, formerly referred to as the Anasazi, who lived in southern Colorado during the Late Prehistoric Period of native occupation. The Ancestral Puebloans thrived in the Four Corners region from approximately A.D. 1 to 1300. Large settlements existed throughout southern Colorado, New Mexico, Arizona and Utah. These people were not mobile like their predecessors. Instead, they developed a very complex farming society, probably traveling into the high wilderness only occasionally to hunt. Ancestral Puebloan activity has been documented at elevations above 11,000 feet in the San Juan Mountains through unearthed pottery shards and other artifacts. Two other uses of high Colorado mountain regions by prehistoric cultures have been explored by Archeologist James Benedict on the eastern Rocky

Chimney Rock Archeological Area
*Courtesy of the USFS*

Mountain slopes. They include vision questing and the trapping of eagles.[7] It is believed that the Ancestral Puebloans could have entered the Weminuche Wilderness for these purposes, and in time such sites will probably be found. They were a very religious people, and visits to the mountains must have been a source of spiritual power. Additionally, their communities located near Chimney Rock and Spring Creek/Sauls Creek areas would have had easy access to the Weminuche Wilderness along nearby river corridors.

The Ancestral Puebloan culture collapsed around A.D. 1300. Speculations about why these people disappeared are numerous. It is possible they used up the timber, game animals and vegetation immediately surrounding their communities as their population expanded. The nearby lands that are now the San Juan National Forest and Weminuche Wilderness, however, remained essentially untouched. For some reason they did not utilize this wealth of food and materials. Perhaps the agricultural lifestyle altered their expectations for hunting or straying too far from the village centers for food. Or perhaps conflicts with remnants of Archaic tribes still living in the mountains restricted access. No specific answer can explain their limited use of the rich mountain lands or the reason for their disappearance.

The Ancestral Puebloans were followed by the Ute peoples of the late Prehistoric period. The Ute tribes are related linguistically to the Shoshone tribes that inhabited the Great Basin and plains region of the United States. Most research locates their origin as Southern California and Nevada. Though archeologists suggest they migrated to Southwestern Colorado before the sixteenth century, the Utes believe they have always lived in the region. They might even be the descendants of the early Archaic people. Speculation continues about their origins.

History reports the Utes of southern Colorado lived in three distinct bands. The *Capote* band occupied the San Luis Valley east of the San Juan Mountains. The *Mouache* lived in what is now southern Colorado and northern New Mexico, extending as far south as Santa Fe. The *Weeminuche* inhabited the San Juan River Valley in southwestern Colorado.

Most written information about the early Utes comes from the journals of eighteenth century Spanish explorers. Historians now acknowledge the Ute people as the oldest continuous residents in the State of Colorado and the San Juan Mountains. Many of the trails we travel in the Weminuche were trampled into place during their summer hunting excursions as they followed the Los Piños River, Vallecito Creek, Ute Creek, Animas River and other drainages into high country from April through October to gather food.

The mountain vistas must have been a welcome sight to these hunter/gatherers after wintering in the lowlands of northern New Mexico and southern Colorado. Their loosely knit communities would split up each spring into family units or small bands to hunt in the Weminuche, according to Ute historians.[8] They traveled on foot, since they acquired horses only after the Spanish entered their country. From spring to fall they followed a circuit of

Weminuche Pass encampment area
*Courtesy of B. J. Boucher*

familiar places. Perhaps in late April they sought the first tender shoots and roots of cattails growing in riparian areas along the Los Piños River drainage. Streams were flowing rapidly, and the trout and waterfowl would be easy prey in bogs and high lakes. Wild onions, dandelions and lettuce would be a welcome change from winter's diet of dried foods. The first old marmot who stretched lazily on a rock to bask in the spring sun might have become fresh meat. Summer's wild fruits like raspberries and strawberries were found in abundance in the high country.

Clear evidence of Ute encampments is sparse, since our feet have trampled their trails and campsites in the river valleys. Though their artifacts do not withstand time as well as Ancestral Puebloan artifacts, archeologists have found tools shaped from objects of European origin as well as "scarred" ponderosa pine trees in the Weminuche Wilderness resulting from the removal of inner bark which was used for food.[9] Campers today pitch their tents in the same meadows and groves they enjoyed. Their alpine trails along the Continental Divide and across the Rio Grande/San Juan National Forests became roads for mule trains packing supplies to miners in the late nineteenth century. Their annual summer encampment along the Animas River in Baker's Park near present day Silverton ended only after the discovery of silver and gold by American citizens in the 1870's.

Few place names in the Weminuche bear resemblance to the names used by these Prehistoric people. Instead, Spanish explorers and American settlers dotted the mountains and valleys with Spanish and English titles. Even so, the Weminuche Wilderness is named after one of the bands of Utes--the *Weeminuche* of the San Juan River valley. The descendants of that band now live near Towoac, Colorado, having been relocated in the late nineteenth century. Today they are called the *Ute Mountain Utes*. The *Southern Utes* who reside closest to the Weminuche Wilderness in Ignacio, Colorado, are descendants of the *Capote* band from the San Luis Valley.

Other contemporary Native American tribes like the Navajo, Apache, Jicarilla Apache, Sioux, Cheyenne, Kiowa and Arapaho, who lived near the Rocky Mountains, are thought to have been occasional visitors to the Weminuche area, where they traded with the Utes and hunted for wild game. They did not remain in the San Juan Mountains for any length of time, however.

SPANISH INFLUENCES ON THE UTE CULTURE

Spanish colonization in northern New Mexico during the eighteenth and nineteenth centuries changed forever the lives of the Ute Indians. With the introduction of the horse, the Ute people could travel great distances to trade with other tribes and with the Spanish settlers. Horse travel also changed community patterns. Expert horsemen could visit the high country when necessary, while other family members remained in permanent communal groups and camps located in the river valleys.

The New Mexico territory was claimed by Spain in the sixteenth century, though early Spanish travelers came not for land but for gold and silver. The Tierra Amarilla Land Grant of the 1800's brought permanent Spanish and Mexican settlers to Southern Colorado, and their legacy gives us many place names in the Weminuche Wilderness. The Animas River, Rincon La Osa, Cañon Paso, Mesa Lato, Rio Grande, Los Piños--a quick scan of the Wilderness map testifies to the Spanish influences.

Early Spanish conquistadors actually set foot on Ute land in northern New Mexico in the later part of the sixteenth century. Coronado, traveling from Texas into New Mexico, Colorado and Kansas encountered several bands of Utes along his route. In 1598 an explorer named Juan de Onate organized an expedition to search for the rumored gold at the "Lake of Copala" in northern New Mexico.[10] No gold was found, but a profitable trade was begun with the Ute people in the region.

The first recorded Spanish penetration into the San Juan Mountains of Colorado was made by the Juan Maria de Rivera expedition in 1765. Rivera came to the La Plata Mountains, located northwest of present day Durango, to investigate reports of silver and gold and to trap for furs. Rivera led three separate expeditions into Ute territory. Eleven years later, in 1776, the Dominguez-Escalante Expedition, seeking a land route to the Pacific Ocean, crossed through Southern Colorado under the snowy peaks of the San Juan Mountains. They had journeyed up the Chama River from Tierra Amarilla in northern New Mexico to present day Pagosa Springs, where a military post would later be established by the U.S. government. They then followed present-day U.S. Hwy. 160 west, crossing through Ute lands and into Utah. These journeys into the interior of Ute country strengthened trade between the Spanish and the Ute tribe.

As a strong trading relationship was solidified between the Utes and the Spaniards, they lived in relative harmony. The Utes traded meat, hides, tallow and other wild animal products for horses. As they became proficient horsemen, the Utes reportedly took captives from surrounding native tribes and sold them as slaves to the Spanish settlers.

Ute encampment on Pine River near Ignacio, Colorado ca. 1900
*Courtesy of the La Plata County Historical Society*

## AMERICAN INFLUENCES ON THE UTES

In 1848 the Treaty of Guadalupe-Hidalgo transferred the San Juan Mountains and surrounding forests from Mexican to U.S. ownership, and American fur trappers and mountain men, who had been in the area since 1821, began trapping the high river corridors in and around the Weminuche Wilderness. The Utes took advantage of this to trade buffalo robes and beaver pelts for flour, cloth, tobacco, trinkets and whiskey. They shared their knowledge of the mountain topography--the passes and paths of least resistance through the high country. Later, miners, road builders and railroad men would use this knowledge to construct routes which brought permanent American settlement into the San Juan Basin.

The lure of mineral wealth for prospectors in the San Juan Mountains finally pushed the Utes out of their homeland. As American penetration increased, a treaty establishing land rights was needed. The first treaty between the Utes and the United States was signed at Abiquiu, New Mexico, in 1849. The Utes agreed not to leave their accustomed territory without government permission. Their accustomed territory, however, included all of Colorado as well as lands in New Mexico and Utah. In return, they were guaranteed perpetual peace and friendship with the Americans.

Military posts were established to protect settlers now flocking to Colorado, and friction erupted. In 1854 the Utes attacked Fort Pueblo located on the Arkansas River in eastern Colorado. Meanwhile, routes were being sought for construction of a transcontinental railroad, causing further infringement and conflicts in Ute land. John C. Fremont attempted crossing the San Juan Mountains through the heart of Ute country in 1848, searching for a suitable rail route to the Pacific Ocean. Fremont and his party met with disaster that winter and had to be rescued by mountain men from Taos. Though no route for a railroad was discovered, a route for mineral hungry explorers to enter the San Juans was popularized.

The U.S. government created the first Ute reservation boundaries in 1863 when Chief Ouray and other leaders signed a treaty which guaranteed them the western part of Colorado. Eastern Colorado was experiencing an influx of settlers, and the U.S. government wanted to eliminate Indian occupation in that area. It was the Brunot Agreement of 1873, however, which removed the Utes from the San Juan Mountains and the Weminuche Wilderness. Gold was discovered at Baker's Park, the location of present-day Silverton, in the 1870's, and miners demanded ownership of the high country. Baker's Park had been a

Ute summer camping site for centuries. The Brunot Agreement, negotiated by Felix Brunot and Otto Mears of railroad building fame, with Chief Ouray of the Ute people, further restricted the Utes' hunting territory, limiting them to the valley lands south of the San Juans. Thousands of miners began to rush into the mineral rich mountains, and further encroachments occurred in the valleys as communities like Durango were established and settlers claimed squatter's rights to the land along river valleys.

Attempts were made to change the Ute lifestyle and train them as farmers. This they resisted. In what came to be known as the Meeker incident in 1879, an Indian agent was shot for attempting to force them to plow the earth, their mother. The Utes were nature worshipers who believed

Chief Ouray and Chipeta ca. 1860's
*Courtesy of the La Plata County Historical Society*

that all animals, plants, trees, rivers and rocks have spirit, and the sun is their source of energy. The earth was not to be broken by a plow. This was the final blow that caused their demise as wilderness hunters and resulted in complete removal from the San Juans and the Weminuche Wilderness.

In 1881, special allotments of privately held land were made to individual Indian families in an attempt to break up bands and assimilate the Utes into Anglo culture. These lands are essentially their home today. The Weeminuche band refused the allotments and subsequently were relocated in the western corner of Colorado near Towoac.

PROTECTING PREHISTORIC INFORMATION

Today the U.S. Forest Service is severely limited in its ability to inventory, evaluate and protect prehistoric cultural sites in the Weminuche Wilderness. Archeological funds too often must be spent conducting cultural resource surveys on forest land where timber sales, fence line construction or prescribed burns occur. Only three archeologists are presently available to conduct such work on the San Juan/Rio Grande Forests and the Weminuche Wilderness.

Protection of cultural resources is desperately needed as recreational activities increase. Prehistoric campsites and trails are becoming less recognizable with time, and illegal collection of surface artifacts and projectile points by back country visitors destroys the evidence needed for research. A policy of "benign neglect" has left archeological sites undisclosed to the general public, which is good; yet the unscrupulous person still seeks them out.

Protection and preservation of all archeological resources on public lands and Indian lands is mandated by the Archeological Resources Protection Act of 1979. Congress, recognizing the increasing loss of archeological resources because of commercial value, prohibited the excavation, removal, damage or defacement of any archeological resource on public lands and established a severe financial penalty as well as imprisonment for any person who knowingly violates the law.

Another issue which haunts archeologists is that of managing a growing conflict between recreational use and traditional cultural places. Many landmarks in the Weminuche Wilderness, such as La Ventanna and the Rio Grande Pyramid, probably had spiritual or ceremonial significance to Native Americans. The privacy of those sites is now compromised by non-Indian wilderness users who "re-create" near them. Their sacredness must be considered by each of us as we visit these remote areas and use them for our purposes. The cultural history of indigenous people who lived near or traveled in the Weminuche Wilderness adds to our experience as we travel through their ancestral hunting grounds. Knowing their story deepens our appreciation of the Weminuche Wilderness and reminds us of changes we have wrought in just 300 years.

# 4

# Anglo Settlement Near the Weminuche

The rugged peaks of the San Juan Mountains lured Europeans in search of riches as early as the sixteenth century. In 1541 Coronado paraded across their southern foothills reportedly accompanied by as many as 350 Spaniards and 800 Indians. The conquistador was convinced that great wealth could be found on the North American continent, but his long journey turned up nothing. By the eighteenth century strong Spanish settlements such as Santa Fe and Taos had been established in the New Mexico Territory claimed by Spain. In 1765 the governor of this territory  dispatched a party to prospect for metals and fur trapping under Juan Maria de Rivera. This was the first formal expedition sent out specifically to the San Juan Mountains. Rivera circled around their western edge toward the La Plata Range and traveled up the Dolores River drainage. He did not approach the area of the Weminuche Wilderness.

Land grants made by the Mexican government in the nineteenth century brought permanent Spanish settlers into the valleys of the San Juan Mountains, but prior to this Spanish miners and traders traveled regularly to the mountains from Taos, New Mexico, seeking wealth. Evidence of Spanish presence in the high San Juans and the Weminuche Wilderness has been found in carved dates and crosses left on trees, according to San Juan National Forest history.[11] Many place names  tell of their presence. Vallecito, meaning "little valley," was named by the Spanish because of the beautiful open section just above the confluence of the Vallecito and Los Piños Rivers. La Ventanna, a window-like rock formation overlooking the Ute Creek drainage, was a landmark for their travel routes. Old tree blazes left by the Spanish along the Continental Divide have been scientifically dated to around 1750.

Legends remain of a rich lode between Vallecito and Ute Creeks  under La Ventanna that was supposedly abandoned  by Spanish miners because of a Ute Indian attack. Evidence of smelting works near the Dolores River drainage and an old Spanish coin found near Howardsville on Cunningham Creek above Silverton suggest Spanish miners ranged widely throughout the area. Silverton historian Allen Nossaman has published three extensive volumes[12] that share these tidbits and others about early explorations in the area of the Weminuche Wilderness.

U. S. Forest Service records also tell of a group of 300 Frenchmen who rode into the San Juan Mountains from St. Louis, Missouri, just prior to the French Revolution of 1789, bringing supplies with them. They placer mined near Treasure Mountain and Summitville, located south of Wolf Creek Pass. They, too, reportedly abandoned their stashes of gold when attacked by Utes, and legends still claim their gold lies hidden, awaiting a finder someday. Summitville, located high in the mountains at 11,000' elevation, would later become a thriving mining center from which much rich ore was taken. The highest mining town in Colorado, this community in the 1880's had a population that exceeded 1,000 residents with fourteen saloons located in the city limits.[13]

Serious efforts by U.S. citizens to find wealth in the San Juan Mountains began in the second half of the nineteenth century after the California gold rush. Prior to this, however, wealth was sought in the form of animal furs. American mountain men began traveling north from Taos on what would become known as the Old Spanish Trail, trespassing on Mexican territory in search of beaver pelts. In 1831, an American contingent of sixty men led by Commodore William G. Walton rode north from Taos to trap beaver.[14] They had been sent by the St. Louis Fur Company. U. S. Forest Service employees have found evidence of such trapping efforts along streams in the Weminuche Wilderness. History also tells of an early group of mountain men under the leadership of Antoine Robidoux journeying south from present day Delta, Colorado, to trap beaver in the upper streams of the San Juan Mountains in the 1820's. Robidoux constructed a fort near Delta which would later be burned by the Ute Indians.

Such early activity in southern Colorado, which became a territory of the U.S. government in 1848, stirred the interest of a country anxious to build a transcontinental railroad to connect California with the east coast. In late 1848 Captain John C. Fremont led a group of thirty-six men with one hundred-twenty mules to explore the San Juan Mountains, looking for a rail route across the Rocky Mountains. Fremont, guided by mountain man Jim Baker, traveled up the Rio Grande River from Del Norte, Colorado, and into the San Luis Valley. When fall turned to winter he encountered increasingly bad weather as he attempted to cross a high, snow packed ridge in the La Garita Range. His expedition became snowbound around Christmas, and the men survived by eating the mules that died. Some members of the group retreated, dropping into the San Luis Valley and returning to Taos to form a rescue party for those left behind. Fremont lost eleven men and all of his mules on the expedition. A permanent exhibit recalling

Highland Mary Mine near Silverton, Colorado
*Courtesy of the San Juan County Historical Society*

Fremont's trip in the San Juan Mountains is located at the Rio Grande County Museum in Del Norte, Colorado. Starvation Gulch in the Weminuche Wilderness is sometimes credited as the place Fremont met his Waterloo, but recent study of journals and a research expedition of 1929 have proven that wrong. Starvation Gulch, located just south of Beartown is the site of nineteenth century mining efforts that failed. Miners of the Bear Creek district, discouraged by their efforts, called the area "starvation gulch."

When gold was discovered in 1860 at Baker's Park, named after Charles Baker who was the first American to view the wide open Animas River Valley as a potential settlement area, word of the discovery spread among prospectors. Historian Nossaman tells of the use of newspapers to publicize the country and lure people into the Baker's Park area. Though the Civil War staved off a major onslaught of miners for a dozen years, by 1874 the town of Silverton was platted on two 160-acre homesteads filed on by Thomas Blair and William Kearns. An enterprising group of businessmen organized the Silverton Town Company and incorporated the community in 1876. By that time Silverton already had 200 structures and a population of 600 people in its city limits.

Southwestern Colorado was opened up to permanent American settlement by the Brunot Agreement of 1873. The treaty called for removal of the

Cairns left by surveyors and wilderness travelers dot ridgelines
*Courtesy of B. J. Boucher*

Ute Indians who were fighting to keep their homelands from Anglo occupation. Publicity of rich strikes in the San Juan Mountains brought miners flocking in from Denver, Colorado Springs, Leadville and other mining centers in the state. Roads were needed for the oxen and mule trains to transport supplies to miners and settlers. So entrepreneurs like Otto Mears built toll roads around the circumference of the San Juan Mountains. Mears, a Russian immigrant, was responsible for opening toll roads and railroads to many southern Colorado communities. Because they were privately constructed, the owners of supply trains had to pay to use them. In 1874 a road was completed from Del Norte to Lake City. Shortly thereafter, another was built connecting Lake City to Silverton over Stony Pass. This road skirted the eastern boundary of the Weminuche Wilderness just below Beartown and followed Cunningham Gulch to the mining community of Howardsville, then to Silverton. Stage routes would travel these roads, bringing mail and settlers to the area. Much of the route is now a four-wheel drive road. The Stony Pass road was heavily traveled until the railroad connecting Durango to Silverton was completed in 1882. After that its use diminished. Many wayside stops that were thriving businesses for half a dozen years disappeared quickly. Cathy Kindquist's book *Stony Pass: The Tumbling and Impetuous Trail* [15] tells an exciting story of travel across Stony Pass in the 1870's.

Several surveying groups entered the San Juan Mountains in the 1870's seeking to establish geographic mapping of the area, one by the Army Corps of Engineers in 1873. In 1874 the U.S. government commissioned an expedition by the U.S. Geological and Geographical Survey of the Territories. Under the direction of Ferdinand V. Hayden, the expedition was supposed to document the nature of the mountainous terrain and its potential mineral resources. Hayden set up triangulation stations, using Howardsville as his base for supplies, and surveyed peaks throughout the area, naming some of them after members of the survey team. Endlich Mesa is named after the geologist who accompanied the group, Frederick M. Endlich. Wilson Peak is named after Allan D. Wilson, another team member.[16] Mt. Sneffels, west of Ouray, was named after an Icelandic volcano of Jules Vernes fame, the Snafellsjokull. Snowden Peak was named for Colonel F.M. Snowden of the Silverton Town Company.[17] Hayden and his men traveled through sections of the Weminuche Wilderness, probably climbing some of the peaks they named. They left rock cairns still visible along many of the ridges. The observations and altitude measurements of the Hayden expedition today form the nucleus of the USGS triangle maps we use when traveling in the Weminuche. The Hayden group, like most early groups in the area, withstood Ute Indian attacks, since the Utes still roamed their native lands despite the Brunot Agreement. Forest records recount how Hayden was attacked just outside the city limits of Durango near the Durango Reservoir.

The year 1874 was a momentous one in the Colorado territory, with the counties of La Plata, Hinsdale and Rio Grande all being organized. Other counties that encompass part of the San Juan Mountains and Weminuche Wilderness were organized shortly thereafter--San Juan County in 1878, Archuleta County in 1885 and Mineral County in 1893. Colorado officially became the thirty-eighth state in the union in 1878.

All of the settlement activity around and in the San Juan Mountains necessitated a military outpost on the western slope, and in 1879 the Fort Lewis military reservation was established in Pagosa Springs. *A History of Pagosa Springs* by John M. Motter tells the story of military activities and settlement in that area.[18] Four companies of infantry and one all black cavalry troop were stationed at the new fort. The military post remained in Pagosa Springs for only two years. Then it was moved to the present Fort Lewis site on the La Plata River just south of the La Plata Mountain Range. Lands that had been part of the Fort Lewis military reservation were opened up for settlement. The army post on the La Plata River was abandoned permanently in 1891, becoming a school and agricultural experiment station in the twentieth century.

Durango, Colorado ca. 1889
*Courtesy of the La Plata Historical Society*

When a group of eager businessmen saw the potential for a thriving community in the open Animas River valley forty-five miles south of Silverton, they struck a deal with the Denver and Rio Grande Railway to build a route from their site to the Silverton community where wealth was being mined from the surrounding mountains. Thus Durango came into being. Though Animas City, two miles north of Durango, had already been established, its refusal to "play ball" with the railroad owners and donate land for their use meant it would ultimately be absorbed by Durango. Durango became the central hub for area mining activities after its incorporation in 1880. Fort Lewis College historian Duane Smith's books[19] tell of early Durango days and of one William J. Palmer, the founder and first president of the Denver and Rio Grande Railroad. Palmer was a community developer, and it was his early planning that established the parks, church sites, residential and business districts in Durango. Palmer not only brought the railroad to Durango; he was responsible for bringing the smelter, which became the city's major industry for the next fifty years. He also helped open the coal mines in the area, so integral to the railroad. By 1885 a census of Durango showed 2,254 people living within the city limits.

Though a toll road connecting Durango and Silverton had been constructed over the rough terrain from Coalbank Pass to Rockwood and then along the Indian trails that skirted the Animas River to Silverton, the railroad took over this route, basically following its right-of-way. The railroad reached Rockwood before winter halted its construction in 1881. It was completed to

Early railroad construction
*Courtesy of the USFS*

Silverton by July of 1882, and the lucrative smelting industry that gave Durango its firm hold on success was begun.

Another toll route constructed over Molas Pass between Durango and Silverton would ultimately become a public highway when the state assumed responsibility for its upgrade. A toll road was constructed to link Durango to Pagosa Springs in 1876. The stage route followed this and other early roads into the area. Pagosa Springs was connected to Del Norte on the east side of the Continental Divide by a route over Windy Pass and around the east side of Treasure Mountain near Summitville. This was the major highway route over the San Juan Mountains from east to west until a state highway was later built over Wolf Creek Pass. There is no complete history of these early roads, though the San Juan National Forest commissioned a full study of the route connecting Rockwood to Rico in the western area of the forest in 1985.[20]

Durangoans began prospecting for gold in the high reaches of the Weminuche Wilderness at the same time Silverton miners were digging their glory holes along Cunningham Gulch in the vicinity of the Highland Mary Lakes, Cunningham Gulch and Red Mountain. Frank Trimble of Trimble Hots Springs fame prospected in the Needle Mountains, according to forest records, and a community called Hewitt, now known as Logtown, grew up near his mine in 1879. Logtown, located above City Reservoir in the Weminuche Wilderness, is close to the head waters of the Florida River. When word spread of Trimble's

The author in Chicago Basin
*Courtesy of B. J. Boucher*

success, people flocked to the Needle Mountains. Because Logtown was so inaccessible, prospecting could occur only in the summer months. The community became large enough that it actually had its own post office for a while. Supplies were delivered from Durango to Needleton by train after the railroad was completed, and then carried by pack mules up Needle Creek, through Chicago Basin and over the pass to Logtown. Chicago Basin became an active camp during this time. Old mining holes dot the mountains near Columbine and Trimble Passes, and foundations of old cabins can still be seen along Needle Creek. The cost of hauling in supplies and packing out ore were enormous, so mining efforts at Logtown ended quickly, particularly when no rich discoveries were made.

Another mining area in the western reaches of the Weminuche Wilderness near Cave Basin was also prospected from Durango. Ute Indian Chief Weasel Skin, according to San Juan National Forest history, guided a group of miners into this basin above Emerald Lake, but again, no major ore discovery was ever made.

Prospectors on the eastern slopes of the San Juan Mountains sought pay dirt from Summitville, located south of Wolf Creek Pass, to Beartown near Stony Pass. Creede became a mining boomtown in the 1890's when Nicholas C. Creede and his partners found gold in the mountains above the Rio Grande River. A wild community with its population reaching several thousand at its height, Creede reportedly "never slept." The panic of 1893 when silver was demonetized dealt Creede a severe blow, however.[21]

Beartown, established in 1893, was connected to both Creede and Silverton by a stage line. Severe weather limited Beartown's population, though it, like many mining settlements that were later abandoned, had a postal service. Numerous mining communities sprang up on the eastern slopes of the San Juans and were ultimately abandoned as the costs for mining increased and limited quantities of precious metals were found. The national panic of 1893 and resulting drop in silver prices contributed ultimately to the decline of mining throughout Southern Colorado.

Though the search for precious metals in the San Juan Mountains continued into the twentieth century, little ore was actually taken from the area now included in the Weminuche Wilderness. The early prospectors "lived on hope and died in poverty," says Durango historian Duane Smith. The high inaccessible mountains and short summers presented challenging difficulties that even the heartiest succumbed to ultimately. Permanent settlers would be much more attracted to the grazing industry that began developing simultaneously with mining.

RANCHING IN THE SAN JUANS AND WEMINUCHE WILDERNESS

Following close behind the miners came farming settlers. Families homesteaded in the river valleys and the prime bottom lands south, east and west of the San Juan Mountains. Though miners utilized the abundant wild game, ranches and farms became the permanent source of food. Much of the land was initially held by squatter's rights, and as mining declined ranching and farming became mainstays in the local economy.

Large scale grazing in the San Juan Basin started in 1878 when Ike Cox arrived in the area with large herds of cattle driven up from Texas. This was a time of open range, since national forest reserves had not yet been designated. Forest records say that Cox's range extended from Cedar Hill, New Mexico, on the east to Bluff, Utah, on the west, and north into the San Juan Mountains. His cattle grazed over 8,000 square miles of mountain and valley lands. Cox was very powerful, since the largest ranching operation could control the most land, but disputes over grazing rights were frequent. The H.D. operation near Bayfield was considered only mid-size compared to Cox's spread. When southern Colorado

Early cattle branding operation
*Courtesy of the USFS*

was opened up to homesteading, more conflicts occurred over land as farmers split and fenced the open range.

The first sheepmen arrived in 1882, and range wars broke out over grazing in the San Juan Mountains. Forest records report an imaginary line called Missionary Ridge being drawn in the Piedra drainage near Pagosa Springs, with sheep grazing allowed to the west and cattle to the east of the line. Huge herds of sheep and cattle grazed in the mountains each summer. Prior to the establishment of the San Juan Forest Reserve in 1905, a report written by one Coert DuBois[22] estimated that 268,100 sheep and approximately 19,000 head of cattle were grazing in the area. By 1910 almost 40,000 cattle were in the area, and that number or more continued until after the Taylor Grazing Act of 1934 established restrictions and directed improvements on public lands. In 1930, San Juan National Forest records reported 41,968 cattle and 216,684 sheep grazing on the forest. These figures do not include calves and lambs.

Though cattle are generally restricted to grazing below timberline, sheep were trailed by Spanish and Navajo herders into the most remote areas of the Weminuche Wilderness. Aspen art carved by the early herders has been found in different locations. Archeologist Phil Duke[23] has documented early carvings in the Elk Creek drainage where large flocks of sheep were brought in by train each summer.[24] Grazing on the forests began as soon as the snows melted and continued until fall weather pushed the animals to lower elevations.

Early forest rangers who were hired to manage the newly created national forest in 1905 worked hard to settle disputes between ranchers, but only after years of effort was any systematic plan established which clearly directed where ranchers could graze their animals and the number they were allowed on an allotment. Grazing was restricted on the forest for a period of time around 1938 because of the severe damage caused by overuse. San Juan National Forest rangers and the Civilian Conservation Corps (CCC) began rehabilitation at that time, reseeding some areas, developing check dams to control erosion and building fences and water projects to restrict animal movement. The allotment and permit system developed by the Forest Service designated certain sections of public land for use by ranchers who qualified for grazing permits only if they owned private land to which the animals could be moved for winter grazing. Ranchers were also assessed fees per animal for each month it grazed on the forests. This arrangement of animal unit months (AUMs) and fees still exists today.[25]

Ranchers developed cattle and sheep associations early in the twentieth century that helped resolve grazing disputes and established brand identifications for animals on the forest. Stock driveways into the San Juan Mountains were constructed by CCC and Forest Service workers, and by the 1940's these became the designated entryways for animals onto the forest. Old yellow markers designating these routes can still be found in the Weminuche Wilderness. As herds reached their allotted range area, they were turned into their grazing section and controlled by fences. These sixteen-foot or wider routes were located along the divides between drainages, often climbing straight up steep inclines. The driveways became muddy paths during rain, and dust beds when the season was dry. Significant vegetation changes occurred as a result of so many animals following the same routes, and those changes are still obvious today. As many as a half dozen driveways entered the Weminuche Wilderness, and sections of them have since become hiking trails, such as the Four Mile Stock Driveway north of Pagosa Springs and the La Garita Stock Driveway near Creede.

Not until after World War II were significant reductions made in the number of animals allowed on many grazing allotments on the San Juan National Forest and Weminuche Wilderness. As forest management practices strengthened and more rangers were hired, sustainability became the primary goal of the U.S.

Forest Service. Over the years animal numbers were reduced and rotation plans developed which limited their length of stay on any one section.

Today, grazing is still permitted on certain sections of the Weminuche Wilderness because of historical use as specified by the Wilderness Act of 1964. Though no new allotments can be added, the Act specifically says "the grazing of livestock where previously established prior to the effective date of this Act, shall be permitted to continue subject to such reasonable regulations as are deemed necessary by the Secretary of Agriculture." No cattle allotments exist on the San Juan side of the Weminuche Wilderness, but seven sheep allotments are still actively grazed each summer. These are located in the areas of Endlich Mesa, Virginia Gulch, Tank Creek, Burnt Timber Trail, the Highland Mary Lakes, Crater Lake and the upper Piedra area.

Currently sheep that summer in the Weminuche Wilderness are assessed a fee of thirty-one cents per AUM of grazing, and cattle are assessed $1.55 per AUM. These rates are determined by the U.S. Congress and can vary from year to year. Twenty-five percent of the funds collected remain with the forest where the animals graze, and are used for management and forage improvement.

Today allotment permits are issued to ranchers for a ten-year period and are subject to modification as forest planning requires change. They are automatically renewed upon expiration and after evaluation. These allotments are considered a major asset by ranchers. They can be inherited or acquired by purchase of the livestock permitted on the specific allotment along with the base property used to support the animals off the forest. Since 1980 the number of animals allowed on allotments has continued to decrease, and detailed management plans are now developed for each range area.

Efforts are made by the San Juan/Rio Grande National Forests to balance the numbers and times of use with sustainable forest conditions. Today's management strategy requires that sheep and cattle be moved to different grazing areas on a regular basis so that vegetation is not heavily impacted. Sheep are allowed on the Weminuche Wilderness each year around the fifteenth of July, and they are removed by mid-September. Because of the vast amount of forage in the high alpine meadows, the U.S. Forest Service reports no major conflict for forage between domestic and wildlife grazing. Sheep are restricted, however, from grazing in areas where elk concentrate in the summer. One dramatic problem with wildlife has developed, and that is the possible interaction between big horn and domestic sheep herds. There is a strong suspicion among biologists that a bacterial infection called *pasteurella haemolytica* which causes a lung disease similar to pneumonia, is transmitted by domestic sheep to the wild animals. Since researchers are divided on this question, domestic sheep have been restricted from areas known to be inhabited by big horns, and the Colorado Division of Wildlife (CDOW) does not transplant big horn sheep in areas now grazed by domestic animals.

At the present time there are approximately 7,000 ewes accompanied by their lambs on the San Juan side of the Weminuche Wilderness each summer. This number continues to decrease as the market demand for sheep diminishes. Additionally, as allotments are vacated on the wilderness, the U.S. Forest Service maintains them in that state. Fewer and fewer domestic animals are seen in the Weminuche Wilderness as time passes. The development into subdivisions of private ranch lands and river valleys that previously offered winter grazing plays a significant role today in eliminating ranching.

Big Horn Sheep
Robert A. Watson ©

TOURISM AND THE WEMINUCHE WILDERNESS

There has always been a scarcity of accommodations for visitors and newcomers to the San Juan Basin. Early mining settlements were jammed with boarding houses and temporary living spaces for the transient population. In 1938 San Juan National Forest Ranger Lewis E. Coughlin, a wildlife specialist, lamented the visit of Will Rogers to Durango and his subsequent newspaper column praising the town. Coughlin said in his report, "When the roads are made there will follow discovery of the area by the Great American Tourist, who will arrive in mobs seeking recreation, sport and investment opportunities, even if he has only $7.00, ten kids and five dogs".[26] Coughlin's prediction has proven true, and tourism is the major source of economic support in many Southwestern Colorado towns.

Early hunting camp
*Courtesy of the La Plata County Historical Society*

Sportsmen were visiting the forest long before it was set aside as public land, and the deer and elk population were decimated by early settlers who hunted indiscriminately or by suppliers who carried food to mining camps. One professional hunter supplying meat to Leadville in 1878 claimed to have marketed 35,000 pounds of elk meat during a three-month period.[27] Antelope and big horn sheep that had lived along the Rio Grande River south of Creede disappeared as their winter grazing areas were settled by homesteaders. In 1906 after the Colorado legislature decreed an end to all elk hunting in the state, San Juan National Forest Supervisor H. N. Wheeler recommended that a game refuge be established in Hermosa Creek north of Durango to protect the small herd still living there. Word came back that the president could not set aside game refuges. Shortly thereafter the elk completely disappeared and had to be reintroduced, with herds brought in from Wyoming by CDOW in 1913. As populations increased, elk hunting became a legal sport again.

Hot springs on the eastern slopes of the San Juan Mountains were discovered by early settlers, and they were developed into popular vacation spots, particularly as rail and stage lines made them accessible.[28] Forest records tell of tourists coming from Texas, Oklahoma, New Mexico and Kansas in great numbers to erect summer cabins in the Rio Grande River valley in the early twentieth century. Fishing on the Rio Grande was also a big draw, and by the beginning of the twentieth century native trout had been fished out of many streams, and stocking was necessary.

In 1917, a group of Pagosa Springs businessmen formed a rod and gun club to promote good hunting and fishing. The group developed small lakes on the San Juan National Forest, constructed cabins nearby and stocked the lakes with fish. The club was active for ten years, but with a land exchange in 1932 the sportsmen lost their hunting preserve. Thereafter, local sportsmen became active promoting the increase of fish and game resources. The introduction of exotic fish species in wilderness waters began in the late nineteenth century when individuals would transport fingerlings to the high country. Rainbow trout, the most prevalent and popular of Colorado's game fish, were introduced to the state in 1882 from California.[29] This stocking practice was adopted by CDOW many years before the 1964 Wilderness Act established protection for native species, and it continues today as historically acceptable. In an agreement with the International Association of Fish and Wildlife Agencies the U. S. Forest Service manages the habitat while CDOW is responsible for maintaining the fish population. Today, CDOW almost exclusively stocks native cuthroats in the Weminuche Wilderness.

Improved highways along with railroad lines and spurs to small towns opened the San Juan Mountains to many visitors. With the completion of the new U.S. Highway 160 across Wolf Creek Pass in 1937, tourism opportunities grew. Campgrounds at West Fork and Wolf Creek on the western slopes of the

Automobile on Wolf Creek Pass ca. 1920
*Courtesy of the La Plata County Historical Society*

mountains were completed a year later. The Civilian Conservation Corps (CCC) developed trails and built campgrounds for visitors. Vallecito Campground was constructed in 1942, shortly after the Vallecito Reservoir was completed, and it became a popular haven for summer visitors.

Professional outfitters began collecting fees for guiding hunters into the forests of the San Juan Mountains early in the twentieth century. In 1942 the American Forestry Association conducted its first trail ride, carrying a group through the Vallecito country. During World War II tourism increased as America's love affair with the automobile grew, and with the end of the war it increased again. The Sierra Club joined the guiding activities in the San Juans in 1957, bringing hikers into the Vallecito and Chicago Basin areas. Today professional guiding and outfitting services continue to carry many visitors into the Weminuche Wilderness.

Skiing on the San Juan Forest began in 1948 with construction of Stoner Ski Area near Dolores. In that same year Coal Bank Hill highway (U.S. 550) was completed, offering a good auto route into the region from the north. Purgatory Ski Area was developed in 1965, and has continued to grow since its establishment.

The movie industry added to the discovery of the San Juan/Rio Grande National Forests by tourists. The movie "Sand" was filmed in Hermosa Park near Purgatory in 1948 and "A Ticket to Tomahawk" in Silverton shortly thereafter. Since then many filmmakers have used the San Juan Mountains for a movie location.

A 1966 forest report records 2,240,000 visits to the San Juan National Forest. The writer says "[Tourists] did their part to keep this region green--by bringing money." Today the visitor days in the greater San Juan Basin far exceeds the 1966 number, and as many as 150,000 people enter the Weminuche Wilderness annually.

WATER DEVELOPMENT AND THE WEMINUCHE WILDERNESS

Early settlers in the valleys that surround the Weminuche Wilderness very quickly discovered the importance of capturing and controlling the waters that flowed from the high alpine country. Private groups created ditch companies and began diverting water from traditional stream beds into ditches and reservoirs for use in the valleys surrounding the San Juan Mountains.

Durango City Reservoir
*Courtesy of B. J. Boucher*

In 1882 a pumping plant was installed to transport water from the Animas River to the small reservoir located just east of Durango. This was the beginning of water diversion projects that would ultimately be developed throughout the region. In 1901 a pipeline to transport water to Durango was installed from the Florida River. The first power plant in the region was completed in 1890 just east of the mouth of Lake Fork Creek north of Silverton. Known as the Ames Hydroelectric Plant, it provided power to Telluride. Tacoma Plant was constructed by the Western Colorado Power Company in 1906 to bring electrical power to Durango.

Early agricultural needs for water required the building of many ditches and water diversion projects. Williams Reservoir (now known as City Reservoir) located near the head waters of the Florida River in the Weminuche, was built for this purpose around 1902. The Williams Ditch Company, builder of the reservoir, filed for the water rights in 1899, then sold them to the city of Durango for municipal water. The city paid $4,000 to the U.S. government for the land surrounding the lake, and $60,000 to the ditch company for the water rights.[30] Durango still owns this in-holding and the water rights.

Numerous high country lakes in the Weminuche Wilderness were augmented and shorelines were changed in order to create water holding facilities for livestock. The Raben Lohr Ditch located near Weminuche Pass was constructed in 1935 to divert water to the Rio Grande and San Luis Valleys from the western watershed and the Pine River.[31] The Fuchs Ditch, also located in the same area, was constructed in 1935, water rights having been appropriated by the ditch company the previous year. Irrigation waters were also diverted to the San Luis Valley through the Don LaFont Ditches located at the head waters of the West Fork of the Piedra River and Turkey Creek. These waters were appropriated in 1940.

Dam construction on rivers began to reshape the flow of waters from the Weminuche high country. Vallecito Dam which captures water from the Los Piños River was begun in 1938 and completed in 1941. The capacity of the reservoir was set at 126,000 acre feet, and the water was designated for use by the Pine River Irrigation Ditch Company. The irrigated valleys were planted in grasses to help sustain the cattle industry. The CCC, while working on the dam, constructed roads in the Vallecito area and built the Vallecito/Pine Guard Station located above the reservoir in 1940. They cleared much of the area around Vallecito Reservoir between 1941 and 1944, constructing the campgrounds that became very popular with tourists. Lemon Reservoir, which captures the Florida River water flowing from the wilderness, was begun in 1936 and completed shortly thereafter.

Tacoma Power Plant ca. 1915
*Courtesy of the La Plata County Historical Society*

Though the Wilderness Act of 1964 prevents the development of additional water projects on the Weminuche Wilderness, these early appropriations remain in effect. Today the watershed of this area has become a political issue, with disputes still erupting between Colorado and the U.S. government over who should manage its flow. Walking beside high alpine streams today, we seldom recognize that they carry "liquid gold" whose value will be immeasurable in the twenty-first century.

# Part II

# Designating and Caring for Public Lands

"*Wilderness* is now -- for much of North America -- places that are formally set aside on public lands - Forest Service or Bureau of Land Management holdings or state and federal parks. Some tiny but critical tracts are held by private nonprofit groups like The Nature Conservancy or the Trust for Public Land. These are the shrines saved from all the land that was once known and lived on by the original people, the little bits left as they were, the last little places where intrinsic nature totally wails, blooms, nests, glints away. They make up only 2 percent of the land of the United States." Gary Snyder, *The Practice of the Wild*, North Point Press, 1990.

# 5

# Forest and Wilderness Designations

Mining, grazing and logging brought numerous settlers to Southwest Colorado, and they were leaving major scars on the forests of the San Juan Mountains. Federal forest reserves were first set aside by the U.S. government in 1891, in an effort to preserve watersheds and timberlands brutalized by American westward expansion. Management was non-existent, however, since the Washington, D.C. headquarters were so far away. Recognizing the importance of conserving public lands, President Theodore Roosevelt created the present National Forest system in February, 1905, and appointed Gifford Pinchot as U.S. Forest Service Chief to establish management operations on the forests. Four months later the San Juan and Montezuma Forest Reserves in Southern Colorado were designated. Within six months, active steps were taken to hire a ground crew located near their boundaries.

Forest Service records tell of numerous boundary and name changes before the San Juan and Rio Grande National Forests became established as we know them today.[32] The original San Juan National Forest extended from San Miguel and Disappointment Valleys in the Dolores River drainage eastward through the San Juan River Basin and into the San Luis Valley. The first Forest headquarters were in Durango, in the 700 block of Main Avenue across the street from Gradens Mercantile Company. In 1906, shortly after his appointment, the new supervisor of the San Juan National Forest was moved to Monte Vista on the eastern slope of the San Juan Mountains, and further additions were made to the western side of the San Juan National Forest. At the same time the public lands east of the Continental Divide were consolidated into another forest, the Rio Grande National Forest. The public lands of western La Plata, Montezuma and Dolores Counties were renamed the Montezuma National Forest, and the forests around Pagosa Springs became the San Juan National Forest. Such changes were to continue for some while before the boundaries would be established as we know them today.

In 1911, President William Taft, by executive order, created the Durango National Forest from portions of the Montezuma Forest and lands surrounding Durango and the public lands around Pagosa Springs continued as the San Juan National Forest. Finally in 1918 the Durango and San Juan National Forests were consolidated, and the executive order making this official was signed by President Woodrow Wilson in 1920. The Montezuma National Forest surrounding Mancos and Dolores remained separate until 1947 when it was finally reconsolidated with the San Juan Forest. Gross acreage of this 1947 public holding was 2,101,247 acres. Extending across five counties, the Forest had nine ranger districts overseeing management at that time: Animas, Engineer, Pine, Piedra, Pagosa, Mancos, Dolores, Rico and Glade. Today there are three ranger districts: Columbine, Dolores and Pagosa Springs.

Local cow punchers or sons of miners and prospectors who knew the region were hired as rangers on the newly established forest lands, and if they proved trustworthy they advanced rapidly in the ranks. Charles B. Mack, a logger before being hired by the San Juan National Forest in 1908, advanced to assistant supervisor before retiring. The first supervisor of the San Juan National Forest was Frank C. Spencer, appointed in 1906. Since the U.S. Forest Service was a new division in the Department of Agriculture, Forest Chief Gifford Pinchot quickly transferred experienced rangers to newly created forests. Spencer was replaced within six months by H. N. Wheeler who lasted for a year before being

Early Forest Service Ranger
*Courtesy of the SJNF*

transferred to another Colorado Forest. Wheeler would later become the Chief of Information for the U.S. Forest Service in Washington, D.C.

Horses were as much a part of the early Forest Service staff as people. Though Wheeler was only with the San Juan National Forest for a year, it was his horse packing trip in the summer of 1906 that brought an additional one million acres of western Colorado into public holdings. Starting from Durango, he rode through Mancos, Mesa Verde, Dolores and into Lone Cone country over Ophir Pass, then to Silverton and back to Durango, surveying the country so he could make recommendations to Washington. The trip took approximately two weeks.

Stockmen who had ranged their animals freely across open country since arriving in the 1870's were not pleased with the creation of national forests. Supervisor Wheeler had to initiate contact with the truculent group as quickly as possible. In the summer of 1906 he called a meeting of stock men in Dolores to explain the concept of animal grazing applications. Faced with 200 stockmen, Wheeler reported he didn't bat an eye when "a man named Pat McKenna from the Disappointment country got up and announced that the first Ranger who came down in their country would be laid in the brush." Wheeler responded as recalled in his report, "If any rangers were killed, we would probably put two in the place of each one that disappeared, and furthermore, that I intended to spend a week or two during the summer in that section of the country." The cattleman backed down and invited Wheeler to stay with him. Such stories abound in the early memories collected in forest records.

Wheeler's replacement in Durango was Ernest Shaw, the first field ranger appointed to the San Juan National Forest. Shaw continued as supervisor until 1915. Shaw quickly gained a reputation as a strong leader. He was frequently involved in settling disputes between cattlemen over grazing areas. Forest records tell how in 1908 when rancher Ike Cox shot cattle rustler Bill Truby at the mouth of the Florida River, Shaw, as supervisor of the forest and one of only two employees, had to investigate the shooting. Shaw determined that Cox had shot in self-defense, verifying this by traveling to the scene from Durango on horseback and studying the tracks.

Though the concept of ranger districts on the forests was initiated by 1910, very few "on the ground" people could be hired, since funding was limited. (This is a refrain familiar to field rangers today.) To become a ranger one had to pass a written office exam that lasted a full day as well as a field exam demonstrating horse and gun skills. An early ranger, relating his many responsibilities stated, "The District Ranger is the representative of the Forest

Service and the greater part of the transactions with the public are conducted by him. These men have settled disputes, halted trespass, established plans for and supervised the carrying out of timber and grazing plans, fought the many forest fires and insect attacks that plagued them and provided the recreational facilities, roads and trails and other necessary improvements."

The ranger by necessity was a jack of all trades. In 1906, rangers were supplied with a map and a use book. With these tools they set out to enforce new management strategy on land that had previously been used freely and indiscriminately by ranchers. Supervisor Shaw commented about the book. "The use book is a good guide, but if you haven't a head of your own, you are not worth a d--- to the Forest Service."

Early rangers performed duties similar to those of today's field personnel; though specialists are now assigned to each task, one individual did everything at that time. The field ranger helped set up fire tool boxes in remote locations for fire control use. He traveled the backwoods on horse and studied burned timber conditions. He settled trespassing problems with miners and cattlemen. He rode the forest, noting potential timber sales and then presided over the sale and clean-up. During World War II, he traveled across the forest collecting scrap metal from old mining sites for the war effort. He counted cattle going on and off the forest. He became proficient on skis, using them to access remote areas during the winter. He maintained snow scales or snow measuring boards scattered over the districts, and read them monthly during the winter.

"It took a lot of chewing and spitting," reported an early ranger, " to get from one place to another," because the horse was his primary means of travel, and chewing tobacco was a staple. So was the gun.

Days were long and strenuous, and often included unexpected tasks. In the 1920's, one ranger recalled: "During a big game hunting season a few years ago, Garland Neel and I were riding down Corral Draw Canyon on the Hermosa drainage when we saw a man on a horse riding around and around on a little flat area at the mouth of a side canyon. When we came to him we found that he was a Texan and was lost. He asked if we knew where Bob Christy's camp was. We told him that we did and that he could get to it by merely following the trail down the creek. He said, 'Which way is down the creek?'"

Even after the automobile became a means of transportation on the forest, the ranger's duties involved long days and unexpected challenges. A U.S. Forest Service bulletin of 1931, as excerpted from Ranger W.I. Wilson's diary states: "July

Granite Peak Guard Station
*Courtesy of the USFS*

2, 1931 - left for--- in car at 8:00 A.M. and met some men hunting for a lost man. I joined the hunt. About 25 men on the hunt and finally found man hanging in a tree on the side of the canyon. Coroner came and took charge of body. I got to camp at 8:00 P.M. General overhead -11 hours."

Lookout towers and guard stations were constructed in remote sections of the forest as early as 1915, when the Granite Peak Guard Station was constructed nineteen miles up the Los Pinos River. The ranger who worked from the station was often joined by his family. Harry Norris, a ranger during that era, recalled: "As I remember it was the winter of 1924-25 we were stationed at the old Square Top Station, 14 miles southeast of Pagosa Springs. Our two children were small. My wife made her last trip to Pagosa the latter part of October and it was the first of May before she got to town again. The nearest neighbors were one mile over a snow road. Our only means of transportation was saddle horses. I brought in all our groceries on pack horse that winter."

In 1921 Ranger Paul Lundell who manned a fire tower deep in the forest had this to share about his experience: "One lone pine on top of hill with top cut out and wooden platform. Living quarters--one room shack at foot of tree. No lightning protection. Packed water on your back from one-half mile down the slope. Washing and bathing held to a minimum."

Denver & Rio Grande Rail Road ca. 1880's
*Courtesy of the La Plata County Historical Society*

The Rio Grande National Forest on the eastern slopes of the San Juan Mountains, having officially been established as a separate entity to the San Juan National Forest in July, 1908, also experienced difficulties curtailing overgrazing and logging similar to the San Juan. Most of the land in the eastern valleys of the San Juan Mountains was patented before the Forest was designated. Heavy logging of Douglas fir and ponderosa pine trees for railroad ties and mining timbers began in the 1880's. Rio Grande records report that "lumber operators cut what they wanted and how they wished without any interference or regulations. They made no attempt to acquire title to timber lands. They simply moved their sawmill into the selected area and started to cut. In many instances, only the clear logs were taken and anything with limbs was not skidded or sawed; in other words they not only high-graded the stand, but also high-graded the logs."[33]

The railroad from eastern Colorado was built to Antonito on the Colorado State line in 1880, and then connected with Durango by 1883. It extended to Creede by 1891, and spur lines were built to other small communities. Railroads opened valleys for settlement and played a key role in resource extraction before public lands were established.

Large herds of sheep spread across the Rio Grande National Forest during summer months as early as the 1860's, and overgrazing was a fact of life. Spanish herders from the New Mexico Territory drove sheep and cattle into the valleys and forests long before Southern Colorado was settled. The first law

Sheep in the San Juan National Forest
*Courtesy of the SJNF*

placed upon the statute books of Colorado concerning the grazing industry was passed by the territorial legislature in 1871. It prohibited the trailing of cattle and sheep from New Mexico into Southern Colorado for grazing purposes. A statewide cattlemen's association was formed that same year to help with stock registration and legal round ups on open range. Even after allotments designating specific areas were established, one early forest employee explained the challenge of controlled grazing in this way: "On the Rio Grande Forest we had a sheep man, Loren Sylvester, who had strong ideas how to get ahead in this world. He let his large flocks go wherever he pleased. If he got caught off his allotted range, he paid the customary grazing fee; if he did not get caught, he had the grass in any event."[34]

Civil Conservation Corps (CCC) workers constructed roads, ranger stations, reservoirs, water systems and fences across the Rio Grande Forest in the 1930's. They also worked with range revegetation, rodent control and poisonous plant eradication. Seventy-five percent of the men who worked with the CCC out of the Blanco station, located south of Pagosa Springs, were of Spanish descent.[35] Irrigation ditches and water facilities such as the Rio Grande Reservoir were constructed to control the water from the Weminuche Wilderness by private ditch companies soon after settlement in the Rio Grande valley. Today the Rio Grande Forest spans 1,962,917 acres, with headquarters in Monte Vista, Colorado. The San Juan National Forest encompasses 2,107,564 acres, and its headquarters are located in Durango, Colorado.

Early logging operation in the San Juan National Forest
*Courtesy of the USFS*

DESIGNATING A WILDERNESS NAMED THE WEMINUCHE

Despite the designation of national forests, logging operations were chewing up the lands with roads and clear cuts. Early efforts to preserve some western lands in their natural state resulted in the concept of designating "primitive areas" under Forest Service L-20 regulations in 1927.[36] A national inventory of all remaining roadless areas greater than 230,400 acres was undertaken by the agency in 1926. The San Juan National Forest proposed the San Juan Primitive Area for the southern slopes of the San Juan Mountains in 1927. It would take four years and two revisions before approval was given in 1932 by the regional supervisor. Forest Supervisor Andrew Hutten urged primitive designation in the San Juan National Forest, saying, "There are numerous reasons why this particular area should be designated and administered as a 'primitive area.' Primarily, the area is a wilderness, untouched by man except for the construction of the barest necessities in the way of protective and administration improvements. Its forests are virgin and unmarred by fire. For natural beauty of the grand and rugged mountain type, it cannot be excelled."

Writing to support creation of the upper Rio Grande Primitive Area on the eastern slope of the San Juan Mountains at the same time, Supervisor R. E. Clark stated that the area "...presents all the environmental features which would make its classification ... possible and desirable ... virgin and as near original primitive conditions as may be found any place within Colorado." Both areas were set aside as primitive areas. No act of Congress was required for these early primitive designations. The L-20 Primitive Areas Regulation gave responsibility for the decision to the regional forester. In 1975, these two primitive areas, plus some additional acreage, were combined to form the Weminuche Wilderness, named after the band of Weeminuche Ute Indians who originally claimed it as their summer home.

EARLY STRUGGLES FOR WEMINUCHE DESIGNATION

Sculpting the Weminuche Wilderness boundaries and winning approval for its designation were not easy tasks. Only after a seven-year struggle between pro- and anti-wilderness advocates did it finally take shape into a 405,031-acre preserve spanning the San Juan and Rio Grande National Forests. The 1964 Wilderness Act was the vehicle used to seek Congressional designation of the former primitive areas. Disputes arose among ranchers, recreationalists, environmentalists, biologists, geologists and agencies over what areas to include, how grazing allotments should be managed, what would happen with patented mineral claims and the possible impacts on a thriving logging industry in Southwest Colorado.

In 1968 when local U.S. Forest Service employees first began to draft the proposal, sheep grazing permits allowed 24,754 animal unit months (AUMs) of annual grazing in the western area of the Weminuche. San Juan National Forest Supervisor R.K. Blacker expressed concern for Weminuche designation, stating that 16% of local sheep grazing was carried out on the acreage proposed to be set aside as wilderness. Sheep ranchers were fearful that a wilderness designation would not only restrict their grazing numbers but also invite a growing population of wild animals to prey on sheep.

Local sheep rancher Victor A. Paulek, then president of the Wool Growers Association of Colorado, wrote in protest, "Wilderness Area means breeding ground for thousands of savage, hungry, wild dogs [coyotes], turned loose on the helpless antelope, deer, elk, sheep, calves, grouse, prairie chickens, squirrels, rabbits, and in fact, all forms of wildlife, even the nesting birds and their eggs. WAKE UP, CITIZENS! Stop this ridiculous encroachment on our wonderful Colorado recreation area."

Attorneys entered the fracas representing clients who expected impacts on water rights and ditch maintenance on private property adjacent to the wilderness. Mining companies demanded that their claims within the proposed boundaries be honored. Approximately 3,000 people submitted testimony, both written and oral, in the series of public hearings that began on October 6, 1969.

In an effort to involve the entire region in the discussion, *The Durango Herald* published a special newspaper supplement prior to the hearings which included opinions from the timber, mining and cattle industries, as well as local sportsmen. A "Citizens for the Weminuche Wilderness" group shared their arguments, and the names of all members were published, as well as the full text of the 1964 Wilderness Act.

Ian M. Thompson
Fourth Generation Coloradoan
*Courtesy of the Durango Herald*

Newspaper editor Ian M. Thompson passionately supported the wilderness designation. Thompson stated in the supplement, "The 'Wilderness' effort we are engaged in at this time is, in one respect, a pitifully futile struggle. Earth's total atmosphere is man-changed beyond redemption. Earth's waters would not be recognizable to the Pilgrims. Earth's creatures will never again know what it is to be truly 'wild.' The sonic thunder of man's aircraft will increasingly descend in destructive shock waves upon any 'wilderness area' no matter how remote or how large. We are attempting to save the battered remnants of the original, work of a Creator. To engage in this effort is the last hope of religious men."

Eloquent pleas to designate the Weminuche as wilderness were penned from around the country. Considerable debate waged over inclusion of Chicago Basin, an area already heavily impacted by the mining industry, where mining claims were continuing to be analyzed. The U.S. Forest Service recommended its exclusion while the Colorado Division of Wildlife and Citizens Group argued that it was prime elk calving ground and so, should be included.

Ruby Holcomb of Nebraska wrote on August 27, 1969, "I am dismayed at the thought of the Chicago Basin being omitted when the new San Juan Wilderness area, called Weminuche, was set aside. Here is an area of unsurpassed primitive beauty within walking range of the middle-aged and elderly, a place where they, too, can escape from the rush and turmoil of daily life. I know--I'm a 55 year old woman who last year backpacked into that basin with my husband for a week's peaceful rest. Please! Help save the Chicago Basin from the roar of motors and the erosion caused by those who seek only to pit their machines against the mountains."

All government agents and agencies had to be informed of the proposal --county commissions, city councils, tribal councils, state and national representatives--and all responded, including the Southern Ute Tribe who supported wilderness designation of lands that had formerly been their summer hunting range. The U.S. Forest Service printed and distributed brochures to the public at large, and the proposal was fine-tuned as responses flooded in.

The 1971 proposal that was finally submitted to the U.S. Congress spelled out recreation opportunities including camping, hiking, mountain climbing, horseback riding, backpacking, fishing, hunting, nature study, solitude and enjoyment of a unique environment. "A population of over 2,000,000 people has access to the area within 250 miles drive by automobile," claimed the document.

Even as it praised recreation, the proposal downplayed mineral and timber resource utilization, even though 196 patented land claims and 425 located claims were within or adjacent to the area. In summary the document claimed, "The proposed area embodies all of the characteristics of a wilderness. Evidences of man's intrusion, except for the trails that make it accessible, are few. Clear, placid lakes, fast-moving streams, tranquil meadows, rugged mountains and varied vegetative types give unusual opportunities for the challenge and excitement of unconfined outdoor recreation."

Hikers in the San Juan Mountains ca. 1920
*Courtesy of the La Plata County Historical Society*

Located in the proposed boundaries, according to the environmental assessment, were 46 lakes, 290 miles of trails, 147 miles of streams, and large populations of deer, elk and bear that were hunted annually. The wildlife population also included bighorn sheep, coyote, bobcat and mountain lions. Smaller mammals living in the area included the snowshoe rabbit, cottontail, pine and Abert squirrels, beaver, badger, marten, weasel, fox, skunk, chipmunk, pika, marmot and field mouse. The bird population, both year-round and migratory, was described as diverse. None of the wildlife, according to forest biologists, would be adversely affected by man's activities or wilderness designation.

Besides recreation opportunities, proponents of wilderness designation argued the proposed wilderness would protect the quantity and quality of water flowing from its boundaries to the surrounding communities and others miles downstream. Several transmountain water diversion ditches carrying water from west to east slope drainages and five manmade lakes were in place in the proposed wilderness. Though non-conforming by wilderness standards, it was argued that all could be camouflaged, and they would not diminish wilderness quality.

In 1971 the proposal was finally submitted to the U.S. Forest Service chief for publication in the *National Register*, but it could not be distributed to the public until after release in Congress. For the next three years the proposal wobbled back and forth between Congress and local offices of the U.S. Forest Service for fine tuning, with continuing disputes surfacing. Boundaries had to be adjusted, and the agency recommendation of a 346,833-acre Weminuche Wilderness was expanded to 405,031 acres because of such debate. Western Senators Peter H. Dominic and Floyd K. Haskell sponsored the bill that finally became national law in 1975.

"Wilderness at last," That was the headline of the *Durango Herald* editorial section on December 30, 1974. Both houses of the U.S. Congress had just passed an Omnibus Wilderness Bill that included the Weminuche Wilderness. The bill was signed into law by President Gerald Ford on January 4, 1975, and the San Juan and Rio Grande National Forests were charged with managing the newly established Weminuche Wilderness under the 1964 Wilderness Act provisions.

*The Durango Herald* editorial proclaimed, "The creation of the Weminuche Wilderness Area is an event of great importance to Southwest Colorado and the Four Corners region. The area will rapidly become a major economic asset to the recreation industry and will doubtlessly some day rival Mesa Verde National Park as an attraction." Those words of prophecy have come true, with visitor days in the wilderness boundaries now climbing annually.

NON-CONFORMING ACTIVITIES IN THE WEMINUCHE WILDERNESS

Shortly after the Weminuche Wilderness was set aside, Climax Molybdenum Company, holding mining claims in mountains surrounding Chicago Basin, challenged the rules restricting motorized travel in a designated wilderness. The company was granted permission to use helicopters to access their claims on a limited basis. Only one landing every ten days was permitted in an effort to preserve vegetation. This non-conforming use was allowed because the Wilderness Act of 1964 permitted mining activities in designated wildernesses until 1984. Patented land claims involving private ownership could be developed any time. In 1976 there were an estimated 1500 unpatented mining claims and 196 patented land claims, each about ten acres in size, in the Weminuche. Though exploratory drilling continued on a limited basis, this was halted with the 1984 shut-off date.

Many inholdings of patented land claims remain in the Weminuche Wilderness. These are located across the forest, but some of the most noticeable include the large resort, Tall Timber, located north of Rockwood and accessed by the Durango and Silverton Narrow Gauge Railroad. The land surrounding City Reservoir also remains as a holding of Durango, and several cabin sites near Needleton are still in private ownership. As these lands become available, the U.S. Forest Service will purchase and consolidate them into the wilderness.

Search and rescue operations have at times necessitated helicopter landings within the wilderness, but special permission must be gained from the U.S. Forest Service before they are allowed.

Grazing allotments also remain in the Weminuche Wilderness, but management plans now monitor conditions, and over the years the number of animals permitted has continued to decrease. Few conflicts have surfaced between wildlife and stock grazing, but wildlife biologists are charged with monitoring such conflicts in favor of wildlife.

Since the original designation, two additional congressional acts, one in 1980 and another in 1993, have added acreage to the Weminuche Wilderness, bringing today's total size to 499,771 acres. There are 334,776 acres on the San Juan National Forest and 164,995 acres on the Rio Grande National Forest. The Weminuche, spanning the Continental Divide, is the largest wilderness in Colorado, and its beauty attracts people from around the world to enjoy its high alpine meadows, towering mountains and rushing streams. This wilderness has become the heart of Southwestern Colorado, aiding the tourist economy which supports the small towns surrounding it, while remaining pristine because it is closed to human development.

# 6

# The Wilderness Act of 1964 - Its Origin and Meaning

The concept of wilderness as a wild, fearsome and uninhabitable place has existed in the American psyche since earliest times. It has not always been viewed as a place to fear, however. Indigenous people of the North American continent developed a harmonious and respectful relationship with wild land and survived as hunters and gatherers for thousands of years before being displaced by cultures dependent on agriculture. For most descendants of European ancestors who followed the agricultural lifestyle, wilderness was a wild, unknown, threatening place that had to be conquered. Historian Roderick Nash writes in *Wilderness and the American Mind*, "Ancient biases against the wild are deeply rooted in human psychology and in the human compulsion to understand, order, and transform the environment in the interest of survival."[37]

The word *wilderness* as used in the King James translation of *The Bible* meant a harsh, uninhabitable land. Nash says, "The identification of the arid wasteland with God's curse led to the conviction that wilderness was the environment of evil, a kind of hell." This idea strongly influenced how early Puritans who fled to the "New World" for religious freedom viewed a wild country inhabited by people whom they considered "savages." The Judeo-Christian philosophy placed humans above nature as its rulers. Nature was to be changed and restructured  according to their desire and needs, and native inhabitants had to be removed.

For three centuries, the North American wilderness was tamed, civilized, transformed and made livable by European standards. Wild forests, wetlands, prairies and mountain ranges--1.9 billion acres in all--were conquered and reorganized. The early settlers' philosophy directed them to destroy wild places, use natural resources without thought of their replacement, fence and revegetate cleared lands with European plants, massacre native animals and humans, drain and plow wetlands and scar mountains in search of minerals. American achievement and success were equated with the use of the earth's seemingly inexhaustible natural resources.

Not until the early 1800's did American thinkers begin to question this philosophy of "conquering wilderness." A romantic view of wilderness as a shaper of wholesome character was incorporated into the novels of James Fenimore Cooper, who created a frontiersman named Natty Bumpo. Bumpo, a simple man of great moral integrity, grew up in the wilderness and spoke passionately for its wildness. He won the hearts of American and European readers and cast a new light on nature. Writers like Henry David Thoreau, Walt Whitman and Ralph Waldo Emerson also gained recognition as American literary voices that spoke of divinity in wild places and praised a new way of experiencing nature.

Thoreau argued in his journal, "The kings of England formerly had their forests 'to hold the king's game' for sport or food, sometimes destroying villages to create or extend them; and I think that they were impelled by a true instinct. Why should not we, who have renounced the king's authority, have our national preserves, where no villages need to be destroyed, in which the bear and panther, and some even of the hunter race, may still exist, and not be 'civilized off the face of the earth'...?"[38]

Such thinking did little to halt the American movement west and the continuing transformation of wild places into farmlands, cattle ranches and urban centers where commercial and industrial enterprises demanded more raw materials. The wild and natural resources were stripped from the earth with little heed for consequences or long-term impacts on ecosystems and the creatures that depend upon them.

First automobile enroute to Silverton over Stoney Pass ca. 1910
*Courtesy of the San Juan County Historical Society*

Only in the late nineteenth century, almost 400 years after European colonization began, was there any growing national concern that unrestricted use of forests in the western United States was greatly depleting valuable timber resources and eroding watersheds that supplied major rivers. It was common practice to "clear cut" all the timber around western towns and mining camps with little thought given to long term sustainability of the forest. Cattle and sheep were grazed on public lands and allowed to consume the grass as though it were inexhaustible. The federal government responded to these problems in 1891 with the establishment of Forest Reserves administered by the U.S. Department of the Interior. When the management of Forest Reserves was transferred to the U.S. Department of Agriculture in 1905, the first active effort was made to control indiscriminate waste and direct the future of public lands.

## DEVELOPMENT OF A NATIONAL CONSCIOUSNESS

President Theodore Roosevelt
and John Muir ca. 1903
*Courtesy of the Colby Memorial Library, Sierra Club*

National publications began printing articles that challenged the loss of wild places by the close of the nineteenth century. Tourism was a growing business, and people were traveling west to see magnificent wild places like the Grand Canyon and Yellowstone which was set aside as a national park in 1872. John Muir, a self-taught naturalist and geologist who traveled much of the North American continent on foot, championed wilderness in magazine articles that captured the interest of eastern readers. Muir was concerned that something sacred was being lost, and his life mission became one of alerting people to the importance of wild country. Muir's efforts spearheaded the first designation of a national wilderness preserve, the Yosemite Valley of California in 1890.

Conservation organizations began to be formed. Muir helped establish the Sierra Club in 1892, and he influenced President Theodore Roosevelt to create the publicly owned national Forest Reserves. His belief that "everybody needs beauty as well as bread, places to play in and pray in where Nature may heal and cheer and give strength to body and soul alike" gave impetus to a growing land ethic which valued the natural environment for itself and not just for its resources.

The first U.S. Forest Service chief, Gifford Pinchot, appointed by President Theodore Roosevelt in 1905, advocated the conservation and wise use of forest lands and began creating local forest staffs to oversee land use, thus further contributing to a changing national consciousness. Such thinkers as Aldo Leopold, Arthur Carhart and Robert Marshall who joined the U.S. Forest Service ranks in the early twentieth century, spoke for saving wild places. Leopold's arguments to save natural ecosystems, later published in his book, *Sand County Almanac*, resulted in the designation of the first wilderness area in the West under the management of the U.S. Forest Service. The Gila Wilderness in New Mexico was established in 1924.

Aldo Leopold
*Courtesy of the University of Wisconsin Archives*

EARLY WILDERNESS REGULATIONS

During the 1920's the status of remaining wild unroaded areas on U.S. Forest Service land became an issue and precipitated an inventory of unroaded forests by the agency. This became the basis for the first systematic preservation of wilderness. The L-20 Regulation written in 1929, attempted to establish permitted and prohibited uses on specific "primitive" or unroaded lands. Timbering, logging, grazing and road development continued, however, on many of the seventy-two declared primitive areas in the western states. Nor was enforcement of the L-20 Regulation a major priority for an agency attempting to create management strategies for logging, grazing and water development on all western forest lands.

The L-20 Regulation was replaced by the U-Regulations in 1939. Chief of the U.S. Forest Service's Division of Recreation Robert Marshall helped develop these strategies which more clearly defined wild areas by their size, use and management. Identical management for all defined wild tracts was planned, and recreational use was supposed to be their primary activity. These roadless primitive areas could be designated by the Secretary of Agriculture who supervised the U.S. Forest Service. The staff overseeing the individual forests where they were located had to develop management plans for them. The use of mechanized transportation was banned, but grazing, water resource development and mining continued as acceptable uses.

World War II interrupted the review and designation of wilderness reserves under the U-Regulations, and after the war, the process bogged down in politics. It became obvious to a growing number of people that legal protection of wilderness by the U.S. Congress rather than administrative designations by the U.S. Forest Service was necessary.

DEVELOPING THE 1964 WILDERNESS ACT

In 1935, Robert Marshall, an intrepid outdoorsman and backcountry hiker, helped form the first national organization devoted to the preservation of wilderness--The Wilderness Society. Marshall was a visionary who cared deeply for wild, "untrammeled" places and recognized that they were fast disappearing. He also understood the psychological benefits of wilderness to the human species. The Wilderness Society, still in existence today, became politically active and helped educate an environmentally conscious public to support wilderness designations by congressional action.

By 1955 the American public was ready to consider the introduction of national legislation to guarantee wilderness protection, and savvy leaders stepped forward to champion the cause. Howard Zahniser, Executive Director of The Wilderness Society at that time, gave a speech to Congress that year outlining the national wilderness preservation concept. Senator Hubert Humphrey asked that his speech be recorded in the *Congressional Record*. A year later the first bill was introduced as a study bill by Senator Humphrey. It took eight years of political maneuvering, sixty-six rewrites of the proposed wilderness act, eighteen public hearings around the country and over 6,000 pages of testimony before the bill was finally adopted as the Wilderness Act of 1964. Without its passage, wilderness preservation as we know it today would never have happened.

President Lyndon B. Johnson signed the Wilderness Act on September 3, 1964, and the National Wilderness Preservation System became law. Congress was officially given the authority to designate wilderness areas. The 1964 Act established fifty-four wilderness areas around the country totaling 9.1 million acres, and Congress directed the Secretaries of the Agriculture and Interior Departments to review other public lands during the next ten years for possible inclusion. Twelve years later, the Federal Land Policy and Management Act of 1976 (FLPMA) required the Bureau of Land Management (BLM) to conduct a similar review of the lands it administers and make its recommendations for wilderness designations within fifteen years. Much controversy now exists over wilderness designations on BLM land, both in southern Colorado and Utah, and many areas still remain as wilderness study areas.

President Lyndon Johnson
signs the 1964 Wilderness Act
*Courtesy of the Library of Congress*

The wilderness leaders who deserve credit for the National Wilderness Preservation System include people like:

• Gifford Pinchot - the first chief of the U.S. Forest Service

• Theodore Roosevelt - the conservation president who created national forests

• John Muir - author, founder of the Sierra Club and advocate for Yosemite National Park

• Arthur Carhart - a U.S. Forest Service employee who helped set aside Colorado's first wilderness, Trappers Lake, in 1924 and urged L-20 primitive designations of other public forest lands

• Aldo Leopold - a U. S. Forest Service employee who developed the L-20 Regulation and wrote *Sand County Almanac*, now considered a classic in land ethic and philosophy

• Robert Marshall - a U. S. Forest Service employee who helped develop the U - Regulation in 1939 and The Wilderness Society in 1935

• Hubert Humphrey - the senator who asked that the first wilderness bill be drafted and presented to Congress

• Lyndon B. Johnson - the president who signed the 1964 Wilderness Act

• Howard Zahniser - the principal author of the Wilderness Act

WILDERNESS AREAS TODAY

Since 1964, conservation organizations, concerned citizens, federal agencies and the U.S. Congress have worked together to identify and preserve wilderness areas throughout the United States. The federal government owns 29% of the land in the United States, although the proportion in each state varies widely and the largest holdings exist in Alaska. Most of these lands are managed by one of four agencies--the U.S. Forest Service in the Department of Agriculture, and the National Park Service, Fish and Wildlife Service and Bureau of Land Management in the Department of the Interior.[39] These agencies now manage 20%

of all federal lands as designated wilderness areas. Since 1964, Congress has enacted eighty-eight laws establishing new wilderness areas or adding additional land to existing ones. Today there are six hundred thirty-one wildernesses in the United States totaling 104 million acres. They are found in forty-four states. The largest is the 8.7-million-acre Wrangell-St. Elias National Park in Alaska. The smallest is the six-acre Pelican Island National Wildlife Refuge off the coast of Florida.

More than 55% of all designated wilderness lands are in Alaska, a total of nearly 19% of all the land in that state. In contrast, less than 4% of the U.S. public land outside of Alaska has been set aside as wilderness. The chart below shows the total acreage of public lands in the Four Corners states.

|  | U.S.F.S. | Park Service | U.S. Wildlife | BLM |
|---|---|---|---|---|
| Arizona | 11,247,052 | 2,672,452 | 1,672,499 | 14,254,167 |
| Colorado | 14,471,081 | 591,202 | 63,910 | 8,314,075 |
| New Mexico | 9,323,059 | 372,928 | 326,581 | 12,878,359 |
| Utah | 8,108,302 | 2,021,358 | 100,156 | 22,147,582 |

Of these federally owned lands, Arizona has 4,537,864 acres of managed wilderness; Colorado has 3,264,420 acres; New Mexico has 1,613,263 acres and Utah has just 800,958 acres. Today debate wages in each session of Congress over wilderness designation of BLM lands in Utah. That battle has been waged for years, and because of the controversy, the future of additional wilderness areas in the Southwest is threatened.

WHAT DOES THE WILDERNESS ACT SAY?

Though considered a landmark piece of legislation, the Wilderness Act contains seven terse and very carefully worded sections. Section I simply states the name of the Act. Section 2 legally establishes the wilderness system and states that only the U.S. Congress can designate wilderness areas according to Section 2a. It also calls for the creation of a management system for wilderness areas that "will leave them unimpaired for future use and enjoyment as wilderness, and so as to provide for the protection of these areas, the preservation of their wilderness character, and for the gathering and dissemination of information regarding their use and enjoyment as wilderness." Section 2b establishes that their management will remain under the department and agency that had jurisdiction over the land before its wilderness designation.

Section 2c defines wilderness and directs that human impacts should be minimal. It states: "A wilderness, in contrast with those areas where man and his own works dominate the landscape, is hereby recognized as an area where the earth and its community of life are untrammeled by man, where man himself is a visitor who does not remain." This definition is rooted in philosophical ponderings that date back through the century. Both Aldo Leopold and Robert Marshall had offered similar definitions, and Howard Zahniser was adamant that the word *untrammeled* would remain a part of the definition.

Section 3 contains five parts that describe how the wilderness preservation system will continue to work and establishes the procedures for admitting specific tracts of public land into the system. All areas classified at least thirty days prior to the passage of the Wilderness Act as "wilderness", "wild", or "canoe" areas were included, and legal descriptions were required to be drawn up within a year.

Section 3b directs that within ten years after the passage, or by 1974, the U.S. Forest Service would review all primitive areas on forests to determine their suitability for inclusion. The same direction is given to agencies that manage land under the Department of the Interior under Section 3c. Guidelines for notifying public and local officials of recommendations to be submitted to the president and public hearing procedures are detailed in Section 3d. If the boundaries of any designated wilderness area are to be changed, Section 3e directs that process.

Section 4 establishes the uses appropriate in wilderness areas, but Section 4a places the National Wilderness Preservation System under the cloak of multiple use, thus eliminating many of the conflicts that had prevented its passage for eight years. It directs that the Wilderness Act will not interfere with previously established U.S. Forest Service acts dating back to 1897. Section 4b then states that any agency administering wilderness areas must be responsible for preserving the wilderness character, and says wilderness areas will "be devoted to the public purposes of recreational, scenic, scientific, educational, conservation and historical use."

Specific uses allowed in wilderness areas are spelled out in Section 4c. These are subject to existing private rights that are already in place when the wilderness is designated, however. Specifically prohibited are roads, motor vehicles, motorized equipment or motorboats, aircraft landing and structures or installations. Since established uses existed in some designated areas that contradicted these prohibitions, Section 4d clarifies their acceptance. These include such things as established aircraft or motorboat use, fire control, continued application of U.S. mining leases until December 31, 1983, water resource development, livestock grazing and commercial enterprises like outfitting and guiding.

Since some private land holdings exist within the boundaries of wilderness areas, Section 5 describes the rules and procedures for accessing those lands, and explains how those private properties can be exchanged for other federally owned property in the same state. Section 6 authorizes the acceptance of gifts, bequests and contributions within wilderness areas by the Secretary of Agriculture, and the final Section 7 requires that annual reports be submitted to the president at the opening of each session of Congress explaining the status of the National Wilderness Preservation System.

Since its passage in 1964, the Wilderness Act has remained a significant event in national legislation. Other countries throughout the world have modeled efforts to preserve nationally held lands after its process. The Wilderness Act today continues to be debated and questioned by some public officials who believe all land should be available to every human use. With the growth of an environmental consciousness among so many people, it is unlikely the law will ever be altered.

# 7

# Managing Wilderness – Is It Possible?

How does one manage a wilderness area? This seems like a contradiction--_managed_ _wildness_. Because publicly owned wilderness is open to man's use, it is _human use_ that must be managed if wildness is to be preserved. It has become obvious over the years that if we wish to maintain portions of our earth in an _untrammeled_ or wild and uncontrolled condition, as the 1964 Wilderness Act directs, then we must either stay away from them or teach humans how to exercise the utmost care when visiting them. It has often been said that acts of Congress may establish wilderness areas, but it is the acts of individual human beings who visit and use wildernesses that will maintain or alter them.

Wilderness, according to the 1964 Act, is a resource to be enjoyed as well as a place to be preserved. Human uses of wilderness areas are numerous and are growing each year as small communities located near them urbanize. Additional recreation opportunities on public land are demanded as urban neighborhoods near large cities become more complex and crowded. Hunting, fishing, hiking, climbing, stock travel, nature study and cross country excursions carry thousands of people into Colorado's wilderness areas each year. That magical word _Wilderness_ draws people to wild country where they expect to find solitude in a pristine environment. Yet, as visitor numbers increase, pristine qualities decline and management demands increase.

Every visitor to the Weminuche Wilderness, by his or her very presence, impacts its pristine atmosphere. We gather wood for building fires. The ground where we establish our camps becomes compacted, losing vegetation. We create trails that widen or erode into deep trenches through the years. Our wastes pollute the streams. Our trash litters the earth's surface. Our animals graze on the natural vegetation. We intentionally and unintentionally introduce exotic or non-native plants and animals to the ecosystems, and they spread, altering nature's balance.

Fire pit damage in the Weminuche
*Courtesy of the SJMA*

Besides recreation pressures, there are historical land uses that continue in the Weminuche Wilderness. Grazing allotments and private inholdings granted long before the passage of the 1964 Wilderness Act are still in effect. Many visitors question why grazing occurs on designated Wilderness lands. The 1964 Act clearly states that " ...the grazing of livestock, where established prior to the effective date of this Act, shall be permitted to continue subject to such reasonable regulations as are deemed necessary by the Secretary of Agriculture." These allotments must be overseen by range experts and grazing prescriptions established that will preserve the vegetation. Private inholdings or patented land purchased prior to the creation of the 1964 Wilderness Act must also be honored by the U.S. Forest Service, and they are visited by rangers who must be alert to inappropriate activities. Those inholdings can become public only through purchase or land swaps by the agency.

Activities in adjacent non-wilderness areas also affect the Weminuche Wilderness: nearby cities with their infrastructure of highways, utility lines and water diversion projects; resource extractions like oil and gas on adjacent public land; air pollution from power and energy plants in the region; overhead air traffic that bombards pristine areas with noise; and the increasing introduction on adjacent lands of exotic and non-native species which spread throughout the region. Without the research and recommendations of professionals who monitor natural conditions--stream ecologists who watch for impacts on bodies of water

Sheep herd on Highway 550 North being driven to summer range  ca. 1940's
*Courtesy of the La Plata County Historical Society*

and riparian areas, fire ecologists who argue for the importance of fire as a natural phenomenon in wilderness and wildlife biologists who track what is happening to wildlife habitat--much that is wild today will be destroyed.

MANAGEMENT PLANS FOR THE WEMINUCHE

In 1985, ten years after the establishment of the Weminuche Wilderness, the first management strategy to monitor impacts on this wild place was adopted by the San Juan/Rio Grande National Forests. Since then, Southwest Colorado has continued to grow as an important outdoor mecca, and the Weminuche is now one of the most visited wilderness areas in the state. This growth has affected both the physical and social wilderness conditions significantly, requiring that a new management plan be adopted in 1998.

Such a plan does not happen quickly, however. Both forest teams responsible for managing the Weminuche Wilderness wanted public input into the plan. In 1993 a wilderness study group composed of local environmentalists, business representatives, backpackers, outfitters, hikers and other interests was created. It met in monthly work sessions over a two-year period to study wilderness conditions and share feelings on management strategy. The model for the work sessions came from ideas presented in the comprehensive book

Weminuche Study Group in the field
*Courtesy of the SJNF*

*Wilderness Management* written in 1990 by Forestry Professors John C. Hendee, George H. Stankey and Robert C. Lucas of Oregon State University. The book presents a planning tool known as "Limits of Acceptable Change" (LAC) that establishes a framework for studying existing wilderness conditions and then creating wilderness standards, guidelines, indicators and management actions to preserve acceptable conditions. What is meant by these various terms?

**Wilderness Standards** establish the criteria or techniques used to evaluate social or environmental impacts. In other words, what is actually happening to wilderness lands, and what are the determinants of wilderness conditions that we must monitor? How many campsites are found in a specific area? What group sizes are being encountered on the trails and where? **Guidelines** define the level of impact that is deemed acceptable. How many campsites are realistically appropriate in a specific area, given existing conditions? **Indicators** identify techniques to monitor and determine if the desired wilderness conditions are being sustained. Are new campsites being created despite the effort to restrict their development in an impacted area? **Actions** are the regulations or responses necessary to safeguard the wilderness conditions desired. Will the U.S. Forest Service have to designate specific campsites and create registration for their use? Will permits be required before one can enter the wilderness? Must there be restrictions on numbers of people allowed to travel in a group?

This all sounds very complicated and cloaked in agency jargon. The study group, however, persevered and after hearing from wildlife biologists, range managers, stream ecologists and other U.S. Forest Service specialists, they helped the San Juan/Rio Grande National Forests develop "wilderness management goals" which direct how the Weminuche Wilderness will be cared for in the future. Those goals include the following:[40]

• Manage wilderness so that changes in the ecosystem are primarily a consequence of natural forces, or within a range of natural variability and succession.

• Maintain wilderness in a natural and untrammeled condition while accommodating human uses.

• Provide outstanding opportunities for solitude and a primitive and unconfined recreation experience.

• Sustain wilderness as a place of peace, solitude and sanctuary.

• Preserve natural resources for their inherent ecosystem and biological diversity values and for scientific research purposes.

• Provide the opportunity for challenge and risk.

• Minimize long-term impacts caused by human uses.

• Sustain natural and indigenous life forms.

• Protect and preserve historic and cultural resources found in wilderness.

If these goals are to be met, then every wilderness visitor has to practice a *Leave No Trace* ethic and honor the special wilderness values that have brought them there in the first place. The U.S. Forest Service in turn must determine what management actions it has to take to sustain these values.

WILDERNESS VALUES

Three timeless and general values underlie the philosophy of the 1964 Wilderness Act that directed the creation of the National Wilderness Preservation System and are still the basis for establishing designated wildernesses today.

Those values are (1) **experiential**, meaning the direct value of the wilderness experience to those who visit it, (2) **scientific** or the value of wilderness as a scientific resource and environmental baseline, and (3) **spiritual**, referring to the value of wilderness as integral to human understanding of greater forces at work. Let's consider those values in more depth.

EXPERIENTIAL

The American character has been shaped by the experience of wilderness, whether as a thing to fear or as a place of retreat. Though a limited number of people may spend time in wild places today, historically wilderness has given us solitude, freedom of movement, challenge, access to open and unsettled land and a relationship with wildlife through hunting, fishing or nature observing.

American literature extols the importance of being in nature. Nineteenth century writers who helped create an American literature grounded their work in the importance of experiencing nature. When human development and expansion threatened the extinction of wild places, men like John Muir, founder of the Sierra Club, Robert Marshall, an early U.S. Forest Service Director of Recreation and *Sand County Almanac* author Aldo Leopold protested, and demanded we preserve wildness. Today, natural history and environmental writers like John McPhee, Gary Snyder, Gary Nahban and Ann Zwinger teach us

Backpackers hearing Leave No Trace from WIS volunteer
*Courtesy of the SJMA*

about the wildness we almost lost through misuse and ignorance. They extol its sacredness and mysteries, and whether or not they ever visit wild places, their readers appreciate and support wilderness preservation.

Numerous experiential nature programs carry people into the Weminuche Wilderness each summer. Scouting and religious groups, licensed outfitters, educational programs like Outward Bound, organized clubs such as the Colorado Mountain Club or the Sierra Club and many other programs offer opportunities for personal growth and environmental education in the wilderness. Visitors confront themselves--their fears, strengths and limitations in wild settings--and discover a relationship with nature that is vital to the human spirit. As many as 360,000 visitors may enter the Weminuche Wilderness each year to be with wildness, a phenomenal number when you consider the small population size of surrounding communities and the shortness of the summer season.

SCIENTIFIC

As a relatively undisturbed setting in nature, wilderness can teach us how natural processes sustain themselves, what are the impacts of modern civilization and what changes were set in motion during the years of western settlement and exploration. Wilderness provides a baseline for studying nature undisturbed; its gene pool maintains a diversity unknown in disturbed areas. Certain plants and animals cannot exist outside of wilderness, and the intricate interrelationships they exhibit tell us things we need to know for our survival and the survival of the planet. If we lose wildness there are many questions now unasked whose answers we will never know. Ecosystems that have evolved outside of man's interference have so much to teach us. What wild organisms offer cures to future diseases and maladies on the planet? We may lose these if we fail to protect the diverse gene pool of our remaining wilderness lands.

Nor can scientific understanding be for the benefit of man only. When we assume an anthropocentric view of the earth--that everything is there for the benefit of the human species--we ignore the rights of every other living thing. By assuming a biocentric perspective--that all living creatures are necessary for the health of the whole--we open up to the fact that natural evolutionary processes are of primary importance and man's use is secondary to those processes. We learn to accept wilderness on its terms, not ours. In the past we changed the habitat patterns in the Weminuche Wilderness so radically that two necessary predators, the grizzly bear and the timber wolf, no longer stalk the high country. That alone has altered the balance of species and will have long lasting impacts on the Weminuche. Scientific study of such changes will help us understand future actions needed to preserve the wilderness.

SPIRITUAL

Pope's Nose on the Flint Creek Trail
*Courtesy of B. J. Boucher*

We live in a fast-paced world that draws us out of ourselves. So much so that when we stop to listen to our own inner voices, we become frightened. Wilderness provides a sanctuary for being with ourselves completely. It inspires us with vision; it quiets the chatter that controls our minds; it teaches us humility; it gives us courage to face challenge; it offers us a face of eternity that we cannot witness in our busy lives; it shows us how small and unimportant we are as its impersonal power sweeps over us. Wilderness can bring us home to ourselves and our own beliefs and personal values.

WEMINUCHE WILDERNESS VALUES

With these three central values in mind, the Weminuche Wilderness Study Group developed the following expanded statement of values which, along with the goals outlined previously, direct management actions within the Weminuche Wilderness. These values are the basis that allow you and me to plan elaborate pack trips or short week-end excursions into wild places. Consider them carefully.

> • Wilderness provides an opportunity to experience the magic of nature, the intensity of color and weather. Here we can have the sense of discovery, of what it might have been like for early explorers. We are reminded that the Wilderness is a place that our

grandchildren should be able to see, which then must be reflected in our sense of responsibility to appreciate it and care for it in the present.

• Wilderness, in contrast to our ordinary lives, is a place away from the threats and fears of daily existence. It removes our worries, clears our mind and creates a sense of relief that we are here.

• Wilderness creates an opportunity for us to separate ourselves from the world and its requirements by providing a respite from technology, from cars, TV's and computers. It provides an "escape" from civilized society, allowing us, at least temporarily, to put in order the world we live in. It creates a place to improve our mental and physical health, our spiritual well being. It also provides the struggle and challenge necessary to make us aware of the surroundings.

River valley high in the Weminuche
*Courtesy of B. J. Boucher*

• Wilderness has important environmental values. It sustains wildlife, fauna and flora and biodiversity. It has values for scientific study, and provides learning opportunities where we can learn about ourselves and the environment.

• Wilderness is a place that shows nature's fundamental indifference and demonstrates the human's issues with control. In the Wilderness we can observe both life giving and life taking, or events throughout every moment of existence, in an ever-

Backpacker traveling Upper Turkey Creek Trail
*Courtesy of B. J. Boucher*

changing biosphere, constantly adapting, where a tree may die, but the totality of nature is relatively undisturbed.

• Wilderness has a value in terms of economic market. It provides economic means.... Because it is a draw within a tourist-based economy it provides jobs and income. This is more noticeable at certain times of the year, such as during hunting season, or in communities where the economy is more dependent on back country activities. Services provided by outfitter-guides provide access to the Wilderness for persons who otherwise could not experience it by themselves. For such persons commercial wild land support services may be viewed as minimizing impact for the inexperienced or unskilled back country visitor.

• Wilderness provides a connection to the past, thus giving us a sense of history, of what used to be both in terms of natural and social history.

• Wilderness provides open spaces where we can feel free. It is a place to recreate away from regulations, a place to experience without influence. Nevertheless, Wilderness must be managed in some ways by nature and in some ways by humans. Regulations and management should respect all forms of life and instill respect in all persons who enter the Wilderness. Management practices should educate, inform and teach people how to visit and learn and should nurture in the visitor a sense of responsibility and protection and preserve the challenge and choice that the Wilderness presently provides.

• Wilderness in its present state provides a sense of freedom, a freedom to choose places to go. We are concerned about over regulation and concerned that there will be no regulation in certain areas. The freedom to fail should be maintained and that education should be provided to inform the visitor about duties and responsibilities. Regulation should be something that carries a message about how to properly relate to the Wilderness, realizing that there is a great diversity in people and in their understanding and depth of awareness about wilderness experiences and values."

MANAGEMENT LEGISLATION

Unless the San Juan/Rio Grande National Forests support these goals and values through applied management actions, the Weminuche Wilderness will be altered severely as human use increases. This is why wilderness management must be spelled out in very clear language. The 1964 Wilderness Act directs management by stating:

A wilderness, in contrast with those areas where man and his own works dominate the landscape, is hereby recognized as an area where the earth and its community of life are untrammeled by man, where man himself is a visitor who does not remain. An area of wilderness is further defined to mean in this Act an area of undeveloped Federal land retaining its primeval character and influence, without permanent improvements or human habitation, which is protected and managed so as to preserve its natural conditions and which (1) generally appears to have been affected primarily by the forces of nature, with the imprint of man's work substantially unnoticeable; (2) has outstanding opportunities for solitude or a primitive type of recreation; (3) has at least five thousand acres of land or is of sufficient size as

Pack llama in the Weminuche
*Courtesy of the SJMA*

to make practicable its preservation and use in an unimpaired condition; and (4) may also contain ecological, geological, or other features of scientific, educational, scenic or historical value.

The 1998 management plan adopted by the San Juan/Rio Grande National Forests creates strategies to protect biological resources, including the air, water, soil, minerals, animals, fish, insects and vegetation, as well as specific ecosystems found in the wilderness. Monitoring of conditions by wilderness rangers during the last three years shows that some ecosystems, particularly destination areas such as lakes, 14,000-foot peaks and high alpine meadows, are experiencing increased damage every year. Soil compaction, trash accumulation and loss of fallen and standing dead wood occur at every established campsite. Sterilized soil from campfires is created with each new fire site that is constructed. Some animals, like black bears and mountain goats, are habituating to human presence, thus threatening their future. Fish-stocking and over fishing in high mountain lakes has disturbed the natural balance in the waters.

A true wilderness experience is almost impossible in many areas of the Weminuche today. Crowding, noise, perceived conflicts between backpackers and stock users, numerous impacted campsites and trails, large groups and litter all affect the quality of a wilderness experience. The increasing presence of domestic dogs threatens wildlife habitat and human solitude.

Recreational stock use is on the increase and becomes an issue of concern. Horses and llamas significantly impact trail and campsite conditions as well as riparian and meadow areas. Overgrazing can occur when animals are not properly controlled. It is the belief of most people that regulation is not desirable. Yet when is the use too much, and how will it be controlled?

## MANAGEMENT STRATEGIES

Conditions and opportunities for human visitation and use in the Weminuche Wilderness are not uniform throughout the wilderness. Some areas, in particular those immediately accessible to transportation routes, receive more visitation than others. For this reason management strategies differ depending on how remote or accessible an area is and the kinds of use it receives. By establishing different zones or areas ranging from semi-primitive to pristine conditions, the San Juan/Rio Grande National Forests can monitor and minimize human impact according to a specific plan of action. *The present San Juan/Rio Grande Wilderness Direction Plan seeks to improve wilderness conditions while maintaining existing recreational opportunities.* This means there will be no effort to increase use, and, in fact, the number of people allowed as a group to visit the wilderness is now restricted to no more than fifteen. Forest-wide standards and guidelines have been established.

Ongoing conditions must be monitored in the field to find out what is happening. How many people are visiting specific areas? What are the impacts of their campsites and travel on meadows, streams and wildlife habitat? Is solitude available for users and for wildlife? Are the wilderness ecosystems free of human impact? The philosophy of wilderness management throughout the Rocky Mountain Region supports keeping evidence of man's activity to a minimum.

## WILDERNESS RANGERS

Wilderness rangers are those seasonal employees who walk the wilderness trails during the summer and fall months, greeting the many people they encounter. I have seldom seen a ranger during my years of backpacking, so I puzzled as I prepared to write this book, who is this person called a wilderness ranger? I spent a season wearing the green uniform of the U.S. Forest Service, and I discovered why I saw so few.

When I hiked the trails as an independent backpacker, I could "make tracks", pausing only as desired to enjoy views or identify wildlife and plants. As a ranger I crawled along the trail, stopping often to do trail maintenance and visit with travelers about the conditions or regulations of the area they were entering. One day while hiking the Los Piños River Trail I collected over one hundred pieces of litter in a distance of three miles--pop cans, plastic bags, candy wrappers, pieces of string, broken shoelaces, snap-tops, horseshoes, cigarette butts and even pieces of clothing. Adding other people's trash to my own pack increased the weight of a load already considered too heavy by my weary back.

As a ranger I began to see the well-worn paths with different eyes. There are miles and miles of trails in the Weminuche Wilderness, and on a typical day, the ranger may cover, at most, only five or six of them. I became very conscious of the many huge fire rings that cried out for cleaning. I saw the trails as ever-widening *roads* where travelers skirted the muddy sections, trampling new routes into place and roping the terrain with numerous social trails.

Unless you travel a path early in the summer you will never know the havoc caused by winter's storms and run-off from melting snow. Being the first ranger on a trail for the season seemed like a joy until I discovered how many downed trees have to be cleared and how many rocks obstruct safe travel. As the season progressed I discovered the tedious task of closing social trails with logs and rocks. I also discovered that trees love to fall across newly groomed paths during summer wind storms, and cleaned waterbars quickly fill up with mud and rocks from the runoff. The pulaski, crosscut and shovel became my friends, and the blisters became my enemies.

I began to really see other things I had missed before -- human impacts

Wilderness Rangers on the Continental Divide.
*Courtesy of B. J. Boucher*

Backpacker hiking braided trails in the Weminuche
*Courtesy of the SJMA*

that were destroying the wilderness setting. Before working as a ranger I arrived at a campsite after a long day of hiking and quickly sought the most level spot for my tent. Now my ranger's eyes saw the size and number of impacted bare sites located immediately beside rivers and streams in disregard of the hundred foot restriction. I remember stopping at one campsite on the Los Piños River Trail and spending an hour picking up toilet paper placed under rocks or logs, burying human excrement and sorting the cans and plastic left in the fire pits to pack out in my backpack. How many hours I worked to remove unnecessary or illegal fire sites. I spent an equal number of hours scaling down the size of fire pits where gaping holes and piles of ashes extended wider and wider, as users neglected to remove their burned debris and new campers piled rocks around the circumference.

I wore the hat of interpreter under my forest green hat, and answered questions, if I knew the answers, about everything from history to climbing conditions on high peaks. If I did not know the answer, I suggested a source in the central office. I met with groups and gave special presentations on wilderness history and Leave No Trace ethics. I keenly watched for wildlife and reported my sightings to wildlife biologists. I counted campsites and monitored conditions as I traveled, reporting them for analysis upon return to the office.

Whereas before I might spend a week enjoying leisurely outings in the Weminuche Wilderness, now as a ranger I prepared for ten-day stints, hauling the

Needle Creek Trailhead
*Courtesy of the SJMA*

food and gear necessary for that period in my backpack. I learned well the adage of the wilderness ranger: "Home is where you sleep at the moment." I became skilled at setting or breaking camp in the middle of downpours. I found myself being the example of good trail and camping ethics, and as I represented the land and the public agency that manages it, I felt joy in knowing that perhaps I was really making a difference.

Safety became a major issue to me as a ranger. I noted the conditions of streams and the snow melt on high passes. I reported these and other conditions daily by two-way radio to the central office. Yes, the ranger carries a *four-pound* radio, not a cellular phone, for communication with the central office, in addition to all the survival gear necessary for those lengthy journeys. Though mountains frequently got in the way of transmissions and batteries might die, the radio became my friend and a source of information about the non-wilderness world. I knew that if I encountered a situation requiring search or rescue, I would be responsible for helping in every way possible. Fortunately, this never happened, but I always remained alert to the possibility.

Trailheads became a focal point for my attention when entering or leaving the wilderness. I collected registration sheets, refilled notebooks with new sheets, added new information to the bulletin boards and cleaned up the trash left by thoughtless visitors. Each time I returned home for a four-day break before the next trip, I hastily crammed in the chores of housekeeping, laundry and gardening, while readjusting to the busyness of the civilized world. I discovered the joy and sadness of being a ranger, and I now take my hat off to each of those seasonal employees. Their numbers are few. Perhaps no more than twelve field rangers cover a 500,000-acre Weminuche because wilderness budgets are limited. Their job is worth a million bucks, because they are the true representatives of the U.S. Forest Service.

During the last several years wilderness rangers have played a key role in helping determine management actions in the Weminuche, another one of their responsibilities. Using the statistics collected from rangers, field specialists and volunteers, the San Juan/Rio Grande National Forests determine what management actions will be taken to preserve wildness.

Fire restrictions, campsite limitations and other changes are made in wilderness management only after the field personnel have monitored and studied conditions. Though not desirable, increased use may ultimately lead to a required permit system for every visitor in the Weminuche. This fact became clear to me after working as a ranger, and I even foresee restrictions on the numbers of people and animals allowed in certain heavily used areas. The 1964 Wilderness Act specifically states that wilderness areas "shall be administered for the use and enjoyment of the American people in such manner as will leave them unimpaired for future use and enjoyment as wilderness, and so as to provide for the protection of these areas, the preservation of their wilderness character, and for the gathering and dissemination of information regarding their use and enjoyment as wilderness."

If we are to have a wilderness for future generations, then we must manage the wilderness we have today so that it remains "unimpaired" by our presence. This is the directive that guides the Weminuche Wilderness management plan, and it is necessary that each of us share responsibility for maintaining this spectacular area in its wild untrammeled condition. When restrictions are placed on our actions, we must yield our personal desires to the good of the greater whole. Whether we visit it once, dozens of times or simply read about it, the Weminuche Wilderness is a legacy of unmeasurable spiritual, experiential and scientific values. We must preserve the howl of coyote, the roar of the bear, the quietness of the deer and abundant grazing for the bighorn sheep forever.

# Part III

# Visiting the Weminuche Today

"First we pollute the wilderness, then we pollute our minds with the belief that we've done the right thing. Then we pollute the wilderness more because we've lost our ability to see it. Soon the wilderness ceases to exist. In its place is a garbage dump--vast and purposeless--and we think how wonderful we are to have created a place that speaks so well for what we are." Mark Strand, taken from *Testimony*, compiled by Stephen Trimble and Terry Tempest Williams, Milkweed Edition, 1996.

# 8

# Ecosystems and Wildlife of the Weminuche

*The earth (I am just going to remind us of a few facts) is fifty-seven million square miles; 3.7 billion human beings, evolved over the last four million years, plus two million species of insects, one million species of plants, twenty thousand species of fish, and 8,700 species of birds; constructed out of ninety-seven naturally occurring surface elements with the power of the annual solar income of the sun. That is a lot of diversity.* Gary Snyder, "The Politics of Ethnopoetics."[41]

A U.S. Forest Service employee in 1936[42] related the origin of the San Juan Mountains' ecosystems in this way:

"When Paul Bunyan was laying down the continental divide with his blue ox and he arrived in the vicinity of Engineer Mountain, above Silverton, he took a notion to go to the Texas Panhandle. Getting to Sawtooth Mountain, on this track, he did not like the looks of Alamosa and decided that the Shelter belts would take care of the Panhandle anyway. So he swerved off south toward Tierra Amarilla and into New Mexico, leaving Sawtooth Mountain as the crazy bone, or turning point of a rough rincon into which he set the San Juan National Forest. The blue ox never got over the wooly-calf habit, hence the general course is meandrous.

"The area of the San Juan nestled in this rough rincon is about a million and a half acres. The greatest continuous width (east-west) is eighty miles and length (north-south) fifty-two miles.

"Approximately, at every twelfth mile along the crest of the divide, Mr. Bunyan turned loose a sizable river--or the makings of one--and started it in a general southerly direction to make up the main San Juan. The valleys are narrow and deep. The crests of the divides range for considerable distances, from 14000 to 16000 feet in elevation while the floors of the valleys drop to 8000. The tributaries and lateral ridges are too numerous to mention.

"Mr. Bunyan hoisted timber line to 11,500 feet and having used up all his lodgepole pine seed, he sowed only spruce down to about 8500 feet where he set ponderosa and continued it down to the lower elevations near the edge of the Forest where inside and outside for miles and miles he planted cedars. Also acorns but the latter of poor quality so we have scrub oak mixed with the cedars. I almost forgot the transition zone--that is where you cannot tell whether the tree is spruce or a ponderosa or a Douglas fir, of which he planted quite a bit, because he got the seed mixed. He also put in a small amount of white fir.

"Of course the browse and grasses and aspen were plentiful and likewise the wild life until, just as in other instances, the white brother came along with his progressible misuse of land and destroyed all the yellow pine leaving a population of all white fir."

If Paul Bunyan created the San Juan Mountains, he left an unbelievable legacy for the American people. No one can enter the Weminuche Wilderness and not be awed by the array of lush colors in nature's palette. The green foliage of trees and shrubs is splashed onto the vivid reds, browns, golds, grays and blacks of rocky slopes and high mountains. Distant white snowfields and endless blue skies form the final backdrop of the landscape. This is the environment of the Weminuche in the summertime. Living in this environment are myriads of species--trees, shrubs, herbs, grasses, flowers, insects, birds, reptiles and mammals. They weave a complicated pattern that inspires and teaches anyone willing to observe.

## LIFEZONES AND ECOSYSTEMS

The human specie can live almost anywhere because we can alter our environment. This is not true for most wildlife. Wilderness creatures live in different places because of physical adaptation to surrounding conditions. The most significant limiting factors for the habitat of any living specie are temperature and moisture.

Temperature in the mountains progressively decreases with an increase in elevation. As moist air moves into the high elevations and comes in contact with cold air, precipitation results. More moisture may occur at higher elevations, but shorter summers, severe weather and wind desiccation prevent rapid growth of plants. These climatic changes result in different conditions to which different species are adapted. Biologists say a climb from the foothills of the San Juan/Rio Grande Mountains to the peak of a 14,000 foot mountain is like a journey from Colorado to the Arctic Ocean in northern Canada. Just as you will experience

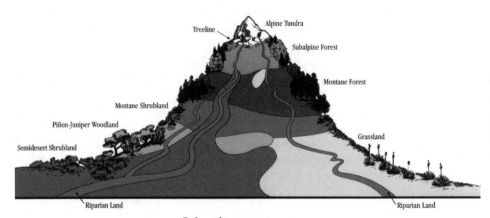

Colorado ecosystem map
© 1995 by the Denver Museum of Natural History, used by permission

climatic changes on that northward journey, so will you also experience change as you gain elevation in the Weminuche Wilderness. These changes are categorized into specific life zones, each with its own characteristic plants and animals.

Ecologists have designated eight life zones in Colorado, three of which are found in the Weminuche Wilderness--the *montane, subalpine* and *alpine/tundra zones*. Within these three life zones are numerous ecosystems. An ecosystem is defined as an area created by the interaction of a specific group of living organisms with their environment. It can also be thought of as a zone in which wildlife species along with their physical and biological environments constitute an interacting unit. Some ecosystems span two life zones, depending on such things as the northern or southern exposure of a hillside, soil conditions and topography. Between two life zones are fringe or edge conditions where the traditional species of both zones mingle. A closer look at the three life zones in the Weminuche Wilderness and some of their ecosystems will help explain the changes one sees when walking in its wildness.[43]

## MONTANE ZONE

This forested region occurs between 6,500 and 9,500 feet in elevation. Two main vegetation types or ecosystems are found here--ponderosa pine and Douglas fir. Aspen forests, by nature, regenerate and are found on specific sites because of disturbance in this zone. The disturbance can be natural caused by wind throw, fire or disease, or manmade such as in clear cut areas. Little if any logging occurred in the Weminuche prior to its designation, however, so natural causes dictate where aspen forests now grow.

1. Ponderosa Pine Forest Ecosystem

Ponderosa pine forests typically exist in parklike conditions created by low intensity fires that burn the lower stories of scrub oak and grasses every ten to fifteen years. Thick orange-brown bark on adult trees make ponderosas fire-

resistant, and as they mature they can reach heights of 150 feet with trunks three feet in diameter. Their needles are long and are arranged in groups of two or three per bundle. The bark gives off a vanilla aroma. Because they like dry, warm, gently rolling country, ponderosa pine forests are frequently found on southern facing slopes in the Weminuche Wilderness. Ponderosa pines are intolerant of shade. Their seeds germinate best on bare, moist mineral soils in open meadows where they can have unobstructed sunlight. Trees only begin producing pine cones after about twenty-five years of life, and a mature tree may produce a good cone crop every three to six years.

Ponderosa Pine Forest
*Courtesy of Chris Schultz*

Ponderosa pines reach maturity at 120 to 140 years of age. Healthy trees can exceed 300 years of age. Wide spacing is important for optimal growth. Human intervention through logging and fire control has altered the nature of most ponderosa pine forests in Colorado, and their denseness now makes them susceptible to fire and disease as well as insects such as the mountain pine beetle. Dwarf mistletoe can also cause damage to a ponderosa pine forest. The San Juan/Rio Grande Forests now are managed under a plan that supports allowing natural fires caused by lightening within the Weminuche Wilderness boundaries to burn unless they pose a threat to human life or private property.

Numerous mammals and bird species find their habitat in the ponderosa pine forest. Certain creatures like the Abert's squirrel, pygmy nuthatch, Grace's warbler and flammulated owl are almost completely dependent on this ecosystem. The Abert's squirrel feeds on the ponderosa pine cone. Old snags provide habitat for cavity dwellers like the flammulated owl and the nuthatch. Charts found in the appendix detail common wildlife and plant life found in the different ecosystems.

2. Douglas Fir
Forest Ecosystem

Douglas fir trees seek out north facing slopes because the humidity is greater there, and they need more moisture than ponderosa pines. They range in elevation from 7,000 to 10,000 feet. Doug firs will be present in the upper reaches of the montane zone to the exclusion of ponderosa pines, and are often found in association with aspen, blue spruce and Engelman spruce, as well as subalpine fir in

Snags provide wildlife habitat
*Courtesy of B. J. Boucher*

transitional or disturbed areas. A mature stand of Doug firs will have a very closed canopy that restricts sunlight from reaching the ground. A pale green lichen known as Old Man's Beard can be found on the lower branches and usually on the north side of the trees. Extensive logging after World War II removed large stands of Doug fir on the San Juan National Forest.

Fir Forest
*Courtesy of B. J. Boucher*

Douglas fir trees have flat, stalked, round-tipped needles. Seed production can occur when the trees are ten years of age. They average 80 to 120 feet in height and can live for over 200 years. Most stands of Doug fir in the Weminuche Wilderness grow in mixed stands of trees. Fires occur infrequently in Doug fir forests, perhaps as seldom as every 200 years; but when they do, they burn very hot, killing all the vegetation. The first trees to reestablish cover in the burned area are aspen groves. You will see them fingering up hillsides in a Doug fir forest. Eventually the aspen forest will be replaced by conifers in a process known as succession.

Though no mammals or birds are restricted specifically to this ecosystem, it provides great shelter for numerous species. Elk, deer and many birds summer here. The great horned owl, a common resident of montane forests, makes a diet of rodents, rabbits and birds found in the Douglas fir forest. The sharp-shinned hawk particularly likes Douglas fir forests.

3. Aspen Forest Ecosystem

Aspen groves are widely distributed in the Weminuche Wilderness, ranging from moist areas in the foothills at 6,000 feet through subalpine terrain above 10,500 feet. They can also be found in narrow strips along riparian corridors. Because they tolerate cold temperatures and late snow, aspen trees grow in all mountain vegetation zones. They are not tolerant of prolonged drought or high temperatures, however. Since most precipitation falls on the windward side of mountains, more aspen forests will be found there.

Aspen understory
*Courtesy of Ted Balchunas*

Ranging up to 100 feet in height, aspen forests are susceptible to wind blow down as well as damage from snowpack and avalanches. But because they grow from rhizomes or root networks that stretch underground, they quickly resprout after damage. An aspen tree reaches maturity between 85 and 100 years of age. Because families of aspen trees are connected by interlinking roots, their beautiful golden and orange leaf colors appear in patterns on the hillside. Aspens are aggressive pioneers, capitalizing on disturbance of other trees by fire or disease. As conifer trees overtake a stand of aspen trees, they reduce the light available, thus causing the aspen stands to decline.

The understory of an aspen grove is luxurious with herbs, grasses and wildflowers. Aspen leaves drop each fall to create a rich soil when combined with the decaying plant matter on the ground. A wide assortment of life is found here, with birds partitioning different elevations in the trees to forage or nest. The quintessential aspen specialist is the warbling vireo. Numerous cavity dwellers such as flickers and sapsuckers love to nest in the aspen tree whose wood is soft. Their abandoned cavities are then used by owls, swallows, wrens, creepers, bluebirds, nuthatches and chickadees.

Beavers love aspen forests, cutting and storing the trees near their ponds for winter food or using them to build new dams. The understory of an aspen forest provides protective cover for elk and mule deer. You may see large scraped areas on aspen trees where elk and beaver have chewed at the bark during winter. Black bears are also common in aspen ecosystems. They feed on the aspen buds and new leaves as well as the berries of understory shrubs. Fall dens are frequently located in the mixed aspen-conifer communities, and you can find their claw marks on aspen trees.

## II. SUBALPINE LIFE ZONE

The subalpine zone is located between 9,000 and 11,500 feet elevation. In this area conifer trees found in the montane zone decline, giving way to forests of Engelman spruce and subalpine fir trees. Growing conditions are more severe here, and summers are shorter. Trees that extend up into the fringes of the alpine zone become twisted and gnarled as a result of severe weather conditions.

## 1. Spruce-Fir Forest Ecosystem

Engelman spruce and subalpine fir trees both grow in a spire shape, possibly an adaptation to heavy snowfalls. Such adaptation allows them to shed snow quickly. The higher the elevation, the more stunted the tree's growth. High summer precipitation provides good moisture for growth even though the season is short.

Mature stands of Engelman spruce and subalpine fir exist in the Weminuche Wilderness since fire  seldom occurs in this high, moist ecosystem. Spruce trees may exceed three feet in diameter, 120 feet in height and 400 years or more in age. Subalpine firs are smaller than spruce trees, reaching a height of about 100 feet and maturing at 150 to 200 years. The canopy of this forest is closed, creating dense shade for a ground floor where old fallen rotting trees provide sustenance for other plant life. Reforestation is extremely slow after a disturbance in these forests.

Because of the short growing season, Engelman spruce and subalpine fir have a compressed timeframe for developing cones and dropping them for germination. Engelman spruce begin bearing cones at about twenty-five years of age, but maximum seed production occurs only after reaching 200 years of age. Good seed crops occur every two to six years. Nor do established seedlings have an easy time maturing since they must withstand a long severe winter as well as damage by small mammals.

The Engelman spruce tree is characterized by a thin scaly grayish-brown bark, dark green four-sided needles and fine soft hairs that envelop the twigs. The needles of the subalpine fir are flat and blunt with whitish lines both above and below. The small cones are purplish in color when immature, but turn brown during their two-month development period. Both species are susceptible to wind blow down because of their shallow roots.

Transmittered Boreal Owl
*Courtesy of Chris Schultz*

Animals which survive in this ecosystem must be adapted to extreme cold. Ptarmigan will burrow in the soft snow under the trees during winter. Bighorn sheep also seek shelter among the trees. Mule deer and elk spend summer days at the upper extremities of these forests. The number of species in the high elevations is much fewer than that at lower elevations. Even so, blue grouse, mountain bluebirds, pine grosbeaks, golden-crowned kinglets, juncos, hermit thrush and many seed eaters love spruce-fir forests. Old growth species that only inhabit mature forests are found here. The pine marten, three-toed woodpecker, boreal owl and red-backed vole are examples.

The spruce bark beetle, a tiny insect which bores into Engelman spruce to deposit its eggs, can cause significant damage to the forest if the outbreak of insects is large. A widespread outbreak occurred in the 1960's in Colorado. Such occurrences are rare, however.

2. Krummholtz Forest Ecosystem

Above 11,500 feet the Krummholtz (a German word meaning "crooked wood") ecosystem begins. Plants intermix between alpine/tundra and subalpine life zones in this area. Since at least five months of the year have continuous below-freezing temperatures in this ecosystem, wildlife is scarce. The most common and easily observed is the white-crowned sparrow. Trees are twisted and gnarled, the windward side receiving brutal punishment. Moisture dries quickly, and there is little energy for reproduction of new trees. Instead, self-preservation with the renewal of needles and the production of a small band of wood uses up a tree's growth energy. Subalpine firs in this ecosystem are more shrublike than treelike, having a bonsai appearance that is stark and beautiful.

### III. ALPINE/TUNDRA LIFE ZONE

"Tundra" is a Russian word meaning "land of no trees." This life zone extends from tree limit at about 11,500 feet, depending on exposure, to the summits of the highest mountains in the Weminuche Wilderness, exceeding 14,000 feet in elevation. This region is defined by extremes in temperatures, winds, weather and growing conditions. The role of climate in shaping this life zone is readily apparent. Storms can occur any month of the year, and snow remains year-round on north facing slopes and in crevasses. The freezing/thawing activities shove boulders around, create ponds or bogs and carve out valleys. A subsurface permafrost may exist in certain areas. Plants must make radical adaptations to survive.

Though only a limited acreage in the Weminuche Wilderness is located in this life zone, its importance is significant. The moisture stored in this cold region melts throughout the summer providing water to the semi-arid lands that lie at the base of the San Juan/Rio Grande Mountains. If this water were all released at once, it would cause major flooding, as happens during early warm springs. The gradual melting sustains streams and rivers which supply irrigation water to ranches and farms as far away as California. These waters also end up in huge reservoirs where electricity is generated for major western cities.

Moon Lake in Alpine Zone
*Courtesy of B. J. Boucher*

Wind is a demanding taskmaster in the alpine life zone. It sweeps across the surface, eroding the soil, evaporating moisture, lowering temperature and demanding that plants cling tenaciously to the earth for existence. Most alpine plants are small, snuggling close to the ground to avoid the wind and conserve energy. They experience increased rates of photosynthesis and respiration in order to mature during a growing season of slightly less than two months. Flower buds even begin developing at the end of the previous year's growing season to get a jump start on the short summer. Most alpine plants are perennials, having a very stable root system, and are several years old before they flower. Leaves are skinny to avoid being browbeat by the wind, and some are succulent so as to retain water. Human intrusions can be very destructive in the alpine/tundra life zone. The trampling of alpine meadows or the removal of rocks can create impacts that will not be restored for hundreds of years because of the harsh growing conditions found here.

Animal life must make significant adaptations to exist in the alpine life zone. Numerous insects--bumblebees, grasshoppers, ladybugs, metallic beetles, spiders, black flies and mosquitoes--frantically swarm to life during the short flowering season. Pocket gophers, meadow voles, mice, marmots, pika and weasels hurriedly store plants and seeds during the short summer or fatten to

Boulder field in the alpine zone
*Courtesy of Karen Thurman*

hibernate for survival. Only one bird, the ptarmigan, lives in the tundra all year. American pipits, horned larks, rosy finches, white-crowned sparrows, prairie falcons and golden eagles summer in the meadows along with the busy hummingbirds who seek out the fields of flowers for food. Grizzly bears and wolverine used to be regular members of this ecoystem too. Several different ecosystems are found in this life zone.[44]

1. Boulder Field (Fellfield) Ecosystem

*Fell* is the Gaelic word for *rock*. Fellfield refers to distinctive plant communities found on rocky, windswept slopes. The soils in this area are limited, coarse in texture and contain little organic matter. Vegetation is restricted to cushion-forming plants like alpine phlox and moss campion.

The boulder field is also home to the many lichens (a plant form made up of algae and fungi which grow as a unit on hard surfaces like rocks) considered *indicator* species in the Weminuche Wilderness. Indicators reveal more quickly than other species the changes occurring in environmental conditions of an ecosystem. Pollution, drought, predation balance, spread of exotics and other impacts are made obvious by the indicator species.

Yellow bellied marmot
*Courtesy of the SJMA*

In this ecosystem you will find Mr. Marmot, a great scavenger, whose major occupation is to fatten up for the next winter's hibernation. The yellow-bellied marmot has been around in this alpine region since the pleistocene period. His neighbor, little pika, harvests the seedheads of plants and stores them for winter consumption in tunnels that snake beneath the rocks. Breeding birds include the Brown-capped rosy finch.

## 2. Alpine Meadows Ecosystem

Alpine meadows have a profusion of plants that provide an array of beautiful flowers during summer. They are found on gentle slopes and in shallow basins where moisture can accumulate and the soil is less rocky. Early snow melt from the sun's warmth opens up a burst of blooms from the sky pilot, American bistort, mountain hare bell, wallflower and numerous other perennials. These meadows are used by herbivores like the pocket gopher or the vole who feed on the roots and stems of the flowers and grasses and store them for winter use. Breeding birds include the american pippit, white-crowned sparrow and horned lark.

Alpine meadow
*Courtesy of the SJMA*

## 3. Snowbed and Snow Ecosystems

There are areas in the alpine life zone where snow lasts late into the summer. As the snow melts, new rings of plants will green up while earlier ones farther away from the snowfield are in bloom. Within an area of a few feet you will find plants in all stages, sprouting, flowering and going to seed. Though the snow shortens the growing season, it also protects the plants from wind while providing them with moisture. The brown-capped rosy finch breeds here.

## IV. RIPARIAN AND AQUATIC ECOSYSTEMS

Riparian and aquatic ecosystems are found in all three life zones of the Weminuche Wilderness. They are discussed separately for this reason. As you travel at 12,000 feet or higher you will see numerous small lakes or pools of water.

You will also see bogs, sinkholes and marshes. Every stream that flows out of the Weminuche begins in these high elevations where snow accumulations melt and flow from the Continental Divide. Riparian areas extend beside bodies of water but have distinctly different living conditions.

1. Riparian Ecosystems

Mountain riparian areas[45] are the most biologically productive ecosystems of those in the Weminuche. Most species of wildlife are dependent

upon them either for habitat or food. Riparian areas represent a transition zone between upland and aquatic ecosystems. They differ in vegetation according to the elevation at which they are found, but generally they are characterized by plant species that require lots of water and can tolerate a water table at or near the surface during part of the year. They exist in a fragile balance and are very sensitive to disturbance.

Riparian areas are in jeopardy throughout the west as a result of water diversion projects, pollution, grazing practices, mining, reservoir construction and channeling. Not only do riparian areas provide habitat for many forms of wildlife; they also create a buffer zone for the protection and enhancement of aquatic ecosystems. They

Ruby Lake
*Courtesy of B. J. Boucher*

provide transportation corridors for humans and wildlife. They function as living filters to remove debris from surface runoff. They stabilize shorelines of streams and lakes. They insulate the adjacent stream temperatures from significant swings.

The soils of many riparian areas are high in organic or partially decomposed plant materials. The soil buildup from decaying organic matter can form wet meadows, marshes, fens or carrs where shrubs such as the alpine willow dominate. One of the key activities of riparian wetlands is to build up soil, displace water and allow for the growth of trees.

Riparian areas traverse a wide range of elevation, and the flora and associated fauna develop distinct communities according to temperature, elevation, humidity, precipitation, length of growing season, wind and soil condition. *Montane* riparian communities are dominated by forests of narrow leaf cottonwood, mountain alder and river birch. Various species of willow as well as Rocky Mountain maple, twinberry, gooseberry, red elderberry and scrubby cinquefoil predominate in the understory. Willows and cottonwoods characteristic of riparian areas can survive only if their root systems are in close contact with the water table.

*Subalpine* riparian areas are dominated by coniferous trees--the blue spruce or the white fir. Their understory features numerous herbaceous plants such as cow parsnip, chiming bells, bittercress, arrow leaf groundsel, larkspur and monkshood. Along wet seeps one will find parry primrose, yellow monkey-flower, globe flower, bog orchid and marsh marigold. Also willow and bog birch

Beaver dam made of Aspen logs
*Courtesy of B. J. Boucher*

will be present. Subalpine riparian communities may also include herbaceous wetlands dominated by sedges, rushes, different kinds of grasses, buttercups, kingscrown and marsh marigolds.

*Alpine* riparian communities exist in the form of bogs, sinkholes and marshes above tree line. Retreating snowfields leave wetlands that support mosses and ground covers.

With the combination of terrestrial and aquatic resources, mountain wetlands and riparian areas have a wide diversity of residents. The beaver creates his own home by damming water with aspen logs, sticks, rocks, plant material and mud. He builds a conical lodge with an underwater entrance. His pond offers habitat for muskrats, trout, frogs, waterfowl and shorebirds. The highly organic and calm waters breed numerous insects. The Belted kingfisher feeds on small fish in the still waters. Amphibians such as the chorus frog, the boreal toad and the tiger salamander live in these wetlands.

Many butterflies like Titiana's fritillary breed in the mountain wetlands each summer, and the black masked raccoon who eats almost anything, finds an abundance of food in riparian areas. A variety of birds like the warbler fox sparrow, Lincoln's sparrow and olive-sided flycatcher nest near the water's edge in the grasses and sedges, on tangled willow branches or in adjacent forests. They feed on the abundant insect life. Little brown bats begin foraging at dusk for bugs and continue until dawn when they seek sleeping places in nearby trees and surrounding brush.

2. Aquatic Ecosystems

Aquatic ecosystems are found in bodies of water ranging from streams to high mountain lakes, springs, seeps, potholes, wet meadows and marshes. They are found from 6,000 to 14,000 feet in elevation. They can be subdivided into *flowing water* and *standing water*.

*Flowing Waters*

Streams are bodies of moving or flowing water that drain steep terrain. The physical and biological characteristics of a stream vary as water moves to lower elevations. Changes in biological communities are related to changes in gradient, velocity, width, depth, temperature and streambed content. Streams

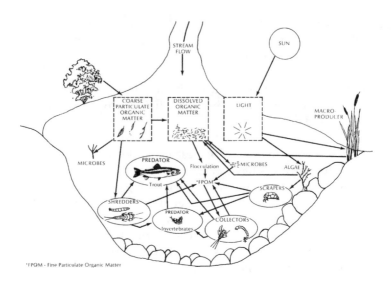

Diagram of typical stream food chain
*Courtesy of the Colorado Division of Wildlife*

vary in size, depth and velocity. High mountain streams often form steep channels through bedrock, cascading in falls over rock and debris. As they reach lower elevations they decrease in current rate and increase in water volume as small streams enter a main channel. Residual soils begin to form, and habitat potential increases. Large streams or rivers form in alluvial valleys, and volume increases even more as intermediate streams converge. This is where the American dipper "dips". Found only in fast flowing streams, the American dipper eats acquatic insects found on the stream floor. It nests in cliff crevices overhanging the streams.

The acquatic inhabitants of streams are classified according to how they feed, whether *shredders, collectors, scraper-grazers* or *predators. Shredders* like the caddisfly and mayfly nymph feed on plant decay that enters the stream from adjacent riparian or terrestrial areas. They break down the organic material into finer particles. The *collectors* such as net-spinning caddisflies and blackfly larvae take the fine particles produced by the shredders and sieve them as sediments on the bottom of the stream. The *scraper-grazers* such as snails and caddisfly larvae specialize in chewing the algae growths attached to rocks and other surfaces in the water. *Predators* like fish, nymphs and water striders capture live prey such as any of the above named species.

*Standing Water*

Nourished by streams, ground water or runoff, marshes develop in poorly drained areas. Natural lakes and ponds are common in the higher portions of the mountains, forming in cirques and gouges left by glacial and rock action. Water also collects in basins at the foot of melting snowfields or draining moraines. The Weminuche Wilderness's natural lakes range in size from one acre to 280 acres (Emerald Lake), and vary greatly in depth as well. Most are found above 9,000 feet in elevation.

Solar radiation is the energy source for mountain lakes. Light penetration is critical to the water's inhabitants. Oxygen is greatest near the surface, decreasing in the deeper waters. The decomposition of organic matter on the bottom of a pond or lake produces a black mud that has a foul smell and further depletes oxygen in the water. Summer sunlight triggers photosynthetic activity in the aquatic plants found in the water, especially the algae, resulting in the production of oxygen. Because of this effect, oxygen levels in a body of water are highest in the late afternoon.

A lake's community is made up of *producers* and *consumers*. The producers are the tiny plants and algae, as well as surrounding large plants in shallow waters. Consumers are those organisms that feed on other organisms whether plant or animal. They can range from microbes to fish. The high mountain lakes are important as a fish resource for wilderness visitors. Because summer use is short, high quality fisheries can be maintained in the Weminuche Wilderness despite reduced productivity of fish.

COMMON BIRDS AND ANIMALS IN THE WEMINUCHE

When I am in the Weminuche Wilderness, all of my senses are heightened. I listen to a bird song in the distance or the rustling sound in nearby brush. My eyes peer into the trees along the trail, attempting to spot a chattering squirrel who is warning everyone of my presence. I smell the evergreen trees, and I catch a hint of herbal fragrances wafting on the wind.

I go to the wilderness partly to experience the wildlife that inhabits it, but I have learned that it takes a special awareness to see wildlife and to understand why different species live in different areas of a wilderness. The ecologist helps me understand why specific species can exist only in certain places and what influencing factors guarantee their survival. Though it would be great to have the trained ecologist's vast understanding, there are particular bits of information that will help prepare anyone for wildlife watching. The more closely we observe, the better our chance of being in the right area at the right time to see an elk, a bear or a wild red lily.

Observing surrounding conditions can heighten the senses, no matter where you are. First, notice the specifics of the terrain. What types of trees, shrubs, grasses or herbs are nearby? What is the elevation? What about sources of water? Wildlife stay in the vicinity of bodies of water. Are there open meadows or riparian areas? What is the season and time of day? All of these, plus many other variables will influence who lives in a particular area. It helps to know something about the tracks of common animals, the songs and calls of birds, and the feeding habits of small and large mammals.

What about sounds and physical clues? Can you recognize the warning calls of the pika, the yips of Mr. Coyote, the whistle of a marmot? What is the difference between bear scat and coyote scat left on the trail? Who slept on a flattened grass spot under a tree? Who might have left the dandelion flowers strewn on the rocks? What about that piece of fur clinging to a bush? Carefully observing the world around you is the first rule for seeing wildlife.

Next, consider the feeding and sleeping habits of wild creatures. Some are *diurnal*, meaning they are active during daylight and rest at night. Mountain goats, wild sheep, vultures, hawks, eagles, songbirds and squirrels are examples. Eighty percent of all animals are *crepuscular*, which means they are active at dusk or dawn and seek cover during the day. Examples of these are deer, elk, rabbits and bears. If they are *nocturnal*, like raccoons, bobcats, bats and owls, they prefer to feed at night and hide during the daylight hours.

Seasons also affect where wildlife will be. Seasonal migration patterns find many creatures summering in the Weminuche Wilderness and going elsewhere during the chill of winter. Many species of songbirds--warblers, bluebirds and sparrows, for example-- move back into high country in the spring, having wintered at lower elevations or even out of the country. Many species summer in the Weminuche because it provides great habitat for breeding and raising their young. Herds of elk will winter in lowland pastures along rivers, but come spring you'll see them moving across high alpine meadows where they break up into smaller bands for summer feeding.

Certain creatures such as bears and marmots remain year-round, but hibernate as cold sets in. Others, like the bighorn sheep and mountain goats, remain active at high altitudes throughout the year, feeding on sparse vegetation and lichen during winter. Pika and voles spend their winters in vast tunnel networks under rocks and snow munching on stored grasses and herbs.

There are numerous bird species in the Weminuche Wilderness, and depending on their feeding and nesting habits, they range at different heights of the same trees. Some like large stands of dead trees. The cavity nesters and raptors particularly seek out old snags or dead trees for nesting and hunting. This means mature forests are a prerequisite for some, and its removal threatens their existence. Learning to observe wildlife species requires patience and a sensitivity to their well-being and environment. Too often we assume that because we haven't spotted certain animals or birds, they do not exist.

RULES FOR WILDLIFE WATCHING

There are certain rules[46] that should be observed when watching wildlife to guarantee their safety and to give you the best experience. They are as follows:

• Never approach any animal too closely. It can cause the abandoning of nesting sites for birds.

• Don't disturb the animal. Move slowly and quietly, using binoculars for close-ups.

• If they act disturbed, move away.

• Never stay at a nest or burrow longer than a few minutes, and never handle eggs or the young of any species.

• Never destroy vegetation in order to have a better view.

• Never flush a species out of its feeding area. Harassment can stress the animal, making it susceptible to disease.

• Never feed wildlife or use bait to lure them closer.

Wildlife viewing is a privilege. We should use it with respect.

Only a field guide devoted to birds or animals can answer all the questions one may have about the many bird and animal species that live in the Weminuche Wilderness. A chart of the more commonly found birds and mammals and the life zones in which they are found is included in the appendix.

Perhaps a short description of some species you are most likely to see will help you identify them as you travel in the Weminuche Wilderness.

Wilson's Warbler
*Courtesy of Chris Schultz*

### BIRDS

*Wilson's warblers* are easy to identify. Bright yellow birds, the male has a satin black cap. They arrive in early spring from wintering grounds in southern Mexico, and nest in willows in riparian areas. Loss of habitat in the areas where they winter is a threat to their future. Cowbirds lay eggs in their nests, and these large hatchlings hog the food and cause the baby warblers to starve, further threatening survival. Different species of warblers forage and nest at different levels of the forest canopy, thus avoiding competition.

*The Broad-tailed hummingbird*, is found throughout the Weminuche Wilderness. The male is recognized by the shrill metallic whistling of his wings. It beats its wings as many as 50 times per second while hovering over a flower and 200 times while in courtship flight. Males have a wide, rounded tail and rose-colored throat. They can fly up to 60 miles an hour, burning large numbers of calories a day. They nest on conifer branches sheltered in the thick boughs, and migrate in late August or early September to warmer climates in the southern states or Mexico.

Broad-tailed hummingbird
*Courtesy of Chris Schultz*

Mountain Bluebird
*Robert A. Watson ©*

*Mountain bluebirds*, recognized by their sky blue plumage, are summer residents in the Weminuche, arriving by the end of March from their southern winter grounds. The bluebird requires a cavity for its nest, but it can't excavate its own; so it uses abandoned woodpecker holes, competing with English house sparrows and Starlings for nest sites. Bluebirds gather in flocks to migrate south in August and September.

*Great Horned owls* are the largest and most widespread of all owl species in Colorado. Their "ear" tufts are large, their bellies finely barred with mottled brown feathers. They nest in juniper, cottonwood and conifer trees, often using the abandoned nests of hawks, magpies or crows. They may also nest in cavities on cliff faces. The great horned owl mates in mid-February, and chicks hatch in mid-March. They have sharp talons to grip prey, and their eyes have a high ratio of rods to cones so as to catch the faintest light. Owls hunt at night, mainly eating rabbits, weasels, squirrels, skunks and birds. Crows and jays will harass an owl during the day as it roosts.

Great Horned Owl
*Robert A. Watson ©*

*Black-billed magpies* have long streaming blue-black iridescent tails, white wing patches and black heads. They raid the nests of other birds, and will eat carrion. They mainly eat insects, berries and fruit. Both intelligent and adaptable, they can be seen as high as 11,000 feet. Magpie nests are sturdy structures, two feet in diameter with a side entrance. The inside is lined with fur or hair. Magpies can have long-term mates, using the same nest year after year. Nests are so sturdy they are often used by other birds like owls, herons and kestrels. Magpies are very sociable, and communal roosts

Black-Billed Magpie
*Courtesy of the Colorado Bird Observatory, Tony Leukering ©*

can be used thought the year. Magpies will mob other birds, forcing them to drop food that they then retrieve.

Blue Grouse
*Courtesy of Chris Schultz*

*The Blue grouse* male is dusk-blue and the female mottled brown, both blending with their surroundings. Mostly they go unseen, yet they are widespread throughout the Weminuche Wilderness. They winter in coniferous forests where they feed on needles and buds, and then move to aspen groves in summer for breeding. Grouse are very territorial in breeding season, the male inflating a throat sack to make a booming sound and announce its territory. Blue grouse nest on the ground. In September, they migrate to lower elevations, feeding on acorns, snowberries and seeds in conifer trees. Predation by coyotes is heavy.

Gray Jay
*Courtesy of the SJMA*

*Gray jay* bold and aggressive birds, are recognized by a black and white pattern on their head and a gray body. They are frequently referred to as "camp robbers" because they are so aggressive around campsites. Gray jay are common year-round residents in coniferous forests. They eat small birds, mammals, carrion, insects and seeds. Because they remain year-round, they store large supplies of food for winter and begin nesting while snow is still deep, lining the nest with fur, feathers, spider webs and bark. Using special saliva glands, they form berries into sticky balls that are stored for future use by sticking them to branches, twigs and lichen clumps. Their ability to remember where dozens of food caches are located around their home range and reliably retrieve them, is quite remarkable.

*Northern goshawks* are larger than crows, with a wingspan of 42 inches. They have a mottled blue-gray underside and a broad white eye stripe. A rapid flier, the goshawk can reach speeds of more than 70 miles an hour for short stretches. They nest in coniferous forests in April or May, using the same nests for several years. Though secretive and difficult to spot, they agressively defend their nests from all intruders, including humans. Goshawks feed on ground squirrels, rabbits, snowshoe hares, mice, blue grouse, mourning doves, flickers, robins and other birds.

Northern Goshawk
*Courtesy of Chris Schultz*

*White-tailed ptarmigans* are found above 11,000 feet. They like alpine tundra and willow patches at timberline. A white-tailed ptarmigan is about twelve inches long, weighing approximately a pound. The ptarmigan changes its plumage with the season, mottled in spring, brown and gray like the rocks in summer, and white in winter. They feed on willow buds, leaves and insects. The ptarmigan stands motionless for long periods when not feeding, and you can walk within two feet and still not spot one. Since the ptarmigan can fly only short distances, blending with its environment while remaining motionless is very necessary.

White-tailed Ptarmigan
*Robert A. Watson ©*

### LARGE ANIMALS[47]

*Mule Deer* range from foothills to canyons to woodlands and high meadows in the Weminuche Wilderness. They were an important food source for the Ute Indians because they are found in more accessible terrain. Every part of the animal was used by indigenous people--the hide for clothing and bedding, the antlers and bones for needles, awls, scrapers and tools. During the late nineteenth and early twentieth century, mule deer were almost wiped out from the Weminuche Wilderness by miners and market hunters who contracted to bring meat to mining camps. Game laws passed in the 1930's allowed their comeback. Deer are browsers who eat shrubs, succulent grasses and forbes in season. They feed between dusk and dawn, bedding down during daylight in thick cover. Deer move into the Weminuche in spring as the snow line recedes. Fawns are born in June, and twins are common. Food in the high country is

Mule Deer
*Robert A. Watson ©*

Early fall snow in the San Juan Mountains
*Courtesy of the Bill Hayes*

Early morning reflections in Emerald Lake
*Courtesy of B. J. Boucher*

Majestic mountain range from high in the Weminuche Wilderness
*Courtesy of the San Juan Mountains Association*

Wilderness information specialists llama packing across Columbine Pass
*Courtesy of Ken Baker*

Endlich Mesa
*Courtesy of B. J. Boucher*

Upper Piedra
*Courtesy of B. J. Boucher*

The Durango and Silverton Narrow Gauge Railroad
*Courtesy of Robert Royem Photography*

plentiful through fall, but early snows drive them to lower elevations. Bucks shed their antlers in February. They do not collect harems as elk do.

Elk
*Robert A. Watson ©*

*Elk*, or *wapiti*, are the largest of Colorado's native deer. The wapiti is brownish tan in color with a yellow rump and a dark mane on the shoulders. Wapiti bulls can weigh almost 1,000 pounds, though cows are smaller. Elk were almost exterminated from the San Juan Mountains and had to be reintroduced through herds brought in from Wyoming in the early twentieth century. Like deer, the male grows new antlers annually and spends each August rubbing off the velvet that covers the new rack. The rack of a mature adult can be five feet wide. Shed antlers are seldom seen because they are eaten by rodents for their calcium. Wapiti are grazers, eating mostly grass. They congregate in high alpine meadows during the summer. Winter range is in river valleys and lower elevations where they feed on bark, twigs and shrubs. Wapiti will move in large herds at certain times, and the males spar for dominance and possession of harems. Bulls begin their distinctive bugling in September, marking the mating season. A single, spotted calf will be born in May or June in the high country of the Weminuche.

*Black bear* inhabit most of the forested ecosystems in the Weminuche Wilderness. They are fond of areas where nut and berry producing vegetation is found, such as Gambel oak, pinon pines and junipers. They love aspen forests where grasses and

Grizzley Bear
*Courtesy of the USFS*

forbes grow. Despite human misconception, the black bear consumes little freshly killed big game. Ninety-five percent of their diet is vegetation, including acorns, service berries, chokecherries and other wild fruits. The black bear will eat ants, grubs, porcupines, rabbits, nesting birds and the young of elk and deer in calving season. Mating occurs in late May or June, with cubs born in January or February and weighing only nine or ten ounces at birth.

The adult bear goes into a feeding frenzy in fall, increasing its body weight by 30% before moving into a prepared den in a natural cave, thick brush or hollow logs for hibernation. The heart rate drops to eight to ten beats per minute, and metabolism slows considerably. The bear remains dormant, living on stored fat through the winter. It emerges from its den in mid-April to late May. Black bears are not always black, often being cinnamon brown or blond in color. Their average weight is around 250 pounds.

*Mountain goats*, weighing as much as 300 pounds, are found in rocky outcroppings, cliffs and tundra. They are not a true goat but are related to the chamois of the Alps and antelope of Africa. A master of climbing prowess with strong hind legs and feet that grip the ungrippable, they graze in very unpredictable places. Kids can climb within hours after birth. Isolation in high rocky areas is their defense.

Mountain Goat
*Courtesy of the The SJMA*

The mountain goat is not native to the Weminuche Wilderness, however, having been transplanted from northern states and British Columbia between 1948 and 1971. The Colorado Division of Wildlife obtained and released fifty-one animals in the northern part of Colorado. Later they were transplanted to the San Juans. In 1993 the Colorado Wildlife Commission proclaimed them a native species. They give birth to young in May and June, usually having one kid. Winter is hard on mountain goats, with below zero temperatures and winds that whip the snow into flurries. Even so, they remain in high country seeking out windblown areas where browse is exposed or pawing through light snow for mosses, lichens or shrubbery.

Big Horn Sheep
*Robert A. Watson ©*

*Bighorn sheep* range above 8000 feet elevation in the Weminuche Wilderness. Grayish in color and weighing up to 350 pounds, males have curling horns that can make a full circle. They are not shed like the antlers of elk and deer. As grazers, their diet consists mostly of grasses, sedges and a variety of plant material that may be available in high rocky regions. Alpine meadows provide perfect habitat. Bighorns prefer remote, rugged country where they are difficult to detect against the rocks. The prominent white rump is a giveaway, however. Mating season is hard on the ram since it takes little time to eat, and mating occurs in late November when winter is at hand. Ewes give birth in May, usually to one lamb.

Bighorn sheep are creatures of habit, using the same feeding, bedding and migration areas year after year. The bighorn sheep of the Weminuche Wilderness are threatened by our encroachment and presence today. Once bighorns migrated to lower wintering grounds, but travel by people has forced them to winter on higher, less favorable sites. Decades of fire suppression have eliminated still more habitat by causing thick forests to overgrow former meadows. Grazing sheep are believed to have introduced disease to bighorn sheep that also causes fatalities.

*Moose* stand five to six feet tall at the shoulder, and the male can weigh as much as 1,100 pounds. Flattened antlers, a drooping upper lip and a dewlap on the throat are distinctive markings. Moose are not native to the Weminuche Wilderness. In 1978 the Colorado Division of Wildlife

Moose
*Robert A. Watson ©*

began transplanting moose into the state from Utah. The population has thrived because of lack of competition. The largest member of the deer family, they are solitary creatures except during mating season. Moose are usually seen where there is water. Aquatic plants such as willows and grasses are their favorite food. Single calves are born in May, and the mother is extremely protective of her young. She can be very dangerous, trampling to death anything that threatens her or her young. Moose stay put in winter rather than seeking lower elevations, since willow, their chief food, is abundant and accessible in the wilderness.

## SMALL ANIMALS

*Chipmunks* are small ground squirrels, and Colorado has several species. The *least* chipmunk, the most widespread, is only four   inches in length. The *cliff* chipmunk, only slightly larger, is found in northwestern Colorado. The *Colorado* chipmunk is found in the Weminuche, and the *Uinta* is found in Colorado's central mountains. It is difficult to distinguish between the different breeds, though range provides a helpful clue.

Chipmunks are primarily seed and berry eaters, but will also eat vegetation, insects and even carrion. They are most active in daylight and live in tunnels underground with openings for access under a rock or brush. Chipmunks can easily become beggars around wilderness travelers, but, like all wildlife, they should not be fed. They store caches of food for winter use in underground tunnels. The young are born in late spring/early summer and are weaned by the time they are 50 days old.

*The Abert's squirrel* relies upon ponderosa pine forests for almost all its life needs. Seed cones, bark of twigs and buds are its food source. It builds nests in high branches, often in mistletoe infestations. The Abert's is distinct because it has conspicuous tufts of hair as long as two inches on its ears. Its coat is light gray to dark black, and it is about 20 inches long. Litters of two to five in number are born between March and May in a nest lined with bark strips and needles. The Abert's doesn't hibernate in the winter, but rather survives on

Abert's Squirrel
*Courtesy of Chris Schultz*

the cones and inner bark of twigs from the ponderosa pine. Old growth pine trees are critical habitat since they are the major cone producers. Goshawks are the primary predator of Abert's squirrels.

*Porcupine,* next to beaver, are the largest rodents in the Weminuche Wilderness. Their quills extend beyond a yellowish coat of hair, and their waddling gait makes them appear fat. Quills can be four inches long, and one animal can have as many as 30,000 quills, each of which is barbed with tiny hooks. An agile climber, the porcupine uses its tail for balance and leverage. Its incisors continue to grow throughout life, so it gnaws to control growth. The porcupine spends much time in the branches of aspen and ponderosa trees eating leaves, seeds and buds

Porcupine
*Robert A. Watson ©*

during summer. It will also feed on the ground, eating grasses and forbes. In winter it peels away bark from tree trunks to get at the inner cambium which

Snowshoe Hare
*Courtesy of the SJMA*

contains starch and sugar. Consequently, it can do extensive damage to trees. The porcupine is a solitary animal, coming together to breed in early winter. The female dens in a rock shelter or hollow log and produces a single offspring. It slaps with its tail as a threat, but contrary to popular belief it cannot throw its quills. Coyotes and bobcat can overcome the porcupine by slapping at its tail and flipping it to expose its vulnerable belly.

*Snowshoe hare* are the prey of many animals. Their most distinctive feature is their back feet which can be six inches long. The snowshoe has thick fur for protection against winter's cold. It prefers areas of heavy undergrowth where it can rest and look for food under cover of darkness. The snowshoe eats grasses, sedges and forbes in summer, and bark and buds of aspen, alder, birch or willow in winter.

This prolific creature can produce up to three litters annually. Babies are born fully furred with eyes open. Birth weight doubles in a week, and the young are soon left to their own care. The fur of the snowshoe hare is white during winter, but the animal molts in April, taking on a mottled brown coat. Change is triggered by daylight length.

Pika
*Robert A. Watson ©*

*Pika* dwell on talus slopes at or near timberline. A close relative of rabbits, they are about eight inches long, approximately the size of a guinea pig, with short round ears. Pika warn each other of danger with a sharp, high-pitched whistle. Well camouflaged, the pika looks like a rock when it halts its fleeting movement. Pika are active during day and usually stay within a restricted territory. Snipped vegetation lying on rocks gives away their presence. This small mammal stores great volumes of vegetation for winter food in tunnels under the rocks. Predators that feed on pika are coyotes, weasels, martens and hawks. The pika breeds in the spring and can have two litters annually.

*Yellow-bellied marmots* (see page 107) are found from 5,000 feet in elevation to above timberline. About two feet long, the marmot can weigh six to nine pounds. Often referred to as a groundhog, it loves to eat and sleep, basking in the sun during summer. The soft hair along its underside is yellow, giving the marmot its name. It has been called "whistle pig" because of its distinct loud warning that carries for a mile. Marmots live in colonies, burrowing beneath boulders, where the female raises four to six young in a summer. Marmots eat constantly when awake, and 60% of body fat is gained for winter hibernation. Their preferred foods are the flowering stalks and leaves of grasses and forbes. Predators include the coyote, badger, bobcat, golden eagle, hawks, owls, weasels and martens.

Beaver
*Robert A. Watson ©*

*Beaver* can be over three feet long, including the large flattened tail, and weigh thirty to sixty pounds. This fur bearer was almost made extinct by trappers and mountain men of the nineteenth century. In l887 the Colorado Legislature placed beaver on a list of protected animals. Nocturnal in habit, this mammal is best seen when sitting near an active beaver pond before dusk. Beaver range from 4,000 feet in elevation to timberline. When habitat is not suitable this animal will create its own ponds near rivers and streams, building log and mud dams over six feet high and hundreds of feet long. It then builds a lodge with underwater access. Water must be deep enough, however, to insure against winter freezing.

The beaver has webbed hind feet, a waterproof coat and oversized lungs that allow it to remain underwater for as long as fifteen minutes when threatened. A colony of beaver needs about eight to ten acres of aspen forest to survive in an area. It eats leaves, buds, sedges and forbes in summer as well as the bark of trees like aspen, willow and alder. In winter the beaver feeds on its cache of twigs and branches since it doesn't hibernate. Beavers mate for life which can be twenty years. They breed in late January, and three to six young are born in the spring. Their habitat is threatened by high-altitude water diversions, pollution and human development.

This sampling of common birds and mammals in the Weminuche Wilderness is meant to whet your appetite to learn more about its inhabitants. Respecting their environment is a key to "walking in wildness" while safeguarding their future. Excellent books are available which offer in-depth information about wildlife in the San Juan Mountains. Check local bookstores for sources.

## ENDANGERED, THREATENED AND SENSITIVE SPECIES

The State of Colorado lists species that are *threatened* or *endangered* in the environment. A third category, *sensitive* species, is also designated on specific forests. Awareness of these species helps one consciously observe their surroundings and be on the lookout for them. Though some of Colorado's listings no longer exist in the San Juan/Rio Grande National Forests or in the Weminuche Wilderness, a complete listing is provided.

**Endangered species** are native wildlife whose prospects for survival in Colorado are in jeopardy. Colorado's endangered list,[48] which is separate to the federal list of endangered species, includes the following: Black-footed ferret, Bonytail, Western boreal toad, Colorado squawfish, Gray wolf, Grizzly bear, Humpback chub, Least tern, Lynx, Plains sharp-tailed grouse, Razorback sucker, Rio Grande sucker, River otter, Whooping crane and Wolverine.

The Federally endangered list includes the Colorado squawfish, Humpback chub, Bonytail chub, Razorback sucker, Rio Grande sucker, American peregrine falcon, Whooping crane, Southwestern willow flycatcher, Black-footed ferret, Gray wolf and the Uncompahgre fritillary butterfly.

**Threatened species** are not in immediate jeopardy of extinction. They are, however, vulnerable because they exist in such small numbers or are so restricted in their range that they may become endangered. Colorado's threatened list includes the following: American peregrine falcon, Arctic peregrine falcon, Arkansas darter, Bald Eagle, Lesser prairie-chicken, Greenback cutthroat trout, Greater prairie-chicken, Mexican spotted owl, Piping plover and the Wood frog. The federally threatened list includes the Bald eagle, Mexican spotted owl, Piping plover, Grizzly bear and the Greenback cutthroat trout.

**Sensitive species** of wildlife recognized by the U.S. Forest Service are native wildlife that are found in very specific areas. Some of them become indicators of the health of a specific ecosystem because they are dependent on that area's well-being to exist. Indicator species have a narrow range of ecological tolerance. Their presence or abundance serves as a barometer of ecological conditions within a specific area. Some examples include: Tiger salamander, Boreal toad, Townsend's big-eared bat, Pine marten, Dwarf shrew, Northern goshawk, Olive-sided flycatcher, Three-toed woodpecker, Boreal owl, Rio Grande cutthroat trout, Colorado River cutthroat trout, Fox sparrow and Black swift.

A more specific look at some of the endangered, threatened and sensitive animal species in Colorado and the Weminuche Wilderness[49] is worth consideration, should you ever spot these creatures in your travel. Remember that classifications are not permanent, however. As the number of a specie increases or decreases it can be re-classified. It is also possible that additional species will be added in the future as human impacts continue to destroy the habitat of wild creatures.

**The lynx**, a cousin of the bobcat and often mistaken for it because of color, a state endangered specie, has a black band that completely encircles the tip of its tail. There is only a slim chance that it still exists in the Weminuche Wilderness. This animal is adapted to life in snowy regions of the far north and at high elevations or "boreal forests" above 10,000 feet in elevation. They need mature forests to provide cover for their dens and kittens, as well as an abundant supply of snowshoe hare, their main prey. The lynx has long legs which allow it to move through deep snow in the winter. Long tufts of fur on the tips of its ears and a flared facial ruff are distinctive features. Though weighing only about twenty-five pounds, their tracks are the size of the mountain lion's, an animal several times larger in size, because of the dense fur on their feet. They are cautious and secretive, avoiding open areas. Large unbroken forests provide them stalking and hiding cover. Fragmentation due to logging, ski area construction and road building cuts into their territory and food source. Trapping led to almost complete extinction. Some states still allow trapping despite their tenuous presence in the west. CDOW plans to reintroduce lynx into the state in Spring of 1999.

**The wolverine**, known for its large appetite, ferocious disposition and strength, is a state endangered specie. A symbol of the wilderness spirit, it makes its living more as a scavenger than a hunter, relying on dead animals for food. The wolverine is the largest member of the weasel family, weighing from thirty to sixty pounds. The adult is capable of dragging the carcass of a large deer or elk because of its heavily muscled body. Wolverines have a reddish-brown band that runs from each shoulder to the tail through shaggy brown hair, giving the appearance of a skunk. They are sensitive to development and require large, roadless forests with an abundance of small and large prey to survive. They are susceptible to traps since they love to scavenge. Wolverines were trapped for their pelts. Only scattered individuals may occur in Colorado, and CDOW will reintroduce them to certain areas of Colorado in Spring of 1999.

**The pine marten**, also of the weasel family, lives in mature subalpine forests. The marten, though fairly common and considered a sensitive specie on the San Juan National Forest, is seldom seen, since it rests during daylight hours. It has a fox-like face, and rears its young in snags, hollow logs or burrows under trees or rocks. It preys on small mammals--birds, voles, squirrels. The marten spends winter beneath the snow in tunnels, depressing its temperature so as to minimize energy exertion. A lean animal with less than 4% body fat, it must eat every day to survive. Voles and mice are its prey. The marten stays in trees, traveling long distances without touching the ground and requires late successional stands of moisture-loving conifers with lots of woody debris near the ground. Its numbers have decreased because of habitat alteration and trapping.

**The peregrine falcon,** a federal and state endangered specie, once soared across the skies of the Weminuche Wilderness. Use of the pesticide DDT, which is now banned in the U.S., decimated the population of this medium sized hawk. As recently as 1972 Colorado no longer had any successful breeding pairs of peregrines left. Today there are over a dozen breeding pairs in the San Juan Basin. This large bird is recognized by the black helmet on its head and slate blue coloration on its back. The adult varies in length from fifteen to twenty-two inches. The peregrine falcon preys on small to medium-sized birds. It nests along steep, precipitous cliffs and in river gorges. Intensive work during the last twenty-five years has resulted in their recovery, but human intrusion near their nesting sites can be detrimental.

**Grizzly bears,** a federally threatened and state extinct specie, were last reported in the San Juan National Forest in 1979 when an old griz was killed in the South San Juan Wilderness after attacking a hunter. Though evaluation by agencies is in process, the Colorado Division of Wildlife believes they no longer exist in the Weminuche Wilderness. The excellent book *Ghost Grizzlies* by David Peterson[50] details the history of the last reported grizzlies in Colorado and an in-depth study conducted in the South San Juan Wilderness by a group of dedicated individuals intent on documenting the existence of grizzly bears in the San Juan Mountains. For this reason it is worth knowing how to recognize them. The grizzly has conspicuously humped shoulders and front legs longer than its back legs. Its color is mostly yellowish to reddish brown, and adults often have white-tipped hairs along the back. Another distinguishing feature is its concave snout.

Grizzlies are not picky eaters, enjoying everything from carrion to fruit to plants and even grubs and insects. Extremely shy, they breed in July, and the young are born to the hibernating female. Females breed at about three years of age, producing cubs every other winter.

Debate still rages over whether the grizzly should be reintroduced, if it no longer exists. Whether it exists or not, the loss of the grizzly in the Weminuche Wilderness casts a grim shadow on human impacts to wild ecosystems.

**The Uncompahgre fritillary butterfly**, a federally endangered specie, is found on northern slopes of alpine peaks above 12,400 feet elevation. Associated with the low snow willow, they are very small butterflies with a two inch wing span and mottled brown coloring. They enter the butterfly stage during late July and early August. These butterflies have not been seen in the Weminuche Wilderness for several years, but biologists continue the search.

This is only a sampling of threatened and endangered species. CDOW's booklets which detail how to recognize animals, birds, amphibians and fish that are disappearing because of habitat loss are worth perusing. It is critically important that we recognize human impacts on natural ecosystems today. Our desire to own and to change nature has caused the extinction of thousands of fellow creatures. We need to understand that every form of life on earth has the right to live. Every living thing, including the human specie, is part of a complex web of life. Arguing the importance of a national land ethic we so sadly lack, the great philosopher/naturalist, Aldo Leopold, described all of nature as an energy circuit which conveys three basic principles: "(1) land is not merely soil;  (2)  the native plants and animals keep the energy circuit open while others may or may not; (3) man-made changes are of a different order than evolutionary changes, and have effects more comprehensive than is intended or foreseen." Leopold also reminds us that "the key to intelligent tinkering is to save all the pieces."[51] Today as our wilderness areas are "loved to death" we recognize the truth of these principles. If we will only remember that the human specie is just one member of "a community of interdependent parts" and we honor that interdependency, then we can continue to know wildness in the Weminuche Wilderness forever.

# 9

# Leave No Trace: Right Actions for Wilderness Visitors

Remember the rules that parents, guides and teachers made establishing standards for actions? They were not always easy to obey. You probably challenged some before you recognized their wisdom. But as you grew more aware, they helped you understand responsibility, integrity, truth and right actions. Ultimately they became guarantees of personal freedom rather than restrictions of it. The idea of standards of behavior in wilderness areas is just as important.

The concept Leave No Trace is a difficult one for the human animal to abide by. We want to make our mark. We want to change what seems unappealing to our eye and "improve" upon it. We want comfort and pleasure wherever we are, and we will alter the environment to create them. Our culture historically has held little reverence for the rights of the other species that share their wild homes with us. Flowers are picked or uprooted for transplanting. Bones and rocks are collected for "show and tell." Trees are used as writing pads, testimony to our having been there. Water is a handy waste disposal system. Birds and animals are available for our delight. We believe mistakenly that the elements and time will weather away the scars we leave. The earth will take care of itself, and we can still have what we want.

When I contemplate the history of our life on the North American continent, I recognize the origins of these attitudes. Why should we want to "leave no trace" in a land we have *conquered*? The trees were there for our taking. The wild game was abundant. Waterways could be diverted and rerouted for use on crop lands planted with European grass seeds, vegetables and grains. Early settlers brought what was familiar and imposed it upon what was already here. Their habits became our own, but we have begun questioning those habits in the last century.

To alter this philosophy requires reviving a sensitivity and consciousness buried long ago by the desire to own, conquer and change. We must recognize that entering wilderness carries with it responsibilities. *Wilderness is wild.* That is its attraction. The mysteries of wildness await us each time we visit the wilderness. What wildlife will I see? How will the weather challenge me? Will I be comfortable in the solitude? How long will it take me to lose myself in the sacred spirit of that wild place?

For many of us it is only in the wilderness that we can enjoy starlit nights where the Milky Way spans the sky undimmed by the city's light pollution. The Pleides dance clearly, and the Big Dipper hangs suspended in its black cupboard, pointing toward the North Star that guided humans for centuries in other wilderness areas now altered by human development. The snort of a deer can startle us, and the rustle of mice and voles may keep us alert as night ebbs away.

As we grow aware of the wildness that surrounds us, we recognize how slight we are in nature's scheme of things.

Through years of backpacking I have learned the art of walking lightly and preparing for the dangers as well as the opportunities that await me in wilderness. Slowly I developed the skills that are now recognized as six basic principles which protect the integrity of wild places. The *Leave No Trace Outdoor Principles* were first consolidated by the National Outdoor Leadership School in 1987 and published in a well written book by Bruce Hampton and David Cole. The book, entitled *Soft Paths: How to Enjoy the Wilderness Without Harming It*,[52] explains the Leave No Trace philosophy and

Wildernes Ranger teaching
Leave No Trace fire prinicples
*Courtesy of the SJMA*

offers a more profound way of "playing" in the natural world while utilizing every sense we possess.

Simply stated, the basic Leave No Trace principles are as follows:

1. Plan ahead and prepare.
2. Travel and camp on durable surfaces.
3. Pack it in, pack it out.
4. Properly dispose of what you can't pack out.
5. Leave what you find.
6. Minimize use and impact of fires.

A closer look at these principles will help you understand the preparatory steps you need to take when planning a trip, and how you can make your visit to the Weminuche Wilderness enjoyable, safe and protective of what you see.

STEP 1: PLAN AHEAD AND PREPARE

**Before visiting the Weminuche, you must learn the regulations of the areas you plan to visit.** Regulations may alter your plans or require the use of special equipment. As travel in the Weminuche Wilderness has increased, special measures have been necessary to ensure its protection and your enjoyment. All of the regulations may not apply to your specific trip, but it is helpful for you to be aware of them. Besides prohibition of motorized and mechanized travel or equipment in a wilderness area, as specified in the 1964 Wilderness Act, other forest-wide regulations are necessary. These include the following. A complete list of regulations is included in the appendices.

**Group Size:** No group larger than 15 people should travel together in the Weminuche Wilderness. No group of people and stock can exceed a combined number of 25 without a special use permit. For information on permits contact the Ranger District office nearest your destination. Those addresses are given in the appendix of this book

**Stock Feed:** All feed must have proof of weed-free certification from Colorado, Idaho, Montana, Nebraska, Wyoming or Utah and be marked with certified twine, packing or transit certificate. Only the following are allowed: weed-free baled hay, cubed or pellitized hay, or steamed grain in a processor's stamped bag.

Large groups create impacts
*Courtesy of the SJMA*

**Outfitters and Guides:** Commercial outfitters and guides must hold a legal permit to operate on public lands. The permit system is set up to make sure these private operations are conducted in a safe and professional manner. Call the ranger station nearest your destination before any money changes hands, to ensure that your guide is permitted. The address for the Colorado outfitter/guide association is listed in the special uses section of this book.

**Hunting and Fishing:** Hunting and fishing are both allowed in the Weminuche under regulation by the Colorado Division of Wildlife (CDOW). Information on licenses, seasons and restrictions on specific streams and lakes is available from CDOW. Additional information is also given in the the fishing section of this book.

**Bear Safety:** It is recommended that all human food, animal food and garbage be stored in a bear-proof manner when not in use or transport. This is a requirement at campgrounds adjacent to the wilderness.

**Site Specific Regulations:** There are site-specific regulations that must also be obeyed. These may change as time passes. It is important to check with the ranger district office nearest your destination, especially when planning a visit to high country lakes. Information is also available at trailheads. See the Appendix for a full listing.

**Know the area and what to expect.** Carry maps and a compass. If you expect to detour from the system trails, obtain detailed topographical maps, and study them carefully first. Consider your skill in backcountry travel before leaving a system trail. The Weminuche Wilderness is vast and rugged. Even experienced backcountry travelers can become disoriented and lost.

**Plan to travel in small groups.** Honor the group size limit, and recognize that traveling in groups of six or fewer will not only cause less damage to the trails, but also allow you and other wilderness visitors a more pristine experience.

**Select appropriate equipment before the trip.**

> • Boots: Hiking puts a lot of demand on your feet, particularly when you carry a backpack. Use boots that are appropriate for rugged terrain, water and mud. They should be broken in, waterproofed and fitted with the right socks to avoid blisters.

> • Backpacks: There are so many models and sizes of backpacks to choose from today. Whether internal or external frame, the pack should conform comfortably to your body size, have lots of zippered pockets and a padded hip belt. Longer trips require packs with a capacity of at least 3,500 to 5,000 cubic inches. A rule of thumb for packing suggests that heavier, denser items be packed in the middle and upper part of your pack, with lighter gear below.

> • Sleeping bags and pads: Choose a sleeping bag rated 10 degrees lower than what you expect temperatures to be. There are advantages and disadvantages to down-filled or synthetic fiber bags. You must be your own judge, but remember, comfortable sleeping means pleasant days of travel. A pad is a must to insulate you from the cold, bumpy ground.

• Tents: A tent is your only dependable shelter when traveling in the wilderness. It holds in heat, blocks out sun and insects, and protects your gear and you from rain, hail, snow and dew. Prices and quality vary, but consider weight and size when choosing one for your trip.

• Water filters and water: Water filters are essential in the backcountry. No streams or creeks are free of giardia risk, no matter how isolated from civilization. Filters range in price from $25 to $250, and they are worth their weight in gold as a preventive measure to serious illness. Water bottles should be kept full. Remember that drinking a minimum of four quarts a day is necessary to prevent dehydration during exercise.

• Rain gear and warm clothing: Whether day hiking or planning an extended trip, always carry good rain gear and layers of clothing for warmth. Summer storms occur frequently in high mountains.

**Repackage food and choose lightweight items.** Reduce bulk by repacking your food in airtight zip lock bags or plastic containers. Even foods like jam, peanut butter or salsa can be carried on a trip when repacked. Pack only the amount you will use, and use leftovers for breakfast or lunch. The range of dried meals now available in grocery stores is phenomenal. Pastas, beans, dried soups, rice dishes -- dinners can be as varied as you choose. Remember to bring food that will not spoil. Tortillas and bagels last for days.

**Take special precautions in packaging your food since you are in bear country.** To protect your food when in camp, carry air-tight, heavy duty plastic bags or containers which can be packed and suspended from tree branches with parachute cord. Remember that smells such as fish, soap and deodorant attract bears. Keep them to a minimum.

**Tell a friend or relative where you are going,** when you expect to return and what to do if you are late. Plan your trip before you leave, and stick to your plan. This special precaution helps alleviate worries and fears.

**For a nominal fee (only $1.00) you can purchase search and rescue insurance** at any sporting goods store in Colorado. Check with local sports shops for information.

Step 2: TRAVEL AND CAMP ON DURABLE SURFACES

ON THE TRAIL

**Double-check regulations at the trailhead** to see if new information is posted. Besides the regulations listed previously, new postings occur seasonally. Hunters, backpackers, stock packers, fishermen and hikers all should stop and check the bulletin boards posted at the trailhead. Closures, fire conditions and special warnings will be brought to your attention.

**Sign in at the trailhead.** Both hikers and stock travelers must sign the register. The U.S. Forest Service uses registration cards to compile visitor statistics and monitor use and conditions. Search and rescue teams also use trailhead information to help locate lost or injured parties.

**Plan to arrive at your destination before sunset.** It takes several hours to reach most campsites from any trailhead in the Weminuche. Setting up camp in the dark is hazardous to both you and the terrain. Give yourself adequate time to enjoy the country without having to rush.

Fragile alpine meadow and riparian areas
*Courtesy of B. J. Boucher*

Wilderness bridges are atypical!
*Courtesy of B. J. Boucher*

Don't cut switchbacks or skirt minor obstacles in the trail, like puddles or mud. High elevation vegetation is vulnerable to the effects of trampling and slow to recover. Mud will come off your boots far more quickly than the plants will grow back. The natural character of a wilderness area is difficult to recover, once disturbed. Walk single file and stay on the path. Traveling abreast creates multiple trails. Trails are designed and maintained to prevent erosion, and switchbacking compromises the design and causes topsoil to wash away, leaving vegetation to die.

Take rest breaks on durable surfaces that are well off the trail. Other trail users will not disturb you, and you will not disturb their solitude. Rocks and bare soil will not feel the impact of your stay as will tender grass and meadows of wildflowers. If you meet other hikers on the trail, move off to the side and stop until they pass. Continuing to walk at the side widens the trail.

Walking parties should yield the right-of-way to stock parties. For the safety of all, step off the trail on the downhill side and speak calmly to the riders as they approach and pass. Backpacking gear can frighten livestock, but your voice will help reassure the animals. Return to the trail only after the riders have passed.

Keep pets on a leash or under control and near you. Better yet, leave them at home! Uncontrolled pets often endanger wildlife and themselves. They can also spook livestock and bother or intimidate other visitors.

When traveling in areas with no trails, spread out your group and follow separate routes to avoid creating a new trail. Travel on durable surfaces--sand, rock, snow, dry grass or pine needles--and avoid wet, marshy areas or tender vegetation. Keep group size small when traveling in pristine areas or high alpine meadows. Plants that grow in alpine areas are fragile and easily destroyed by the human foot. Most take years to mature since growing conditions are so severe. One season of human trampling can destroy them.

**Be careful!** Old mining structures and mines found in the Weminuche Wilderness are often unstable and dangerous. Rock scree slopes can also be very unstable and slick. It is easier to travel uphill than down. When descending on loose scree move cautiously, choosing each step carefully. Stream crossings can be dangerous. Spring run-off in the Weminuche Wilderness can last until mid-July, and summer storms can cause sudden deluges. Because it is wilderness, few permanent bridge structures have been constructed by the Forest Service. Frequently, logs are in place that serve as bridges; but when fording a deep, rapidly moving stream, use a third leg (sturdy stick or pole) to assist you. If you wade wear sneakers or sturdy sandals that protect your feet. These same shoes can be your footwear at camp.

**Take special precautions in high altitude thunderstorms.** June is the month least susceptible to high altitude storms in the Weminuche. Expect daily storms in July and August, the monsoon season in the Southwest. Don't be caught on a high ridge during mid-day, the most frequent time of occurrence. Avoid standing under tall trees and structures that might attract lightning.

**Dense forests can create confusion.** Keep your compass at hand and always note high ridges and mountains for orientation.

**Respect wildlife when traveling a trail.** Animals will travel the same trails at different times of day. Learn about them before you enter the wilderness, their habits, their living and feeding needs, their behavior when confronted with loud noises or sudden movements. Always travel quietly.

AT CAMP

**Select a previously used site when camping in heavily used areas.** At this time campsites are not designated in heavy use areas. This may change as the number of visitors to the Weminuche increases. Though campsite solitude is important, more important is preserving the pristine nature of the wilderness. Compacted soils, social trails and vegetation loss occur when a site is used repeatedly. It is far better to keep that impacted site free of human litter and waste so that it can be used again rather than spread the destruction of nature to other areas.

**Camp away from trails to give yourself and others privacy.** Studies show that privacy when camping is the number one concern. Camp at least 100 feet from the trail to give yourself and others solitude.

**Avoid places where impact is just beginning.** If you must choose between an impacted site and one that is still intact, choose the former. You want to encourage others to use your site rather than damage a new one. You are helping preserve the wilderness by camping on the impacted site.

**Locate your camp, wash dishes and bathe at least 100 feet from streams** to avoid contaminating water sources. Water is a special resource, both for you and for all the creatures who live in the wilderness. It is a focal point for most campsites. Use biodegradable soap or no soap at all for your dishes and bathing. (Soil, sand and pine needles make great scouring pads.) Strain food scraps from cooking and washing water, and pack them out. Scatter gray water away from water sources and camp.

**Bury human waste at least six inches deep in individual cat holes.** Deposit human waste at least 200 feet from water, camp or trails. Cover and disguise the cat hole when finished. Cat holes should be widely dispersed, and always located in a site that will promote decomposition. Organic soil rather than sandy mineral soil promotes rapid decay. Mixing organic material or debris from the surface also promotes more rapid breakdown.

A properly dug cat hole
*Courtesy of the SJMA*

A properly covered cat hole
*Courtesy of the SJMA*

Bear tracks
*Courtesy of Chris Schultz*

**Urinate on rocks, sandy areas or pine duff away from water sources.** Wild animals are attracted to urine salts, and they may defoliate plants or dig up soil where urine is found. Urine can be diluted with water carried to the site, thus avoiding concentration of odor or habituation of animals to urine salts.

**Use toilet paper sparingly, and avoid dyed, perfumed brands.** Pack out or burn all toilet paper. I have picked up discarded toilet paper on every trail in the Weminuche Wilderness. Not a pleasant task! All feminine hygiene products should be packed out also. They decompose slowly if buried, and animals often dig them up.

**Keep an extra clean camp in bear country, and protect yourself and your food from unnecessary wildlife encounters.** The San Juan/Rio Grande National Forests now recommend that all stored foods be bear-resistant as previously mentioned. Lightweight bear-proof containers are available at sporting goods stores. An alternative is to carry nylon parachute cord which can be used to suspend food ten feet above the ground and ten feet away from the tree trunk. Bears are intelligent and will take advantage of any food source in their vicinity. Smells attract them, so all food preparation should be carried out away from your sleeping tent.

**Marmots, porcupines, chipmunks and other small mammals are also attracted to human food.** Pack out all leftovers so as not to habituate them. They live in the wild and must remain dependent on the sources of food that are naturally available to them.

STEP 3: PACK IT IN, PACK IT OUT!

There are four guiding principles behind Leave No Trace sanitation practices:

(1) Avoid polluting water sources

(2) Eliminate contact with insects and animals

(3) Maximize decomposition

(4) Minimize the chances of social impacts

**Reduce litter at the source.** Repackage food into reusable containers or zip lock bags, and remove any excess packaging when preparing your trip. This reduces weight and creates efficiency for packing out refuse. Those same bags become garbage bags as they are emptied of their food.

**Dispose of trash and garbage properly.** "Trash" includes non-food wastes such as packaging, twist-ties, candy and food wrappers, cigarette butts, spent gun shells, toilet paper and other small items of waste. All of these items should be packed out in a double lined plastic garbage bag. Often food wrappers appear combustible, but the foil or plastic component leaves a residual litter once burned.

A messy campsite left by stock travelers
*Courtesy of the SJMA*

"Garbage" is food waste. Reduce such waste by carefully planning and preparing your meals. All food scraps--including particles from food preparation, eggshells, fruit cores and peelings, even dishwater scraps--should be packed out. Burning or burying food is not recommended since burning is often ineffective, and buried waste is dug up by wildlife, especially bears. To habituate them to human food is to create disaster for you and the bear.

**Take everything out that you brought in.** Though we may expect to return to an area, it is never appropriate to leave anything behind for future use. Hunting camps have been left behind, and critters have spread the items across the floor of the forest. I have stumbled on these unsightly messes and stood in helpless anger, unable to carry out all the heavy remains in my backpack. I take careful notice of the campsite, however, and report it to the U.S. Forest Service upon return. Remember, the wilderness has its own system of composting its refuse, and it is very efficient. Downfall is composted by insects and molds. But plastics, cans, paper and other manmade items only accumulate, destroying the pristine wilderness.

STEP 4. PROPERLY DISPOSE OF WHAT YOU CAN'T PACK OUT

**Dispose of fishing and hunting waste appropriately.** Consider taking your fish home and disposing of the entrails there. Otherwise, bury the entrails in a cathole. All game should be dressed well away from campsites, trails and water.

STEP 5: LEAVE WHAT YOU FIND

**Minimize site alteration.** It is not appropriate to dig trenches for tents. With proper planning, you can locate a tent so that natural drainage will keep it dry. Nor should trees or shrubs be cut to construct lean-to's or rough furniture. The naturalness of the site was pleasing to you when you arrived and will be so to others in the future when you leave it that way. If you move surface rocks, twigs, pine needles or cones, and other natural objects, replace them before leaving. If the site you have chosen is in a high-use area, clean it up by dismantling excessive fire rings and picking up any trash left behind by previous visitors. Remember, *good campsites are found not made.*

**Leave flowers, rocks, archeological artifacts and other objects behind.** When we enter the wilderness, we are enchanted by our discoveries. Those same discoveries will enchant future visitors. The natural environment can remain natural only if we honor its sanctity. The cumulative effect of gathering plants can be harmful. The loss of archeological information through thoughtless collecting weakens our understanding of human history.

**Avoid damaging live trees and plants.** Trees have suffered much damage from our misuse in the past. Where we tied our horses they were girdled. We used our knives and hatchets to disfigure them with initials. We created clothes hangers with nails driven into their trunks. We gathered low bows for beds. Such damage is irreparable and completely unnecessary. Equally irreparable is the damage done when plants are repeatedly trampled. Trampling plants by unnecessarily extending the size of your campsite ultimately leads to bare hardpacked soils which can grow nothing.

**Avoid disturbing wildlife.** The wilderness is home to numerous species. Loud noises disturb their solitude and ours. When we chase, feed or attract them we compromise their ability to live in their natural habitat. Left undisturbed they offer us the opportunity to view them from a safe distance while they pursue their natural lives. We visit the wilderness to know its specialness, and one aspect that is very special is its combination of voices--the yip of the distant coyote, the bugling of an elk, the sharp chastisement of the squirrel or the musical song of the warbler. When we tune our ears into the subtleties of the wild, we learn more than we can possibly imagine.

**Reduce your impact on other visitors.** Uncontrolled pets intrude on others' privacy, as do loud music, boisterous conversations and loud noises. Respect the privacy and solitude of other visitors who have journeyed to the wilderness to seek isolation and quietness.

STEP 6: MINIMIZE USE AND IMPACTS OF FIRE

**Campfires cause lasting impacts to wilderness.** Numerous fire rings are one of the most common impacts seen in the Weminuche Wilderness. Rather than constructing a new one, it is better to remove the old pit. Carry a lightweight stove for cooking and a candle lantern for evening conversation. Stoves are usable in any terrain. Fires demand fuel, and overuse of downfall so vital to the revegetation, as well as the thoughtless destruction of standing trees, leaves barren campsites that can never recover. The impacts of campfires increase with elevation. Gnarled old trees in subalpine settings have taken centuries to grow to a stature of ten feet, and one night's fire destroys them, leaving bare areas that will never grow another tree. Without a fire, the starlit nights become magical, and you are no longer separated from the wonderful night world that surrounds you.

Top soil saved for return to fire pit
*Courtesy of the SJMA*

Fire pan for protecting soil
*Courtesy of the SJMA*

**In high-use areas, use existing fire rings, fire pans or mound fires.** Fires, if needed, should be built in existing fire rings in high use areas. Recognize, however, that only small fires are needed. Be frugal with firewood. Remove any residual trash and carry it out. Scatter the ashes and leave a clean fire ring.

**Use dead wood only, and burn it completely to ash.** Fires should only be built where firewood is plentiful, and only downed wood should be used. Never break branches off of trees. Seek wood several minutes from camp, and gather it from a large area, rather than cleaning out one small spot. Use wood that is no larger than the diameter of your wrist, since this can be broken easily and burns readily. Any wood not used should be rescattered on the forest floor.

**When building a fire in remote areas, use techniques that Leave No Trace of its presence.** This means taking care in the site chosen, the size of the fire, the removal of the firesite afterwards and the use of a fire pan. The heat from fires can destroy organic soils. A firepan will protect the soil. They are available commercially, but they can also be made from lightweight inexpensive aluminum pans propped up on small rocks to protect the surface underneath from the heat.

Select a durable site that minimizes trampling by people cooking or socializing near the fire. Rings of trampled grass invite future use, and ultimately an impacted area results.

A FINAL THOUGHT

It is not easy to read such a lengthy list of suggested ethical behaviors in the wilderness. They sound like restraints put on the freedom you are seeking when you visit the Weminuche. But remember, even as we would not welcome into our home someone who destroyed its integrity, so the wilderness, too, is our home. Its beauty and naturalness are what we all seek when we enter it. Its future depends on our care and love. To walk responsibly in wilderness, to honor its needs, to care for the future of its creatures--these are the actions that kindle our hearts and give humility to our sense of personal worth. I ask you to consider the closing quote from the book *Soft Paths* which sums up wilderness ethics:

> *Let no one say and say it to your shame*
> *that all was beauty here until you came.*

# 10

# Special Information
# for Contemporary Users

The Weminuche Wilderness attracts thousands of people into its forests and mountains annually. There are stock travelers, fishermen, backpackers, day hikers, hunters, outfitters and climbers using the same trails and seeking "recreation" in wildness. All of these visitors share in a legacy that cannot be valued in dollars. Each group has specific responsibilities and codes for ethical behavior that should be practiced. Each of us feels the wilderness is there for our specific use, and when we observe the sloppy habits of others we angrily declare they have no right to be there. Yet multiple use is the directive given the U.S. Forest Service for managing wilderness recreation. Respect for all user groups occurs when each practices right actions. To help understand some of the varying concerns each group must recognize, I have included specific information for fishermen, stock travelers, hunters, climbers, professional guiding services and train passengers. The Leave No Trace principles discussed previously apply to everyone. Day hikers and backpackers should review them carefully.

## FISHING IN WILDERNESS LAKES AND STREAMS

Many of the high alpine lakes and streams in the Weminuche Wilderness offer excellent fishing, and some are still the home of Colorado's native river cutthroat. Native trout, however, have been impacted by the introduction and stocking of non-native species such as the rainbow and brook trout, which are more aggressive and adaptable to unpredictable conditions. How many of the sixty-six lakes and 245 miles of streams in the Weminuche contain fish is not known, since fishermen keep their favorite spots secret.

Lakes range in size from less than an acre to the 265-acre Emerald Lake, the third largest natural lake in Colorado. Large rivers such as the Vallecito and Los Piños Rivers flow long distances through the wilderness. The Los Piños River originates near Weminuche Pass and meanders for eighteen miles to its exit from wilderness boundaries. Side streams that enter the major rivers can be less than a mile in length or flow for several miles.

Emerald Lake
*Courtesy of B. J. Boucher*

The Weminuche Wilderness Management Direction document adopted in 1998 calls for the reintroduction of native cutthroat trout in the future, but this will be a lengthy and tedious task as the U.S. Forest Service and Colorado Division of Wildlife (CDOW) work together to cull out exotics and find appropriate native fingerlings that can adapt and become self-sustaining in high mountain lakes and streams. Presently a moratorium is in effect on stocking any fish in the Weminuche because of *whirling disease*,[53] a disease that affects the fish's ability to swim. The disease is now prevalent throughout Colorado's lower streams and lakes. It was found in the Durango Fish Hatchery in 1997, and resulted in its closure until disease free. Once clear, it is anticipated the hatchery will produce native cutthroats which can be placed in Weminuche waterways and lakes.

Many high mountain lakes were gouged out by glacial action over 10,000 years ago. The quality of fish habitat that lakes and streams offer depends on a large number of variables. First, there must be an adequate feeding base for the fish. Spawning gravels where eggs can be laid either in spring or fall, depending on the species, are necessary to sustain the population. Water quality and temperature are significant determiners of fish habitat, as are flow conditions into and out of the lake. Severe weather conditions in the mountains can cause significant variations in the water quality. Geology is also a component of good fish habitat. Sedimentary rock areas are more conducive to fish than igneous rocks where heavy mineral deposits can seep into the water. Run-off from melting winter snow can impact survival, particularly of spring hatchlings. Predation and heavy recreational fishing affect numbers. Introduced diseases such as whirling disease can destroy the integrity of the fish community.

Complicating survival are the challenges of cold winters that occur year after year. Winter is the most stressful season for fish in high mountain lakes. Lakes tend to stratify in terms of temperature, forming layers of varying temperatures at different water depths. During summer the warmest waters are at the surface. As winter approaches the warm temperatures will move to the lower levels, providing open water for fish to survive winter's freeze. Fish feed aggressively during the fall when the shift in water temperature levels occurs. If the lake has lots of organic nutrients, the oxygen level in the water is depleted. The inflow of fresh water, lake depth and the amount of snow cover all contribute to oxygenation of a lake during winter. With the loss of oxygen in the water, the fish die. This is known as winter kill. Without a source of recruitment for new breeders to a winter-killed lake, it will remain void of fish.

When spring thaws begin, the water in a lake reverses temperature stratification once again. The ice cover and snow on the surface melt, and recirculation of the water begins. As the surface warms under the sun's rays, the waters will shift, with the warmest temperatures at the surface.

MANAGING FISHERIES IN THE WEMINUCHE

Wildlife biologists employed by the San Juan and Rio Grande National Forests are responsible for monitoring water quality conditions in the streams and lakes of the wilderness. Impacts are numerous, and wilderness rangers help collect data that biologists use to monitor changes and institute actions which preserve pristine waters. Impacts include pollution and trash left by visitors which destroy water quality. Recreational fishing frequently causes heavy pressure on fish population in certain areas. Trails along shorelines and streambanks can erode and dump silt into the stream. Riparian areas so vital to the health of lakes and streams are trampled by recreational and permitted livestock. Stream flows are altered by rock and log dams. Water development projects constructed before the Weminuche Wilderness was set aside change stream flows. These impacts and others can completely alter a healthy fishing stream, turning it into a barren waterway.

FISHING REGULATIONS

CDOW, the agency responsible for managing Colorado's wildlife since 1897, publishes a guide to fishing seasons, license requirements, creel limits and fishing methods on lakes and streams in the Weminuche Wilderness. This guide is available at all U.S. Forest Service offices in the area as well as CDOW offices. Specific regulations that govern certain bodies of water are also posted at trailheads that enter the Weminuche Wilderness. In general the regulations are as follows:

1. A fishing license is required for anyone sixteen years or older who fishes. Children under sixteen are not required to have a fishing license, but the bag limit is half the daily bag and possession limit for that lake or stream.

2. A resident fishing license costs $20.25 annually. A senior resident license for individuals at least 64 years old costs $10.25. Non-resident fishing licenses cost $40.25 per year. Five-day licenses for both residents and non-residents are available for $18.25, and a one-day license costs $5.25. The twenty-five cent addition covers a search and rescue fee which is well worth the money.

3. Bag and possession limits vary according to the species of fish and the body of water. In general the possession limit is eight fish in one day. Emerald Lake has a special restriction because of the unique strain of fish that has hybridized in its waters. These fish, a hybrid cutthroat-rainbow trout, have adapted in marginal habitat where inflow and aeration of the water is limited. They are a self-sustaining population. Emerald Lake was barren of fish until cutthroat were introduced from the Los Piños River in 1888. Rainbow were stocked around the turn of the century. The following restrictions apply to Emerald Lake: Only artificial flies or lures can be used. Anglers are allowed to keep two trout, 14 inches or less in length. Fishing is prohibited in Lake Creek inlet for 1/2 mile above Big Emerald Lake from January 1 through July 15th because of spawning.

4. Regulations regarding threatened and endangered species prohibit the taking of several species of fish and frogs. For example, it is believed that the Weminuche Wilderness offers habitat for the boreal toad. This toad appears in shallow brackish water at high elevations. During the tadpole stage it is jet black in color. Adult toads are recognized by a white stripe along the length of their back. If seen, its presence should be reported to the U.S. Forest Service and CDOW. The greenback cutthroat trout and the tiger salamander are also endangered.

Check with public offices for additional information about threatened or endangered species.

5. The legal method of take is restricted to the use of a conventional rod.

CDOW can be contacted for specific information at the following addresses:

Colorado Division of Wildlife
Southwest Region: 280 S. Townsend
Montrose, Colorado 81401
(970) 249-3431

Colorado Division of Wildlife
151 E. 16th St.
Durango, Colorado 81301
(970) 247-4755
(970) 247-0855

LEAVE NO TRACE FISHING ETHICS

Every visitor to the Weminuche Wilderness should observe the Leave No Trace principles explained in an earlier section of this book. There are several additional practices for fishermen[54] that will guarantee pristine waters and quality fishing for the future.

**Catch-and-Release-fishing.** Many fishermen now recognize the importance of this practice, and certain waters can only be fished in this manner. Check regulations to be certain when fishing any new stream or lake. Returning fish to the water alive is not as simple as it sounds. There are ways of handling fish that can kill them. Anglers should follow these steps to ensure the best chance of survival for the fish:[55]

• Do not play any fish to exhaustion. Keep the fish in the water as much as possible when handling and removing the hook.

• Remove the hook gently; do not squeeze the fish or place your fingers in its gills.

• If deeply hooked, cut the line. Do not pull the hook out.

• Release the fish only after its equilibrium is maintained. If necessary, gently hold the fish facing upstream and move it slowly back and forth.

• Release it in quiet water.

• If fishing in catch-and-release waters, strongly consider using barbless hooks.

**Streambank and Water Protection.** Fishermen frequently tangle or snare lines, change baits and change locations along the stream. The following practices will maintain a pristine environment:

• Pick up all broken pieces of fishing line. Untangle snared pieces from bushes and trees. Waterfowl frequently become tangled in the line or swallow the hook.

• Carry out all bait containers.

• Treat all riparian areas with care. A riparian area is the green area immediately adjacent to and influenced by water. Healthy riparian areas are essential for quality fish populations Removal or trampling of vegetation causes erosion and reduces cover for fish.

• Dumping wastes and garbage in waters can stress or kill fish. It is also ugly and unnecessary. Clean water is essential for fish and people.

• Altering streambanks or bodies of water with logs and rocks is unacceptable. Nature is responsible for those changes, not man.

• Transplanting fish or any exotic species of plant or animal to the wilderness is illegal. Exotics alter the natural community and destroy fish habitat.

Horse travelers in the Weminuche
*Courtesy of the SJMA*

• Fishing equipment and waders should be rinsed before being used in the wilderness. Whirling disease spore, now found in most Colorado waters, are viable for 30 years, according to fish specialists.

• Contaminated equipment can contaminate pristine waters.

### HORSE SENSE IN THE WILDERNESS

Marvelous opportunities await the stock user in the Weminuche Wilderness. The terrain is varied, the trails are open and vast reaches of wild country are available for travel. Traveling with stock, however, demands responsibility not only for yourself but for the animals. It is tempting to undertake travel on a trail that is too demanding for one's personal expertise or the ability of the animals. Most of the trails in the Weminuche are suitable for riding, but some are not recommended, either because of conditions such as heavy foot travel and lack of camping opportunities or because of difficult travel. Narrow, steep, boggy or rocky sections can be dangerous for animals. Many miles of trails are above timberline where exposure to lightning can be significant. Some trails are heavily used by outfitters who guide groups into the back country throughout the summer. Their permits guarantee their camping sites and use of certain trails. These and other situations must give pause to anyone planning a potential stock trip in the Weminuche Wilderness.

With the freedom to travel accompanied by stock comes the responsibility to care for the environment and to respect the rights of other users. The complex ecological interrelationships in the Weminuche Wilderness have existed for thousands of years and can quickly be destroyed by any careless recreationalist. Destruction can be significantly increased when stock are managed carelessly. Once damaged, many fragile soils and plants may never recover.

Besides the trip planning tips and Leave No Trace information previously discussed which applies to every wilderness traveler, there are some additional ideas that stock users should consider. The National Outdoor Leadership School (NOLS) has written an excellent brochure which carefully explains "good horse sense" in back country travel. The San Juan/Rio Grande National Forests also have brochures and travel information to assist you in your trip planning.[56] Remember, the basic rules that apply to any back country traveler apply to you To reiterate the Leave No Trace principles for stock users consider the following:

- Plan ahead and prepare your stock before you go
- Minimize horse impacts
- In popular areas, concentrate use
- In remote areas, spread use
- Avoid places where impact is just beginning
- Use campfires responsibly
- Pack it in, pack it out
- Properly dispose of what you cannot pack out
- Be considerate of others
- Leave what you find

PLANNING BEFORE YOU GO

*Information:* Contact the local district offices for any special rules, maps and opportunities for the area in which you plan to travel with animals. You will need information concerning permits, campfire use, party size, grazing, weed-seed-free feed requirements, trail conditions and closures. Having adequate information helps you determine the equipment needs for your animals and you. When you consider your route before leaving, you can locate river crossings, mountain passes, trail hazards or use and potential camping areas.

SJMA volunteer Ghost Riders in the Weminuche
*Courtesy of the SJMA*

*Stock:* Know the condition of your stock and whether they are in shape for the trip. Get them accustomed to highlines, pickets, hobbles and temporary corrals before you leave. Carry insect repellent and a first-aid kit for your animals. When animals suffer accidents, they need immediate attention.

*Feed:* Plan to take supplemental feed and get your stock accustomed to it before you leave home. The San Juan/Rio Grande National Forests require that all feed taken into the Weminuche Wilderness be weed-seed-free certified so as to help prevent the spread of noxious weeds on the forests. Ask district offices about potential grazing in the areas you plan to visit, so you know how much supplemental food to take and where to find grazing.

*Nose bags and manger:* Use these to feed your stock hay, pellets or grain. They conserve feed and keep the ground free of food that can attract other animals.

*Packing:* Carry lightweight, compact camp equipment and prepackaged, dehydrated food that is repackaged to save space and reduce weight. The fewer animals required for a pack trip the better. Practice packing animals at home before leaving. This will give them the experience needed before starting up a trail. A shovel and axe are useful for keeping camp clean, clearing brush or trees which fall across the trail and spreading animal droppings before you leave camp.

ON THE TRAIL

*Horse sense:* Your own or your animals' lives can be at risk in rough country. Let your stock pick their way through boggy places, slide zones, on slick and steep trails, and through deep water and snow. Better yet, lead them through treacherous stretches.

*Trail protection:* Stay on the trail rather than cutting switchbacks and trampling vegetation. Ride single file. Keep your stock from skirting shallow puddles, small rocks or bushes, thus preventing the creation of wide, deteriorating trails. Make decisions that will cause the least impact and preserve the trail.

*When resting:* Tie your stock off the trail to a tree at least eight inches in diameter. This is a courtesy to other trail users and helps reduce wear and tear on the trail. Before moving on, scatter the manure and fill in any pawed ground.

*Smoking while traveling:* Careless cigarette use can result in fires as well as threaten your own safety while on the horse. It is best not to smoke while traveling.

*Trail courtesy:* Say hello to other back country travelers, and remember these basics when passing in difficult terrain. Downhill traffic usually yields to uphill traffic, but if you have a better place to pull off, do so. People with llamas or on foot should yield to horse traffic, stepping to the downhill side of the trail. If they don't, smile and yield the right-of-way or ask them politely to step below the trail and wait quietly while you pass.

CAMPING

*Stock needs:* Keep all pack animals at least 200 feet from streams, lake shores, trails and camping areas. This necessitates careful analysis of a site before stopping. Is it well-drained and open? Is the water accessible for the animals? The 200-foot recommendation helps keep water clean, protects the soil and vegetation, and keeps trails and campsites clear of loose stock. Certain lakes like Flint, Archuleta and West Ute have 200 foot restrictions. Check regulations before camping. Rotate stock throughout the area to reduce trampling and prevent overgrazing.

*Securing animals at camp:* Regulations require that animals be restrained at least 100 feet from water. There are several techniques for controlling your stock. They include highlines, hitching rails, picket ropes and pins, hobbles, and temporary fences or corrals. Horses should be tied to trees for only short periods of time. When erecting highlines, use tree-saver straps to keep your stock from girdling the tree. If you create a hitching rail, use a dead or downed pole and place padding under the lash ropes to protect the bark of the live tree. DO NOT CUT TREES TO CREATE HITCHING RAILS. When using the other restraints, consider the terrain and its preservation as well as your horses' needs and safety. A helpful principle to remember is that more confinement generally means more impact.

*Human needs:* Allow enough time at the end of the day to select an appropriate site for you and your animals. A hasty decision can result in shortcuts and destruction to the environment. In popular areas, the best choice is to use existing campsites. This prevents the creation of additional impacted areas. If you must create a new site, an out-of-the-way or screened location is best. You want a campsite that is clean, private and offers a wilderness experience. If you observe the "Pack it in, Pack it out!" rule you will guarantee that the next person has the same good time you had. If the campsite you choose is not clean, why not improve the site? Do not  hammer nails into trees for hanging gear. Carry adequate tents and equipment for storage.

All food must be properly stored so as to make it uninviting and inaccessible to bears. All food should be located at least 100 feet and downwind from your sleeping area. Bear-resistant panniers and containers are available to the stock traveler and make food storage much easier.

Follow all of the Leave No Trace points made previously regarding fires. Remember, fire pans and cook stoves are good alternatives to traditional campfires. Constructing rock walls, log benches, lean-to's, and other human erected structures is not permitted in the Weminuche Wilderness.

**When breaking camp, scatter the horse manure** and fill in pawed holes. Naturalize the setting, and return any rocks that were removed. Existing fire rings should be left since dismantling them only causes further destruction when they are rebuilt. Fire pits should be cleaned for the next user. If possible scatter a covering of needles and cones over the site disrupted by your animals to help recreate its natural appearance.

## HUNTING IN THE WEMINUCHE WILDERNESS

The Colorado Division of Wildlife is responsible for managing the animal population in the Weminuche Wilderness while the U.S. Forest Service manages habitat. This may sound like a weird division of duties, yet the two agencies are vitally linked in their missions and work together to ensure a pristine environment for the deer, elk, black bear and bighorn sheep sought by bow hunters, muzzle loaders and rifle hunters who come from across the country each fall.

Regulations control hunting activities to ensure the safety of the numerous hunters and the preservation of game. Though some are basic and remain the same year after year, new ones are added frequently. Regulations establish seasons, bag limits, legal hunting methods, hunter safety education, license requirements, state residency qualifications and many other requirements for safe and ethical hunting. Every hunter should obtain a copy of the "Colorado Hunting Season Information" published annually and available at all CDOW or U.S. Forest Service offices in order to be current before the hunting season begins.

Hunter in the Weminuche
*Courtesy of Laurie Gruel*

Specific restrictions related to hunting in the Weminuche Wilderness must also be kept in mind. They include:

1. No motorized or mechanized vehicles, including deer carts, can enter wilderness boundaries according to the 1964 Wilderness Act.

2. Site specific restrictions limit stock activity and camping near high country lakes. Check regulations discussed elsewhere.

Though most non-hunters recognize the value of hunting as a management practice in wilderness areas today, many are very critical of the sport because of the thoughtless and inhumane approach taken by a few hunters. Ethical behavior cannot be mandated by law. It must be a part of the individual's personal sense of right and wrong. Respecting the land, the integrity of habitat, rights of the animal and the quality experience of other wilderness visitors are vital ethical practices.

The National Shooting Sports Foundation has this to say about ethical hunting:[57]

> • In the time of our beginnings, we were hunters. To succeed and survive, our earliest ancestors had to cooperate in the hunt. That need helped shape our basic societies.

> • To prevail over larger, faster, stronger creatures, those ancient hunters relied on intelligence and invention. With tools of stone and wood and bone, they were no longer inferior to the game....

> • Few of us now hunt in order to survive. Instead, modern hunters work to ensure the survival of wildlife. We have properly assumed responsibility for our natural heritage.... As our tools are now more efficient, we abide by ethical standards to preserve the challenge of the hunt. We avoid the use of technology that would place the game in an unfair situation. We are not wasteful.

> • We know the majesty of wildlife and wilderness. We still wonder at the mystery of our world. We respect the game we take and appreciate the opportunity to continue our ancient occupation.

> • Finally, we understand the difference between right and wrong. We behave accordingly because we must. And because, in the time of our beginnings, we were hunters.

Ethical hunters observe the following guidelines to protect their hunting heritage:

> • Responsible hunters also think of safety first and shoot game second.

Alpine Lake - Weminuche Wilderness
*Courtesy of B. J. Boucher*

• They maintain their equipment so it functions properly and poses no threat to them or others. They prepare well before the hunt so as to be able to handle challenging physical demands.

• They demonstrate respect for private and public property, asking permission to hunt on private land, driving only on developed and open roadways, and following Leave No Trace camping practices.

• Responsible hunters study and abide by the regulations for the area in which they hunt, reporting violations or vandalism to the proper authorities.

• Responsible hunters understand the game they hunt and respect the animal's rights. They never take a shot until certain of the species and clear that it will be a good shot. They hunt only during shooting hours and in season.

• Responsible hunters take care of their game immediately. They never leave wounded animals to suffer. They immediately field dress and transport the game to the appropriate storing facility to avoid spoilage.

• Transporting game from the field in such a way that it does not offend the general public is important to the ethical hunter.

Needle Mountains
*Courtesy of B. J. Boucher*

• Ethical hunters respect the rights of other individuals by preserving wilderness conditions. Other recreationalists in the area may not be hunting. They deserve a pristine environment.

• Responsible hunters involve themselves in conservation efforts that guarantee future hunting experiences.

Individuals who ignore these ethical standards and hunting regulations are not hunters. They are destroyers of the wilderness and its wildlife.

## MOUNTAINEERING AND CLIMBING IN THE WEMINUCHE WILDERNESS

Opportunities for mountaineering and climbing in the Weminuche Wilderness are numerous. Besides Mt. Eolus, Sunlight and Windom Peaks in the Needles which exceed 14,000 feet in elevation, numerous other mountains challenge climbers. The Grenadier Range, accessed from Elk Creek Trail, invites many visitors who enjoy snow and rock climbing on the Trinity Peaks, Graystone, Vestal and Storm King Mountains. The Vallecito drainage provides access to additional climbing areas like the Guardian. The West Needles which lie east of U.S. 550 near Crater Lake, are another favorite area for mountaineering. The Rio Grande Pyramid on the eastern slopes of the Wilderness attracts climbers. Some of the most challenging mountaineering experiences in Colorado exist in the Weminuche Wilderness.

Mountaineering is a growing sport because of the challenge it presents as well as the exhilaration felt after reaching a summit. It is also a demanding sport that requires physical preparedness, skill, mental alertness and a willingness to accept nature's indifference and hardships. Excellent books have been written that instruct the mountaineer in safe climbing techniques and explain the A's to Z's of equipment, route finding and climbing or mountaineering techniques. Perhaps one of the best is the comprehensive *Mountaineering: The Freedom of the Hills* published by The Mountaineers of Seattle. Safety is the primary concern promoted by this book and should be the focus of every individual who seeks the exhilaration of summiting high alpine peaks. The simple code of ethics outlined by The Mountaineers of Seattle expresses the concerns that any climber or mountaineer should understand before entering the Weminuche Wilderness. That code includes the following:[58]

> • A climbing party of three is minimum, unless adequate prearranged support is available. On glaciers, a minimum of two rope teams is recommended.

> • Rope up on all exposed places and for all glacier travel. Anchor all belays.

> • Keep the party together, and obey the leader or majority rule.

> • Never climb beyond your ability and knowledge.

> • Never let judgment be overruled by desire when choosing the route or deciding whether to turn back.

> • Carry the necessary clothing, food and equipment at all times.

> • Leave the trip schedule with a responsible person.

> • Follow the precepts of sound mountaineering as set forth in textbooks of recognized merit.

> • Behave at all times in a manner that reflects favorably upon mountaineering.

Every alpinist should be aware that any disaster which occurs on the peaks in the Weminuche presents a major challenge for rescue.[59] At least every other year, a serious accident has occurred, and, with much hard work, the La Plata County Search and Rescue team has successfully responded to the emergency. Challenges for rescues include inaccessibility, restrictions on the use of motorized vehicles in a designated wilderness and rugged peaks littered with loose debris. Too often inexperienced climbers attempt ascents from Chicago Basin into the Needles where three fourteeners are easily available, and ignore the terrain hazards and weather. As a rule of thumb, any climb in the Needles should be completed and descent made by noon. Alpine thunderstorms are a daily occurrence, and the downsloping ledges are very slick when wet. Additionally, the electrical storms are very dangerous.

Little snow climbing is done in the Weminuche Wilderness. The wilderness is very inaccessible in the winter, and great danger exists in the spring when the snow melts rapidly. Ski mountaineering is possible in some areas, especially in the early morning hours of spring days, but caution should always be taken and consideration must be given to avalanche danger.

Wilderness is meant to remain pristine. Like any other user group, climbers and mountaineers can seriously deface the landscape and endanger themselves through careless actions. By adhering to specific responsibilities for courtesy, mountaineers and climbers can preserve wild mountain slopes for future generations to enjoy.

PRESERVING THE LAND

   • Equipment needs of the mountaineer are very specialized. All equipment should be used in a manner that does not scar the rock. Any anchors or petons set for repelling or safety should follow Leave No Trace guidelines.

   • Bolting is now outlawed in the wilderness. Most climbers philosophically oppose the use of bolts anywhere, but this is doubly so in the wilderness.

   • Old slings used for rappelling by previous climbers should be removed. If possible, always remove your own slings.

   • When mountaineering, recognize that numerous social trails scar the face of a mountain. Always follow the established route rather than creating another. Often cairns mark the routes up mountains.

• When traveling in loose terrain, it is not appropriate to knock away boulders to improve the route. Instead choose your steps carefully.

• Boulders cascading down a mountain cause unnecessary noise, safety threats to other people on the mountain and destruction of the mountainside.

• Chipping out handholds or altering a route to make it easier for your climb is never acceptable.

MOUNTAINEERING COURTESY ON THE MOUNTAIN

• Always be considerate of other people on the same route. Like you, they are there for a wilderness experience. If you find it necessary to pass another group enroute, ask permission and be courteous to their needs. Upon reaching the summit, enjoy the vistas and give others the same opportunity for privacy that you desire. Summit and move on!

High alpine camp
*Courtesy of B. J. Boucher*

• Have a commitment to the safety and well-being of others through the decisions you make. Don't walk away and ignore those who need your help.

EQUIPMENT PLANNING AND CAMPING ETHICS

• Carry the right equipment for the climb, but take only what you need.

• Depend on your skills, not your gear. Speed can often mean safety, since alpine peaks in the Weminuche should be scaled before noon to avoid weather hazards.

• Take care not to leave permanent impacts in the high alpine meadows frequently used by mountaineers and climbers. The setting is fragile and can be easily destroyed.

• Fires are never appropriate in a tundra or alpine setting. The small bushes and old trees of the krummholtz and tundra areas cannot be replaced because they have taken centuries to mature. Always depend on your stove for warmth and cooking.

Summer range for elk and mountain goats
*Courtesy of B. J. Boucher*

• Choose your campsite carefully, since tents in a high alpine setting are very visible for long distances. Consider carefully where you erect your tent so as not to impact others' views.

• Multiple nights in high alpine country are seldom appropriate. Complete your climb and leave the area for others to enjoy.

• Camping is not appropriate on the mountain routes or in heavy traffic areas.

WILDLIFE PROTECTION

• Contact between humans and mountain goats in Chicago Basin has been negative. Having become accustomed to people, the goats now destroy vegetation where the salt from human urine accumulates. Always urinate on rocks to protect vegetation.

• Don't feed the goats. They are dependent on the alpine environment year-round for food. If habituated to humans, their survival is threatened.

• Be aware that large animals such as elk and mountain sheep live in high alpine meadows. Don't disturb their summer range. When disturbed, they often permanently leave areas heavily used by humans.

Mountain goats habituated to humans destroy fragile plant life at Twin Lakes
*Courtesy of SJNF*

The joy of climbing or mountaineering within a designated wilderness comes from knowing that the area is pristine and protected from human impacts. The greatest challenge for any alpinist is to experience the untamed wilderness without altering it. It is a human trait to try new things, to go where others have not been. But this opportunity carries with it much added

Outfitter guiding fishing party
*Courtesy of Tom Koltak*

responsibility in the wilderness. Local sports shops can provide up-to-date information on climbing in the Weminuche Wilderness. Additionally, several books devoted to route descriptions exist. Check these sources before planning any climb.[60]

## PROFESSIONAL GUIDING SERVICES IN THE WEMINUCHE WILDERNESS

Professionally licensed outfitting services offer many individuals who would otherwise have no opportunity to visit the Weminuche Wilderness guided tours into its deepest areas. Pack trips for fishing, hunting, photography, sightseeing, day hiking and leisure time in the remote reaches are offered from mid-June until the snow falls each year. Outfitters also offer drop services that pack in client gear, then leave them to their own devices before being packed out at a later time.

Every outfitter who accepts compensation, whether in-kind or by monetary payment, is required to hold a valid U.S. Forest Service permit to guide visitors into the Weminuche Wilderness. To obtain a permit from the San Juan/Rio Grande National Forests, the outfitter must demonstrate a need for the service, be economically sound and offer longevity to the business.[61] The number of professional guide services or outfitters allowed to operate in any forest depends on the capacity of an area to handle them. Capacity is determined by forest officials who, through analysis of use, determine how many permits are appropriate before major impacts result. At the present time outfitter permits in the Weminuche Wilderness are at capacity. This means that future permitting will occur only when an existing business changes hands through a sale.

Every client who employs a guide service is responsible for determining the legitimacy of the business. Always request to see their permit before contracting with a business. Every client should be aware of the following requirements established by the San Juan/Rio Grande National Forests for guides:

• A guide must possess a state registration. This is not a license. Instead, the registration ensures the visitor that the guide will abide by the state's requirements for bonding and insurance. Bonding and insurance guarantee the customer legal recourse, should an accident occur.

• Every guide must also be permitted by the San Juan or Rio Grande National Forests to operate on the Weminuche Wilderness.

• Every outfitter is permitted for a specific campsite in the wilderness during the season, but the area surrounding the campsite is open to anyone. Usually outfitters are located in areas where there will be limited activity by other users.

• An outfitter's base camp cannot be set up earlier than seven days before the first trip of each season, and it must be taken down seven days after the last trip. Though a seven-day gap is supposed to occur between trips, most outfitters usually allow more time to elapse so as to reduce impacts on the wilderness.

• Group size for every outfitted trip is limited to a combined number of twenty-five people and stock ("heartbeats" as it used to be known), and is not to exceed fifteen people.

• The outfitting season begins June 15th of each year and ends when the snow makes it impossible to enter the area.

• Every outfitter must develop an operational plan that gives a schedule of activities, itineraries for each trip and possible solutions for handling any problems that arise. The plan is approved by the local forest, and a specific ranger is designated to oversee those plans.

• Fees are assessed each outfitter payable to the U.S. Forest Service and based on the outfitter's trip plans and the amount charged to customers.

OVERSIGHT OF OUTFITTERS

Two organizations oversee the conduct and operations of professional outfitters in the State of Colorado. A state license is issued by the Colorado Department of Regulatory Agencies and is valid for nine years. Requirements for registration by the state include first aid training, bonding and insurance. Before renewal the record of the outfitter must be reviewed for any possible reported problems. The Outfitters' Board of Registration reviews any challenges that may have come from customers, whether tickets have been issued, etc. Fines can be imposed by the board or the outfitter can be removed from business for improper actions.

The Colorado Outfitters Association is a voluntary organization to which any professional outfitter can belong. Only 10% of Colorado's registered outfitters presently belong to this self-regulating association. The group serves a very important function as it works with the U.S. Forest Service and Colorado Division of Wildlife on such policy issues as agency/outfitter relationships, changes in game and fish laws and marketing strategies. Members of the Colorado Outfitters Association have adopted a code of ethics that provides guidelines for services and gives clients an idea of what to expect from a quality outfitter. The following have been adapted from their publication.[62]

• An outfitter must have a valid license regardless of the type of trip.

• Compliance with all state and federal laws and regulations is required.

• A permanent base of operation is desirable.

• All livestock and equipment should be personally owned, and the outfitter should be completely certain of their safety.

• An outfitter's camp should meet sanitary conditions at all times with cleanly served, well prepared food, a properly located latrine, garbage bags maintained for the collection and removal of all wastes, bottles or cans and proper attention given to food storage and stock conditions.

• An outfitter should advise all clients or prospective clients of weather conditions, terrain, housing and type of service before booking. The guide should offer advice on guns, equipment, clothing and other gear furnished by the client.

• Rates, accommodations and services should be understood by the client before a deposit is accepted or a client is booked. The good operator will not misrepresent any part of his business.

• All equipment should be in good repair. Animals should be properly cared for and fed before and during the trip. Employees should be courteous at all times and available for service to clients. An adequate number of employees to meet customer needs should accompany any trip.

• Neither the outfitter nor the staff should assume responsibility of hunting for clients.

• The outfitter should make certain that all game is properly cared for immediately after a kill and is delivered to the processor or client according to agreed terms.

• Safety of clients, personnel and stock should be the outfitter's top priority at all times.

• The outfitter should make certain that the use of alcohol either before or during a hunt is not allowed.

• The outfitter should be a good example of Leave No Trace principles, being a model for the clients.

• The outfitter should alert clients to the danger of fire because of carelessness.

• The outfitter should abide by all wilderness regulations.

• Pack stock are always strung together for proper travel along trails.

## EDUCATIONAL OUTFITTERS

Educational outfitters like The National Outdoor Leadership School (NOLS) and Outward Bound are not required to register with the state. They must be permitted with the U.S. Forest Service, however, providing operational plans for their travel and obeying the restrictions on group size. The same is true for all groups that enter the wilderness under the auspices of a church or other organization.

## NON-OUTFITTING STOCK USERS

The public needs to be aware that not every stock group encountered in the Weminuche is a professionally licensed outfitter group. In fact, numerous groups of people use horses as their major mode of transportation. They, like professional stock groups, are limited to no more than twenty-five combined stock and people in a group.

Nor is every outfitter who transports people into the wilderness licensed. Many outfitters are operating illegally, and in fact, it is believed that twice as many illegal operators use wilderness trails as those who are permitted. There are presently approximately twenty-five permitted outfitters operating in the Weminuche Wilderness. The illegal outfitter receives compensation for services, whether from transporting clients or through in-kind repayment of a debt owed another individual without being properly licensed by the state or the U.S. Forest Service.

Consider the following problems which can result if one hires an illegal guide:

1. The customer has no legal recourse or insurance of safety.

2. Because they operate illegally, such outfitters often cause greater resource damage.

3. Unethical hunting practices are often resorted to, causing problems for everyone.

If you wish to find out more about an outfitter, you can write to the following addresses for information:

Colorado Outfitters Association
2400 RBC Road 12
Meeker, Colorado 81641
(970) 878-4312

For licensing information, complaints or other concerns write:

Colorado Department of Regulatory Agencies
Outfitters Registration
1560 Broadway, Suite 1340
Denver, Colorado (303) 894-7778

## RIDING THE DURANGO AND SILVERTON NARROW GAUGE TRAIN

The Durango & Silverton Narrow Gauge Train has been traveling along the Animas River from Durango to Silverton for over a hundred years. It was completed in July, 1882. When it was first constructed, the train was used to haul supplies for the mining operations and the people who worked them from Durango to Silverton. Its return trip brought ore to the smelting plant in Durango. After the mining boom ended, the train continued to be the major transportation vehicle between the two cities, and during the summer months it transported sheep to Needleton and Elk Park where they unloaded to graze on allotments in the high meadows.

Backpackers unloading at Needle Creek
*Courtesy of the SJMA*

In the 1970's the train was sold to a private corporation. It now operates as a tourist attraction, giving its passengers the chance to relive the historic experience of riding on a narrow gauge train while traveling through a spectacular wilderness environment. The train transports backpackers to and from the Needleton and Elk Park stops daily during the summer usually. The 8:30 a.m. train boards backpackers, since it is the main one that makes stops at these two locations. This helps the railroad maintain its schedule of four trains daily. Two return trains are boarded at Elk Park either at 2:30 or 4:10 p.m. and at Needleton either at 2:50 or 4:40 p.m.

The train will stop only if you signal for it to do so. To signal, wave your arms across the front of your body, making an X as your arms cross each other. The Durango and Silverton Narrow Gauge Railroad produces an up-to-date schedule each summer which details current train schedules and fares. These are available by contacting:

Durango and Silverton Narrow Gauge Railroad Co.
479 Main Avenue
Durango, Colorado 81301
(970) 247-2733
(888) 872-4607

# 11

# Traveling Safely in the Wilderness

Wilderness travel demands knowing what to expect when, and being prepared for the unexpected. When the unexpected happens, and it probably will, you will be able to survive and recall the experience as a great story to share with others if you are prepared. Here are some basic survival skills and tips that can be of help to every visitor. Don't consider them all-inclusive, because only you know your own special needs when you are away from civilization.

**Be conscious of the weather as you travel.** On an average, the temperature drops about four degrees Fahrenheit for every 1,000 feet of elevation gained in the Weminuche Wilderness. This means you can experience a 16 to 24 degree change as you go from the 8,000 feet to 14,000 feet elevation. Temperature variations at different elevations can be extreme during storms or at night. Frosts will occur in the high alpine meadows of the Weminuche throughout the summer.

Storm clouds gathering in the high country
*Courtesy of B. J. Boucher*

Lightning is dangerous
*Courtesy of the USFS*

Mountains shape the weather in the wilderness, which arrives in fronts from the Pacific Ocean. When you first spot wispy cirrus clouds on the western horizon, anticipate the possible approach of a storm. Winds blowing up and over the mountains create an "up slope" effect in which the rising air expands and cools, condensing its moisture content into clouds and precipitation. This can mean snow, hail, sleet, rain or cold biting winds any month of the year.

Thunderstorms, usually short-lived, often produce strong gusty winds as well as precipitation and intense lightning. Thunderstorms are associated with dense rain clouds which billow and tower like the high mountains themselves. Mountain ridges are notorious for generating thunderstorms. The mountains force the air to rise. In the summer the earth mass collects heat from the sun, then discharges it into the cooler air mass that surrounds the mountains. Strong updrafts of air carry moisture to the cold upper parts of the clouds, and the interaction of water and ice particles causes the electrical charge. Most thunderstorms occur during the early afternoon and evening hours when the temperature is warmest. Cold fronts that move in can also generate thunderstorms. Daily thunderstorms are the norm in the Weminuche Wilderness, and high ridges are most dangerous after noon because of lightning strikes.

The weather throughout the summer months varies, but generally you can anticipate that June will be the sunniest and driest month in the Weminuche Wilderness. Spring run-off is in full force, however, so streams are usually quite full. Many snowfields will not melt until mid- to late July, particularly around high lakes, on northern exposures and at mountain passes. July and August usually experience heavy moisture in the high mountains because of southwestern monsoons which blow in from the tropical Pacific over the Mexican Baja Peninsula and up to Colorado. As this humid air sweeps in, afternoon thunderstorms blaze lightning from cloud to ground and pound the wilderness with rain and hail.

Late August and September experience a slackening of thunderstorm activity. September is usually cooler and drier, but by the first of October winter weather is returning, with high alpine snowstorms blanketing wilderness travelers and cold winds sweeping across the high passes.

The weather is always a consideration when traveling in the Weminuche Wilderness. Appropriate rainwear and warm clothing, including an umbrella, can prevent hypothermia. Rocks become slick and dangerous when wet. Good footwear and careful steps prevent an accident.

**Lightning and severe weather must be respected, no matter your plans.** You do not want to be caught above treeline in a thunderstorm. Crossing high passes and scaling the fourteeners should be done by noon. An electrical charge that is close at hand often announces itself. You may hear an insect-like buzzing noise. Your hair may stand on end and your scalp tingle. You can determine the distance to the center of a thunderstorm by counting the time in seconds between when the lightening strikes and when you hear the thunder. That number divided by five (five seconds equals one mile) tells you the distance to the strike. If you are caught in an exposed area by a sudden storm, consider doing the following:

• Avoid open areas, water, caves and ridges during lightning storms.

• If caught in an exposed area, distance yourself from metal objects (pack frames, poles, etc.).

• Avoid lone trees and boulders.

•Place an insulating material such as a poncho or a foam pad on a small rock and sit on it with only your buttocks and feet touching the material. Clasp your hands around your knees.

**Know where you are going and how to get there.** Map collections are essential, and should include a detailed map of the wilderness as well as appropriate topographical maps. Plan your route before you leave. Determine where you will be each day. Share your plan with friends who are not going on the trip and stick to the plan. Discover as much as possible about the area you are venturing into and what might be demanded of you when there. What is the terrain like? What kind of stream conditions can you expect? What weather is predicted? How physically prepared are you to endure the challenges along the route? Don't let members of your group stray too far, and if they do strike out alone, have them leave word of their plans.

**Know how to use a compass.** If you leave your route at any time, you may become disoriented. Use your map and compass to get back on track. If you become lost, stay calm, carefully reason where you are, then backtrack, if possible. Practice orienteering with your compass and map before leaving. Have someone set up a route that you must follow using your skills of map reading and compass orienteering.

Wilderness travel is challenging !
*Courtesy of B. J. Boucher*

**Be prepared for your own safety, since wilderness travel implies risk.** In the event you become lost and cannot retrace your steps, stay put since the route description you left with a friend becomes the vehicle for your rescue. The different county sheriffs' offices have rescue responsibilities in the Weminuche Wilderness. Each county has its own search and rescue team, but their operations are limited by distance, severity of terrain, manpower and time. Additionally, the 1964 Wilderness Act prohibits the use of motorized or mechanical transport in a wilderness except in severe or life-threatening situations. You can support local search and rescue efforts by purchasing a special license for only $1.00 from any sports shop in the area before leaving on your trip. This special program, begun in 1995, allows all outdoor enthusiasts to help pay for search and rescue efforts which can be extremely expensive. The search and rescue group is reimbursed by the state for the expenses they incur.

**There are certain pieces of equipment that you should carry at all times.** Always have a knife, compass, maps, survival food, rainwear and first aid equipment with you on overnight trips or day hikes. It is a temptation to set up camp and take off for a short hike free of any burden. A small day pack supplied with these items can often help you return safely to your camp when the unexpected happens.

**Remember that travel at high elevations can have serious health consequences.** Hypothermia, exhaustion and altitude sickness result from over-exposure to the elements. No matter the month you visit the Weminuche, be prepared for rain, hail, snow, freezing temperatures and harsh wind. Recognize the early symptoms of hypothermia, a drastic drop in body temperature which can be life-threatening. They include uncontrollable shaking, inability to think rationally and sleepiness. The only treatment is warmth and dryness. Never venture out without rainwear, extra food and drink, your first aid kit, maps and a compass.

**Just as threatening is exposure to heat.** Hard exercise in intense heat at high elevations can elevate the body's temperature quickly. Clammy moist skin and disorientation can result. Dress in layers which can be removed or added as needed. Wear fabrics that breathe to keep you from sweating profusely. Always wear sunscreen and a broad brimmed hat. If you feel exhausted from heat, seek shade and bathe the body with a moist cloth. Better yet, recognize your capabilities and honor them.

Wading a swift stream demands caution
*Courtesy of B. J. Boucher*

Elevations in the Weminuche range from 8,000 feet to above 14,000 feet. **High-altitude sickness is a potential problem** for individuals unaccustomed to the thin air. Spend several days acclimating before traveling to high elevations. During the trip, rest often, drink lots of water and monitor yourself. Symptoms include raspy breathing, a rapid heartbeat, irritability, headaches, dizziness, nausea and difficulty in sleeping at night. Seek lower elevations for relief.

**Be prepared with the proper first aid equipment, whatever your length of stay or journey.** Your kit should include, at a minimum, sterile bandages, band aids, moleskin, first aid cream, pain relief medication, a bandanna or ace bandage, gauze, adhesive or duct tape, flashlight, insect spray, sunscreen, chapstick, safety pins, tweezers, water-proof matches, parachute cord, emergency food, space blanket, electrolytes, candle, whistle and water-purifying tablets. Sounds like a lot, right? If you look carefully at the list, you will probably remember a time when one of the items could have been extremely helpful and saved energy and time.

**Fording high water can be dangerous.** The Weminuche Wilderness is crisscrossed with hundreds of streams and rivers. Most of them carry water year-round, and during run-off in the spring or after thunderstorms, they can be treacherous and swift. Special considerations are necessary when you have to cross swift streams.

• Choose a place to ford the stream that is shallow and offers the most secure bottom material. Look for stable rocks and fallen trees that span the water, and test them before putting your weight on them.

• Be careful of slippery rocks. Wading in sandals or sneakers can help prevent falls.

• A stick is always helpful as a third leg for balance.

• Loosen your pack waistband before crossing so that if you lose your balance you can free yourself of the pack weight.

• Don't expect children to cross dangerous streams. They do not have the body weight to withstand the swift water!!!

**Giardia is always a threat in the wilderness.** TREAT ALL WATER EITHER WITH FILTRATION, BOILING OR CHEMICAL TABLETS. Giardia lamblia is a waterborne protozoan found in streams and lakes and introduced by fecal matter deposited in the water by humans or animals upstream. Though giardia is not life threatening, this bacteria-caused illness which manifests as an intestinal disease can be of long duration and requires medical intervention for cure. Symptoms are not felt for six to 20 days, but they are extremely debilitating to the body, once they do occur. They include chronic diarrhea alternating with constipation, abdominal cramps, bloating, fatigue, appetite and weight loss and fever. A water filter that removes particles larger than 0.1 microns is necessary. Water must come to a rolling boil, if this is the method used for killing the protozoa.

**Equipment needs must be carefully considered.** A rule of thumb with clothing is to carry items which can be layered. Lightweight fleece apparel is easy to carry. So is a windbreaker. Gloves and a warm hat are a godsend when the temperature suddenly drops 20 degrees. Large plastic bags make instant backpack or equipment covers. They then convert to garbage bags for hauling out trash.

**Care must be taken to provide safety for yourself and any wild animals you might encounter.** The Weminuche Wilderness is the home of wildlife, and care must be taken to protect them. Bears, mountain lions and moose roam the

Mountain lion at rest
*Courtesy of Tom Koltak*

wilderness freely, and their presence can be a challenge. If you travel with stock, they can be easily spooked by wild animals. Always keep children and pets with you.

**Mountain lions are secretive,** and your chances of encountering them are very slim. Deer are their main prey. If you cross paths with a mountain lion:

• Remain calm and speak firmly.

• Do not run! This may trigger the lion's instinct to chase prey.

• Give the lion an escape route so it doesn't feel trapped.

• Increase your body size--raise your arms, open your jacket, etc.

• Fight back with any accessible object if a lion attacks.

**Bears have an acute sense of smell and are tempted by human food.** They prefer riparian zones though they are sometimes spotted at high altitudes and along the trails. Most bears will avoid human contact. Conversation, whistling or singing will help alert them of your presence. If they come into your camp they can be very destructive. Although they rarely attack human beings, these large unpredictable animals can be dangerous.

The following tips will bear-proof your wilderness visit:

• Be alert, travel in groups and do not approach bears.

• Keep a clean camp. (See the Leave No Trace section.)

• Suspend items whose odor might attract bears (food, garbage, grease, pet food, toiletries) off the ground at least 100 feet from camp.

• Use unscented, biodegradable soaps and toiletries.

• Never store food in a tent, even in bear-proof containers.

• Check your pockets and saddlebags for forgotten food before going to bed.

• If a black bear charges you, stand your ground and look "big."

• Black bears often "mock charge" before leaving.

• A bear standing upright is not necessarily showing aggression.

• Always keep in mind that bears do not like surprises. Never approach a bear.

• If you encounter a black bear, remain calm, speak softly and back away, avoiding eye contact. Never turn your back on a bear or kneel. Avoid sudden movements or running. If attacked try playing dead, lying in a fetal position with knees pulled tightly against the chest and arms protecting the head.

**Insects will annoy and bite you** when you visit the Weminuche Wilderness. They play an important role in the wilderness ecosystems, even though you consider them unfriendly. At any elevation you will be visited incessantly by flies. They seem to swarm particularly during the heat of the day or after a rainstorm. Houseflies are a nuisance only, but deer and horse flies bite and leave severe welts that can become inflamed. Mosquitoes and gnats are prevalent during the rainy season, and they breed in bodies of stagnant water or riparian areas. Expect to find them near any body of water and at any elevation.

**Ticks are also residents** of the Weminuche. They carry bacteria that cause Rocky Mountain spotted tick fever, Colorado tick fever, Lyme Disease and tularemia. They are not plentiful in the wilderness, though I have experienced a larger outbreak during extremely wet years. They can be lurking on logs or rocks that you brush against or sit upon. Check your body carefully each evening for ticks. They love warm moist places on the body. If you find one attached, use tweezers or your fingers, grasping close to the attached point, and pull gently to remove it. Treat the bite wound with an antiseptic, save the tick in a small container and record the date of removal. If you experience illness within two weeks, see your doctor and bring the tick for diagnosis.

**Insect repellent or citronella oil is an absolute necessity** to help insure protection from bugs. Use it liberally on exposed parts of your body. You can also retard stings by wearing long pants, long sleeved shirts and high socks.

**Poisonous snakes are unlikely to be found above 8,000 foot elevations.** You will see water and grass snakes which are not dangerous.

**Poison ivy, oak and sumac grow in some areas** of the Weminuche Wilderness. If you suspect that you have come in contact with these plants, wash the skin thoroughly with a good soap. Wash clothes that may have brushed against the plant with hot soapy water. If you know you are allergic to these plants, take proper precautions before visiting areas where they are found.

Safety in the Weminuche Wilderness requires alertness, careful planning, proper precautions and coolheaded responses when a special situation arises. Part of the joy of wilderness travel is facing the challenges that come your way when all the conveniences of civilization are not available. The joy of accomplishment is a long-lived gift that the wilderness gives every person who chooses to experience the unknown.

# Part IV

# Trail Descriptions

"As humans develop more and more sophisticated tools, as they travel more and more deeply into areas uninhabited by technological cultures, the diversity of America is threatened. And here we do not worry only about the loss of one species, though each loss is regrettable, but also about losses in the variety of associations that species inhabit; for it is the variety of associations in which plants and animals participate that forces them to face multiple evolutionary regimens, to develop varied adaptations and, eventually, to create new species.

"If natural diversity survives and flourishes here, it will be because we leave some areas largely alone, letting the forces that create and sustain life continue, forever wild. " Bryan G. Norton "The Spiral of Life", taken from *The World of Wilderness*, edited by T. H. Watkins and Patricia Byrnes, Robert Rinehart Publishers, 1995.

# - 12 -

# Rating Systems and Trail Maintenance

There are approximately 490 miles of U.S. Forest Service maintained trails in the Weminuche Wilderness. There are many additional miles of non-system trails not maintained by public employees which are traveled by wilderness visitors and wildlife. Only system trails that are maintained by U.S. Forest Service crews, contract employees or volunteers are described in this book. There are thirty-one trailheads which provide access into the Weminuche Wilderness. Some have campgrounds, corrals and loading ramps. Others only have parking lots. Most have educational and informational bulletin boards as well as registration materials. Registration at trailheads by all visitors is extremely important, not only for safety reasons, but also to help the U.S. Forest Service determine adequate management strategies for trails.

Trail bridges over streams in the Weminuche are limited. There are three on the Pagosa District, eight on the Columbine District and five on the Divide District. Otherwise, all streams and rivers must be waded. None of the trails in the Weminuche Wilderness are considered wheel-chair accessible because of steep grades, exposed rocks or roots and stream crossings.

Rating the difficulty of a system trail is a very subjective process. The most difficult route for one person can be a stroll in the park for the more physically fit individual. Even a moderately flat trail can challege anyone not in condition or not acclimated to high altitude travel. Poor weather conditions and improper clothing can combine to create extreme difficulty for the prepared and the unprepared visitor alike. Wilderness travel is always challenging. Radical temperature swings can occur between midday and midnight. A beautiful sunny day can suddenly become a winter snow scene.

Wilderness travelers should be alert to changing conditions, whatever the trail, and be prepared to face them. Every trail in the Weminuche Wilderness begins at over 8,000 feet. For these reasons, no trail should be considered easy.

The following criteria influenced the ratings I have suggested:

- Overall elevation gain and loss
- Length of sections with severe elevation gain or loss
- Ease in route finding
- Changing travel conditions and maintenance
- Travel above timberline and along exposed ridges
- Severity and number of stream crossings
- Access
- Camping opportunities

I have applied four basic categories to the Weminuche Wilderness Trails described in this book. These categories are somewhat similar to the San Juan/Rio Grande National Forests' ratings throughout the forests. They suggest three categories--easiest, more difficult and most difficult. I have expanded that to four, and changed the easy category to moderate because the trail is in the wilderness. As you travel the trails, devise your own rating scale that helps you remember <u>your</u> criteria for difficulty.

1. *Moderate* - trails requiring wilderness awareness and physical stamina with **limited overall challenges** to travel. Limited challenges can include stream crossings, rolling terrain with maximum grade pitch of 15% for no more than 200 feet, and encounters with many other users.

2. *Difficult* - trails requiring wilderness awareness and physical stamina with **some challenging travel conditions**. Challenging conditions can include difficult stream crossings, sections longer than 200 feet that sustain a grade of 15% to 20%, travel above timberline, trail length and possible camping limitations.

3. *More difficult* - trails requiring wilderness awareness and physical stamina with **a greater degree of challenge to travel**. More difficult trails have grades that may be 20% to 30% in pitch and longer than 300 feet. The above conditions apply, plus trail width and passing may be a challenge for pack animals.

4. *Most difficult* - trails requiring wilderness awareness and physical stamina with **a high degree of challenge to travel**. All of the above conditions exist, plus the grade pitch may exceed 30% for 500 feet or more. Route finding may be a challenge on some trails, and exposure at high elevations is possible.

Regarding the depth of description I have given for trails, I have chosen to give essentially factual, straightforward information that can help you make a decision whether or not to travel a route. I believe the Weminuche Wilderness should be a place of challenge and discovery for everyone who visits this special place. If I tell you everything you can expect to see--wildlife sightings, spectacular views, breathtaking waterfalls, unusual rock formations--you will be seeing the Weminuche through my eyes. All of these things and many more await you, but I want you to discover the magic yourself. Where appropriate I have included historical data that is relevant or of interest.

Wilderness visitors should be able to read a map and use a compass. These skills allow you to take note of elevation and changing topography. You can locate your position at any time during travel. Therefore, I do not tell you much about the changes in elevation along a trail. My elevation figures, rounded off to the nearest hundred foot mark, alert you to the difference between trailhead elevation and the elevation at the end of the trail. Most trails gain and lose elevation as they travel deeper into the Weminuche or countour around mountains, over passes and through river valleys. Map study before visiting a specific trail is of utmost importance. You should carry an overall wilderness map plus USGS topographical maps specific to the area you plan to visit. *The Weminuche Wilderness Map* published by Trails Illustrated, a subsidiary of National Geographic, is keyed to the trails discussed in this book. An alert traveler will frequently peruse the maps, note the names of surrounding peaks or streams and seek to make appropriate decisions that ensure safe travel. Remember, traveling in a wilderness area is risky, but the risk is part of the pleasure.

You are given extra space to make your own notations at the end of each section of trails. Your notes may include your memories of travel, the challenges you faced and the special experiences you had. Personalizing wilderness travel in this way helps you know the joy of being in a wild place and keeping that place wild. Your notes are for you and your friends.

### Trail Maintenance

The how's, when's and why's of trail construction and maintenance in the Weminuche Wilderness often puzzle visitors. Many people expect well-groomed, easy-to-travel routes wherever they go, forgetting that designated wilderness is an area whose main reason for existence is to sustain wildness. Many recreation trails used today were created by ranchers driving stock to summer range, miners packing supplies to diggings, indigenous people accessing summer camping areas and game moving across the forest. They often follow the shortest route between two points without consideration for steepness or ease in travel. Many parallel streams and rivers, accessing alpine meadows and passes. These trails have logically become the routes traveled and maintained today. As conditions demand, new sections may be constructed to help preserve the wilderness. Otherwise, new routes are not developed. Many social trails created by humans and animals exist. Some are in excellent condition, in fact sometimes better than the system trails. These are open for travel, but the U.S. Forest Service doesn't inventory or maintain them.

You may travel a very muddy trail and wonder if it was ever touched by a trail crew. Believe me, it was! Crews of public employees, contract labor and volunteers spend numerous hours each summer grooming and improving trail conditions.[63] Sudden summer rains and heavy use can quickly change a trail just groomed by conscientious workers into a quagmire almost overnight.

Though more time consuming and labor intensive, the U.S. Forest Service requires all work be done by hand tools. The agency feels that using power tools, such as chain saws, to maintain trails violates the intent of the 1964 Wilderness Act which prohibits the use of mechanized equipment. All crews, therefore, work

A muddy trail in the Weminuche Wilderness
*Courtesy of B. J. Boucher*

with hand tools transported either by foot or animal, to complete all trail maintenance and construction. Not all federal agencies feel the same, and some allow the use of mechanized tools.

The first priority for trail work each summer is to correct unsafe conditions. In the early months this means removing trees that have blown down during the winter. Each year this becomes an unbelievably big task since fall and winter winds cause severe damage in many areas. Snow avalanches can wipe out a hillside of aspen trees and leave deep piles of rubble to be cleared. Crews use hand tools such as crosscuts, axes, shovels and pulaskis. Removing downed trees and brush from every trail in the Weminuche Wilderness takes many hours. Without their quick removal, people will make new trails around them and damage the land further.

Crews then concentrate on correcting conditions that cause trail damage --erosion, seepage, standing water puddles, collected debris and washouts left by storms on steep sections. Building water bars that re-direct water flow from the trail is tedious and backbreaking work. If time permits, attention is given to appropriate signage and route markers. Trails over time can become hazardous to travelers and necessitate reconstruction or re-routing. When erosion, washouts and other safety hazards limit safety for people and stock, specific trails are reworked.

"All trails are not created equal," according to one trail construction manual.[64] Each has specific maintenance requirements according to its planned level of usage. Trails are, therefore, graded to help determine a maintenance schedule. Certain ones, like the Los Piños and Vallecito Trails, which are heavily used by every kind of wilderness travel, receive more attention than remote trails that see few people. Long term plans are developed according to a trail's level of use and direct how much maintenance each will receive.

When you see deeply rutted trails that hold water during a rainstorm, the tendency is to seek a more comfortable route. This results in numerous paths running side by side and causing braided trails. When the mud looks too deep to walk through, the average traveler tiptoes along the side of the trail, contributing to a widened path. When rocks are in the way, they are often skirted rather than removed. If every visitor did a little bit of trail maintenance, the conditions for travel would be greatly improved and maintenance by professionals might be more timely. Kicking away stones or rocks that have rolled onto the path can be a small help. Chopping the log that the last storm brought down across the trail may take time, but it helps the next traveler. A small axe or shovel carried in one's gear can open a plugged water channel or remove debris. Staying on the path and slogging through the mud always helps preserve the route. Boots can be dried in a few hours. Trail maintenance is an unending task but a very necessary one, which, if assisted by each of us, will contribute to our safety and pleasure when we visit the Weminuche Wilderness.

Braided trails in the Weminuche Wilderness
Courtesy of B. J. Boucher

# 13

# Columbine Ranger District Trail Descriptions

The Weminuche Wilderness is a very special and spectacular piece of country composed of approximately 500,000 acres of forests and high alpine peaks, making it the largest in the state of Colorado. The Columbine Ranger District encompasses the western portion of the Weminuche, north to the Continental Divide near Silverton and east to the Los Piños River. This geographic area has a wide variety of terrain--from the granite walls of the Grenadiers to the more gentle, wide, open valley of the Los Piños River. The western portion of the Columbine District is steep, rugged country with narrow V-shaped valleys and numerous high mountains, including three 14,000 foot peaks. The eastern portion of the district is gentle, with open river valleys shaped by ancient glacial action.

As a wilderness manager responsible for this section of the Weminuche Wilderness, I feel a great obligation to the American people to provide for the wilderness setting directed by the 1964 Wilderness Act. This proves to be no easy feat. I often feel torn between providing for, on the one hand, an "outstanding opportunity for solitude," primitive recreational experiences and protection of the resource from human degradation (an area "untrammeled by man"), while managing the existing uses that often result in crowded trails and heavily impacted camping areas. The spectrum of management philosophies runs from highly maintained trails and detailed signing which offer a more secure wilderness experience, to the removal of trails, bridges and signs to provide a more adventurous wilderness experience. Somewhere in between these two extremes lies an appropriate level of management.

In addition to supporting the philosophy of wilderness, there is the day-to-day mangagement of users who come with their own ideas of what wilderness is to them. There is the job of educating the wilderness users to care for and be responsible for the land, to understand why a large group may impair the experience of other wilderness users and to utilize Leave No Trace camping practices. These are only some of the continued challenges I face in management and seasonal wilderness rangers encounter daily as they hike the trails.

In the broader picture, I am grateful for those organizations with the vision and goals of setting aside and protecting wilderness. It is important that they lobby Congress to protect America's invaluable and precious jewels. It is a credit to those individuals who have given and continue to give their time and energy so that future generations may have an area of land unimpaired by civilization's mechanization and expansion. The intent of Congress, when establishing wilderness areas, is "to assure that an increasing population, accompanied by expanding settlement and growing mechanization does not occupy and modify all areas within the United States" (Section 2a, Wilderness Act). As the world's population continues to grow and the demand for goods and services increases, the protection of these pockets of designated wilderness becomes vitally important and increasingly difficult. I ask that you as a wilderness supporter and user become an active voice for the preservation of wilderness. Become an educator to your friends, family and acquaintances. With a collective voice, we will continue to have places where people can find mental and spiritual restoration in our fast paced, high tech and often stressful world. Tread lightly and enjoy your visit to the Columbine District.

Nancy Berry
Columbine District Wilderness Manager
Columbine Ranger District
San Juan National Forest
Durango, Colorado 81401
(970) 385-1282

CUNNINGHAM GULCH TRAIL
FOREST SERVICE TRAIL 502

| | |
|---|---|
| Length: | 2.5 miles |
| Trailhead elevation: | 10,400' |
| Ending elevation: | 12,200' at Continental Divide |
| Difficulty: | Most difficult |
| Cautions: | Steep ascent up switchbacks |
| | Sheep grazing allotment |
| | High alpine storms |

Access: Take Colorado 110 north from Silverton 4 miles. Turn right on FDR 589 and proceed around 3 miles, keeping right as the road divides for Stony Pass. Park along the roadside and walk through the old Highland Mary mine site, wading Cunningham Creek to the trailhead immediately left after the crossing. The creek can be quite high during runoff.

Stock tips: Stock users can access the alpine Continental Divide Trail above timberline via this trail. The tundra grass, though grazeable, is very fragile, and care must be taken to move stock frequently. Water may be limited.

Cunningham Gulch Trail is essentially an access to the Continental Divide Trail (FS 813) and the Colorado Trail. The trail quickly climbs above timberline, so be conscious of mid-day electrical storms. It provides opportunity for a loop trip and return to your vehicle via the Highland Mary Trail (FS 606). As you begin the steep ascent, be prepared for switchbacks that can be quite slick during rain. You will be traveling through country included in an active sheep grazing allotment, and during the months of July and August you may hear or see them. Herders rotate their grazing areas daily so the animals will not severely impact the alpine terrain.

As you near the Continental Divide Trail, you will have a spectacular view of the mountains surrounding Silverton. It was near Cunningham Pass in December, 1889 that Melanie Ressouches almost lost her life. Mrs. Ressouches, 60 years old, had moved to Silverton to live with her sons. When a son took ill in Denver, she set out alone to walk to the capital city. She became disoriented in the deep snow drifts and turned back. Her faithful dog helped her return, and she was rescued approximately a half mile up the trail. She later ran a boarding house in Silverton.[65]

Upon reaching the Continental Divide Trail, you can see Stony Pass in the distance, the major wagon road to Silverton for years. In 1910 the first automobile brought to Silverton was hauled over this pass by a team of draft horses (see photo on page 60). Camping is available only after reaching the Divide Trail above timberline. Water is found in small lakes and bogs along the Continental Divide. During dry seasons, these may be dry.

HIGHLAND MARY LAKES TRAIL
FOREST SERVICE TRAIL 606

| | |
|---|---|
| Length: | 4 miles |
| Trailhead elevation: | 10,400' |
| Ending Elevation: | 12,100' at Verde Lake |
| Difficulty: | More difficult |
| Cautions: | Alpine topography around lakes is fragile |
| | Firewood is not available |
| | Limited campsites near lakes |
| | Severe alpine thunderstorms |
| | Sheep grazing in the area |
| | Lakes may not thaw until mid-July |

Access: Follow the route described for accessing Cunningham  Gulch. After wading Cunningham Creek follow an old road to the right along the stream to the trailhead.

Stock tips: This trail is not recommended for stock. They will have difficulty ascending the trail because of its rocky, steep, narrow terrain. To access this country, use Cunningham Gulch Trail (FS 502). Grazing for animals is not available near the lakes, and the fragile meadows necessitate frequent movement of animals.

The Highland Mary Trail is a steep rocky route that demands some stamina. It climbs to the left of the creek for the first half of the trip, then crosses two streams and winds its way through scrubby willows before reaching a talus slope. Don't be confused at the double stream crossing by what appears to be the main trail heading up the hill between the two. This only leads to a heavily impacted camping area.

After crossing both streams, the trail continues through the willows and becomes somewhat obscure in the upper rocky area. The trail turns left over a talus slope and returns to the stream which you will follow to a crossing. You may encounter snowfields on the talus until late July. Upon crossing the stream you emerge in between the two lower lakes which are surrounded by lush, rolling, green hills. Immediately below the lakes is a manmade rock dam whose origin and date of construction is not clear. It was probably built in the early 20th century to enlarge the natural lake and augment water supply for mining operations. As you continue beyond them you will climb a grassy hill and view the largest of the Highland Mary Lakes. The trail circles above the large lake and gently ascends alpine slopes to reach Verde and Lost Lakes. Many social trails connect all the lakes. Do not expect isolation here because many people day hike to the lakes.

You may continue beyond Verde Lake, following post markers, to a junction with the Continental Divide Trail. All camping near the lakes must be at least 100 feet from shoreline as per wilderness regulations, and no fires should be anticipated since wood is unavailable.

MOLAS TRAIL
FOREST SERVICE TRAIL 665

| | |
|---|---|
| Length: | 4 miles |
| Trailhead elevation: | 10,400' |
| Ending elevation: | 8,900' at Animas River |
| Difficulty: | Difficult |
| Cautions: | Numerous switchbacks |
| | Limited water supply along trail |

Access: Molas Trail is accessed 1.2 miles north of Molas Pass and 46 miles north of Durango on U.S. 550 en route to Silverton. Park in the graveled parking area east of the highway, and cross the gravel road to an old road that descends to the trailhead immediately before the path descends a hill.

Stock tips: This trail offers access to the upper reaches of the Animas Valley. Grazing can be limited.

Molas Trail offers a walk through a beautiful dense forest after descending the first half mile through open meadows. Views of the Grenadiers and Needles are available from the meadows. Though the switchbacks are numerous as the trail descends to the Animas River Valley, they are moderate in steepness and well maintained. It is a temptation to cut switchbacks when you can look below or above and see the trail so close to you. Please don't! Short cutting switchbacks carves out open paths which water courses through, causing erosion, scarring the hillside and destroying plants and trees.

At different points Molas Trail offers superb views of the Animas River Canyon below, and as you descend you may hear the train chugging along the railroad track which follows the canyon floor. You will cross Molas Creek as you enter the valley and the Animas River bridge shortly afterwards. You can then continue up the hill on the other side of the river and railroad track to access Elk Creek Trail (FS 503).

If you follow the tracks south you will come to Elk Park where the train stops for passengers to Silverton or Durango. In 1880 David C. Hershie started a hotel and ranch at Elk Park. Hershie ran a dairy herd in the area until the Durango and Rio Grande Railroad began operations in 1882 and his hotel was no longer needed. During the early 20th century sheep were hauled to Elk Park by train, then trailed into the high meadows that extend over to the Highland Mary Lakes. Elk Creek Trail also heads uphill at Elk Park and intersects with the other loop within a half mile. Campsites are available along the Animas River south toward Elk Creek.

CRATER LAKE TRAIL
FOREST SERVICE TRAIL 623

| | |
|---|---|
| Length: | 5.5 miles |
| Trailhead elevation: | 10,800' at Andrews Lake |
| Ending elevation: | 11,700' at Crater Lake |
| Difficulty: | Moderate |
| Cautions: | Sheep grazing during summer |
| | Late snows obscure trail |
| | Heavy day use |
| | Limited campsites at Crater Lake |

Access: Drive approximately 45 miles north of Durango on U.S. 550, and turn east at the Andrews Lake sign on a paved road. Parking is provided for day use at Andrews Lake. Others should turn left just before the road end to the upper long-term lot. The trail register is located at the southern end of Andrews Lake.

Stock tips: This trail is easily negotiated by stock, but camping at the lake is very limited. Campsites exist prior to reaching the lake. Stock users should park in the upper lot as the stock trail begins at the bulletin board.

Crater Lake Trail offers many photographic opportunities, since the lake is nestled at the base of North Twilight Peak in the West Needles. This area was added to the Weminuche Wilderness in 1993 because of its scenic quality. Engineer and Potato Mountains loom on the southwestern horizon. The oldest Precambrian rocks of the San Juan Mountains are exposed in Twilight Peak. Deposited almost two billion years ago, the rock layer is called Twilight Gneiss. This gneiss is the foundation for all later rock deposits and intrusions.

Be prepared to meet many people on this trail, since day hiking from Andrews Lake is popular. Though the trail begins with switchbacks, it soon eases into a gently rolling route that passes alternately through timber and open meadows. Numerous old snags attest to the fire that consumed this area in 1879. The fire, according to some storytellers, was started in Purgatory Flats by a careless group of miners. Old snags still standing a hundred years later provide homes for birds and other wildlife.

Expect to encounter lots of mosquitoes in the summertime at the lake. Take your insect repellent with you. Because of heavy use, wood supplies are limited near the lake, so take your stove with you. Be on the lookout for campsites before reaching the lake since campsites are limited in its vicinity.

ELK CREEK TRAIL
FOREST SERVICE TRAIL 503

| | |
|---|---|
| Length: | 9 miles |
| Trailhead elevation: | 8,900' at Animas River |
| Ending elevation: | 12,800' at Continental Divide |
| Difficulty: | Most difficult |
| Cautions: | Severe elevation gain in upper sections |
| | Limited campsites |
| | Train access increases usage |

Access: Elk Creek Trail may be accessed in two ways. The Durango and Silverton Train makes a stop, allowing backpackers to by-pass the hike down Molas Creek Trail, the other access. One saves money, however, by walking in on the Molas Trail. See directions above for Molas Trail access.

Stock tips: Camping is limited and grazing opportunities are sparse.

After climbing out of the Animas River Valley, either at its junction with Molas Trail (FS 665) or at Elk Park, the trail skirts along Elk Creek, at times descending to its banks, and at others climbing high above. You will begin to have fleeting views of the high Grenadiers as you hike along the trail. Campsites are non-existent for the first 3 miles. Only when you reach the Beaver Pond at mile 3.5 will you find sites. Good camping is located immediately behind the pond, but you must cross the talus pile on the eastern shore to reach them.

Climbers cross the roaring Elk Creek to ascend hand over hand on a very steep hillside into Vestal Basin in the Grenadier Range via an unmaintained non-system trail. No campfires are allowed in the entire Vestal Basin area. This range is composed of upturned quartzite that has been faulted and wrenched into its present location from distant areas over a billion years ago.

One can also find camping approximately a mile beyond the pond in a flat meadow area. Because alpine meadows are fragile, choose sites already impacted that are located in the trees above the creek.

After leaving the meadow the trail climbs gently through spruce and fir forests. It then begins a very steep ascent through the narrowing valley whose slopes are heavily talused and where marmots and pikas whistle warnings of intrusion. There are numerous stream crossings, though most have fallen logs to accommodate the backpacker. Not so, when you reach the final stream crossing in the upper basin. Expect to wade this cold creek, no matter the season.

At approximately 7.5 miles up the trail you will pass an old miner's cabin, a remnant of failed turn-of-the-century efforts to find gold in the Grenadiers. These sites in the Weminuche are now rare because of human destruction and weathering. Old historical cabins and Indian artifacts are protected by the Archeological Resources Protection Act of 1979. The trail continues past the cabin, crosses the stream and then ascends numerous switchbacks up the steep hillside to the Continental Divide Trail. Camping along the Divide is possible near small alpine lakes to the north or Eldorado Lake to the south. This lake was formerly named Annabell Lake by the historic Bell family of Silverton who worked claims near Kite Lake in the 19th century. Why the lake was renamed Eldorado Lake is unknown.

PURGATORY CREEK / ANIMAS RIVER TRAIL
FOREST SERVICE TRAILS 511 AND 675

| | |
|---|---|
| Length: | 12 miles |
| Trailhead elevation: | 8,800', and 7,700' at Animas River |
| Ending elevation: | 8,300' at Needle Creek Bridge |
| Difficulty: | Moderate |
| Cautions: | Cattle grazing in Purgatory Flats |
| | Heavy day hiking and stock traffic |

Access: Travel 28 miles north from Durango on U.S. 550 to Purgatory Campground located across the road from Purgatory Ski Area. Park in the small gravel lot immediately before the campground. No parking is allowed in the campground.

Stock tips: Day use by stock travelers is frequent. Campsites in Purgatory Flats and along the Animas River offer limited grazing.

The first half of this trail, though popular, offers great day hiking. After the first mile and a half, it enters a meadow known as Purgatory Flats where old mining cabin foundations can be seen. These sites are protected by the Archeological Resources Protection Act. Many side trails have been created as people meandered around the sites and along Cascade Creek, but you should not get lost if you continue east toward the Animas River. The aspen forest which borders the trail and creek is home for numerous birds that summer in the Weminuche Wilderness.

After leaving the meadow, the trail ascends to a promontory point that offers excellent views of the Animas River Valley below. It then descends along the narrow Cascade Creek gorge to its junction with the Animas River in approximately 4.5 miles. It then crosses the Animas River on a suspension bridge near the mouth of Cascade Creek. A post office existed at Cascade before the railroad was built, and a rancher named Levi Carson owned the property further down river that became the site of Rockwood. Carson supposedly made a rich strike in the area, and it later became known as the"Lost Levi Carson mine." You may encounter lots of visitors at Cascade as the Durango and Silverton Train occasionally stops here and lets people take a short walk or picnic by the river.

Beyond the Animas River the trail briefly follows the old wagon and stage road which formerly connected Needleton and Rockwood. This is part of the original toll road that was used by pack trains carrying supplies to Silverton from Durango before the railroad was completed in 1882. The trail parallels the Animas River for 6.7 miles before it reaches the junction with Needle Creek Trail (FS 504). There are several stream crossings which can be difficult early in the summer.

Campsites are available along the river, and fishing is possible, though mineral deposits in the water from early mining days are high. You will cross private inholdings as you head upriver, particularly near Needleton. Needleton had a post office and train stop for many years after most of the former wagon stops closed. Theodore Schoch, of Swiss origin, founded the town in 1882 and had a hotel there. These privately owned properties are now the sites of summer homes. Public access across these properties has been graciously granted by the owners, but visitors should stay on the trail. Camp only on public land, not on private property.

Bears are sometimes spotted by train travelers and trail users in the Animas River Canyon. Since this is bear country be particularly careful to hang your food and maintain an immaculately clean campsite. After crossing the Needle Creek bridge, the trail intersects with Needle Creek Trail.

NEEDLE CREEK AND COLUMBINE PASS TRAIL
FOREST SERVICE TRAIL 504

Length:                8.3 miles
Trailhead elevation:   8,000' at Needleton
Ending elevation:      12,680' at Columbine Pass
Difficulty:            More difficult
Cautions:              Heavily used campsites in Chicago Basin
                       Mountain goats, marmots and porcupines
                       habituated to humans
                       Severe summer thunderstorms, preventing
                       access to 14,000 foot peaks at times
                       Camping prohibited in Twin Lakes Basin
                       Fire ban in Needle Creek drainage
                       Private property restrictions

Access: Needle Creek Trail is reached by two routes, either an 11-mile hike in on Purgatory Trail (FS 511), that takes approximately 5 hours, or a ride on the Durango and Silverton Narrow Gauge to Needleton, taking approximately 3 hours.

Stock tips: Stock are not often seen on this trail because of extremely heavy backpacking use and because of limited grazing in Chicago Basin.

If you want to join a crowd of people in the wilderness, head for Chicago Basin. Though this is a beautiful valley, on an average day as many as 50 people may disembark from the Durango and Silverton Narrow Gauge Train headed for the popularized basin that was once a mining community.

Needle Creek Trail follows along the creek for slightly more than 5 miles until it reaches the lower end or southern mouth of Chicago Basin. You will cross rushing New York Creek en route via a Forest Service bridge at mile 3, and then begin a steady climb that can be a challenge for individuals not acclimated to the elevation or the alpine heat. The trail was once a freight road heavily used by pack animals carrying supplies to the miners in Logtown located just above City Reservoir. This becomes obvious near New York Creek where a wide trail remains.

There are very few camping opportunities until you reach the mouth of the basin. Chicago Basin lies in a glacier-sculpted cirque and is surrounded by towering peaks. Mt. Eolus is a granite peak whose exposed rock is dated at 1.46 billion years of age.

Many impacted campsites in the basin are located too close to the stream. It is of utmost importance that you obey wilderness regulations and camp 100 feet from water unless campsites are designated. Camp only in the impacted sites rather than create new ones in fragile subalpine meadows. Camping at Twin Lakes is not permitted because of user impacts to the high alpine ecosystem.

Please do not feed the wildlife, especially the mountain goats, who have been habituated to human food and will seek you out. Remember, they live there year round and must acclimate themselves to existing food conditions if they are to survive. You won't find a larger or friendlier population of marmots, chipmunks or porcupines anywhere in the Weminuche, and these creatures love the salts in your boots, packs, tents and food. Keep a clean camp, and protect all your gear in packs suspended from sturdy tree branches when away.

A permanent fire ban was placed on Needle Creek and all its head waters in 1989 due to heavy human use that caused resource impacts. A proliferation of fire rings damaged the soils and nearby trees where wood was collected.

As you continue on the trail, you will cross Needle Creek at its north entrance into the basin which is approximately 6.5 miles from the trailhead. You now begin a steep climb to Columbine Pass. You must ascend switchbacks for 2 miles and 1,500 feet before reaching the summit. Ptarmigans spend their summers in the rocky talus slopes here, blending so completely with the rocks that you may miss them as they perch immediately beside the trail.

From the summit the trail descends down Johnson Creek Trail (FS 504) to Vallecito Trail (FS 529) or over Endlich Mesa Trail (FS 534), which takes off to the south below Columbine Pass and crosses Trimble Pass before descending to City Reservoir by way of the old mining camp, Logtown.

CITY RESERVOIR TRAIL VIA LIME MESA
FOREST SERVICE TRAIL 542

Length:                  7.7 miles
Trailhead elevation:     11,500'
Ending elevation:        10,400' at reservoir
Difficulty:              Difficult
Cautions:                Difficult 4-wheel road access to trailhead
                         Sheep grazing allotment in area
                         Lingering snowfields at high elevations

Access: Take the East Animas Road from Durango to FDR 682 or Missionary Ridge Road. Follow this winding mountain road for 17.5 miles to Henderson Lake turn-off. Drive FDR 81 for 5 miles to its end. This four wheel drive road becomes more difficult the further one drives. Horse trailers must park approximately 3 miles before the trailhead. Both Lime Mesa and City Reservoir Trails begin at this trailhead. Lime Mesa cuts north about 1/4 mile from the trailhead, while City Reservoir Trail turns east.

Stock tips: City Reservoir Trail offers stock camping and adequate grazing in the gulches that border the streams prior to the reservoir. Good stock camps are not available at the reservoir itself.

City Reservoir Trail is deceiving. It is more difficult than the beginning and ending elevation figures suggest  because it follows a rolling terrain up and down mesas into meadows and gulches before finally descending to the reservoir. West Virginia Gulch is reached approximately 2 miles from the trailhead. This valley offers camping opportunities that become scarce near the reservoir. Burnt

Timber Trail coming from Lemon Reservoir intersects the trail about a half mile before you descend into West Virginia Gulch.

After West Virginia Gulch you ascend a mesa only to drop down into Virginia Gulch with its limestone rocks and mountain vistas. After leaving Virginia Gulch the trail switchbacks up the forested hillside to West Silver Mesa at 11,800' where you can see lime deposits left from early seas that covered this country millions of years ago. The descent into Missouri Gulch is fairly rugged. A non-system trail heads south along the valley floor, while City Reservoir Trail curves back north through the forest, then downhill to the south end of City Reservoir.

City Reservoir was created in 1902 by a group of private citizens operating as the Williams Ditch Company. They filed water rights on the Florida drainage in 1899 and patented the land around the reservoir. Shortly thereafter, they sold the water rights to Durango for $60,000.

Campsites at City Reservoir are limited. The north end of the lake is more open and flat, but you must cross the river to reach a campsite. Old impacted campsites at the south end of the lake are too close to the river and should not be used unless so designated.

Endlich Mesa Trail continues beyond the reservoir to Marie Lake and the abandoned mining camp called Logtown. Logtown was formerly known as Hewitt, named after one of the military men who accompanied the McCauley army expedition of 1877 to survey the area for access accross the mountains.

LIME MESA TRAIL
FOREST SERVICE TRAIL 676

| | |
|---|---|
| Length: | 4 miles |
| Trailhead elevation: | 11,500' |
| Ending elevation: | 12,600' at overview |
| Difficulty: | Difficult |
| Cautions: | Late snow remains on trail |
| | Limited campsites |
| | Severe alpine thunderstorms |
| | Difficult descent to lakes |
| | Campfire restrictions |
| | Difficult 4-wheel drive access to trailhead |
| | Sheep grazing allotment in the area |

Access: Follow the same route described for the City Reservoir Trail (FS 542). Follow this trail for approximately 1/4 mile to a large open meadow where Lime Mesa Trail will branch to the north while City Reservoir cuts southeast downhill.

Stock tips: Day trips for stock users are possible to overlook areas. Beyond that point, the trail is too steep for animals. No campsites are available at the lakes.

Lime Mesa Trail begins in a meadow, then winds along deeply rutted gullies left from an old four-wheel drive road. The trail crosses through a timbered area before descending to Dollar Lake less than 2 miles from the trailhead. Thereafter, it begins a gentle climb above timberline up the limestone mesa to crest on a ridge that offers views well worth the effort of the ups and downs on the trail. Looking to the east along the ridge you will see large old cairns whose origins are unknown. Perhaps they were erected by the Hayden surveying expedition, since the party headquartered in Howardsville and travled throughout this area. Certainly they were used by sheepherders who began trailing their sheep into this country a hundred years ago. Thunderstorms can move into this high country quickly, so don't linger on the ridge.

After reaching the overlook at mile 4, the trail becomes a social path which winds down a steep talused slope to Ruby Lake and then to Emerald and Pear Lakes. These small alpine lakes are like jewels set in the rugged mountain slopes. Do not descend into the basin unless you have the stamina to climb out again. Snowfields may have to be navigated until late July. Campsites are extremely limited near the lakes and must be 100 feet from water. Fires are not permitted since this area is part of the Needle Creek drainage.

Emerald Lake, which catches the water cascading down to the Needle Creek drainage from Ruby Lake, is bordered by a private inholding and is used by the owners of Tall Timbers Resort as a site to drop their guests via helicopter. Helicopter landings on private property in the wilderness are not illegal.

BURNT TIMBER TRAIL
FOREST SERVICE TRAIL 667

| | |
|---|---|
| Length: | 7 miles |
| Trailhead elevation: | 8,500' |
| Ending elevation: | 11,400' at junction with City Reservoir Trail |
| Difficulty: | More difficult |
| Cautions: | Sheep grazing allotment |
| | Limited campsites |
| | Steep sections |

Access: Travel east from Durango on Florida Road to its junction with FDR 596 which goes to Lemon Reservoir. Continue approximately 5 miles to Florida Campground. Then continue through the campground another 1.5 miles to Transfer Park Campground. The trailhead begins just before the campground entrance.

Stock tips: This trail offers access for stock users to the City Reservoir Trail. Grassy pastures skirt the trail and offer potential grazing. Water can be a limiting factor.

Within the first mile or so of Burnt Timber Trail, so named because of a devastating fire in the area years ago, you gain a thousand feet in elevation as you climb through a lush Aspen forest. After crossing Burnt Timber Creek, you quickly crest to a rolling meadow through which the trail meanders as it continues climbing. Over a thousand feet below is the Florida River drainage, and distant vistas of Endlich Mesa and the peaks beyond can be seen.

The trail slowly ascends along the side hill, skirting through the meadow. After approximately 3 miles it meets with an old logging road which continues north for a short distance as the trail path. During July you may see large herds of domestic sheep grazing in the meadows below the trail. The trail is easily followed as it enters a spruce-fir forest at about mile 4. Within another couple of miles after switch backing through the timber, Burnt Timber Trail will connect with City Reservoir Trail.

Campsites along the trail are limited, though some exist in the forested area at mile 4. Water availability also may be a challenge for campsites in the meadow high above the Florida River, since stream encounters are few.

ENDLICH MESA TRAIL
FOREST SERVICE TRAIL 534

| | |
|---|---|
| Length: | 13 miles |
| Trailhead elevation: | 11,300' |
| Ending elevation: | 12,800' at Trimble Pass |
| Difficulty: | More difficult |
| Cautions: | Severe alpine thunderstorms |
| | Difficult 4-wheel access to trailhead |
| | Limited water along the alpine trail |

Access: Follow Florida Road (C.R. 240) to Lemon Reservoir. Continue past the lake on FDR 596 for 5.5 miles. Then follow FDR 597, an old logging road, which climbs 9.5 miles to its end and the trailhead. The trail ascends a hill to the east, then turns north to follow Endlich Mesa.

Stock tips: This trail offers limited grazing for stock. Campsites are few and far between.

Endlich Mesa Trail is difficult to reach, but it offers breathtaking vistas of distant mountain ranges from its 12,000' elevation. As you walk along the alpine path, you see the La Plata Mountains and distant Utah ranges to the west. Looking east you have views of the mountains that surround Pagosa Springs. To the north are the Needles and the Grenadiers. Don't expect to find many sources of water along this high trail. Go prepared.

The trail begins its steep descent into the Florida River drainage and City Reservoir at approximately mile 5. After a mile it crosses the dam at the south end of the reservoir. It then joins City Reservoir Trail which has dropped down from Lime Mesa.

Endlich Mesa Trail skirts the north side of the reservoir then climbs steeply to Lake Marie at 11,600' elevation. Nearby you will find remnants of Logtown, also known as Hewitt, an old mining town which was founded in 1882. Logtown had a post office for three years, but the 11,400 foot site was inhospitable to settlers and was soon abandoned. After Logtown the trail ascends Silver Mesa, climbing steeply up to Trimble Pass at 12,800'. Continuing beyond the pass it traverses rocky talus slopes, losing slight elevation to intersect Johnson Creek Trail and Columbine Pass at 12,680'. Endlich Mesa Trail passes several old mine sites en route to the pass where one must marvel at the endurance of miners who worked this exposed terrain to extract minerals from the mountains.

Camping is a challenge along Endlich Mesa Trail, but it is possible. You may not find the level spot you are accustomed to, but you will find sites. A greater challenge is finding water sources on the mesa. There will be limited campsites at City Reservoir and below its outlet along the Florida drainage.

VALLECITO CREEK TRAIL
FOREST SERVICE TRAIL 529

| | |
|---|---|
| Length: | 17 miles |
| Trailhead elevation: | 7,900' |
| Ending elevation: | 12,500' at Hunchback Pass |
| Difficulty: | Moderate to difficult |
| Cautions: | Heavy day hiking in first 3 miles |
| | Numerous stream crossings |
| | Heavy stock use |

Access: Take Florida Road (C.R. 240) from Durango to Vallecito Lake. Continue along the lake for 5 miles to a junction with FDR 508, and go left 3 miles to the Vallecito Campground. The trailhead is immediately before the campground.

Stock tips: The first 3 miles of Vallecito Trail are difficult for animals because of exposure. Beyond that the trail is gentler. Campsites and grazing can be found in meadows after the first 6 miles.

Vallecito Trail is very heavily used because of its access to other trailheads. Groups descend Johnson Creek (FS 504) after traveling through Chicago Basin, or enter by way of Rock Creek (FS 655) and Flint Creek Trails (FS 527). The trail was the route of Lieutenant C.A.H. McCauley's military expedition in 1877.

The trail begins with a rocky climb up cliffs overlooking Vallecito Creek far below. It then skirts along a rock outcropping above the creek for a couple of miles before descending to the first bridge crossing of Vallecito Creek. There is one campsite at this 3-mile point along the trail.

The trail now skirts the east side of the creek, crossing several side streams that can be challenging in early summer. It passes through a lush spruce/fir forest where limited campsites are hidden before crossing Vallecito Creek again at mile 5. The trail skirts above the rushing creek for approximately a mile before crossing back to the east shore just beyond Soda Spring.

The trail splits at mile 8, with Johnson Creek Trail (FS 504) heading east at the fourth bridge crossing over Vallecito Creek, and Vallecito Creek Trail continuing north before the bridge crossing. Campsites exist in the valley that surrounds the junction of Johnson and Vallecito Creeks. Please choose a site that is impacted rather than creating another in this heavily used area.

Beyond this junction Vallecito Creek Trail gently gains elevation while skirting the creek. Anticipate wading a fast moving Roell Creek whose head waters originate from Hidden and Lost Lakes. A short distance beyond Roell Creek will be Sunlight Basin to the west. This and other wide meadows offer good stock camping.

The most difficult stream crossing occurs at Rock Creek, 14 miles from the trailhead. When crossing a difficult stream, use a long stick as a third leg. Take small steps sideways, always facing upstream, and loosen pack straps and waist belt so you will not be encumbered should you fall. There are campsites in the Rock Creek area as it joins Vallecito Creek, but they may be crowded since Rock Creek Trail (FS 655) channels people into this area.

Beyond Rock Creek Trail the valley narrows, and Vallecito Trail begins steeply ascending towards Nebo Creek and Hunchback Pass. It intersects the Continental Divide Trail (FS 813) at mile 17, approximately one mile from the summit of Hunchback Pass. Be prepared for steep traveling as you cross the pass. This area was a turn of the century prospecting site, and old "glory holes" may be visible in the rocky peaks.

JOHNSON CREEK TRAIL
FOREST SERVICE TRAIL 504

| | |
|---|---|
| Length: | 6.7 miles |
| Trailhead elevation: | 9,100' at junction |
| Ending elevation: | 12,700' at Columbine Pass |
| Difficulty: | Most difficult |
| Cautions: | Switchbacks with steep grades |
| | Limited campsites |
| | Stream crossings |
| | Severe alpine thunderstorms |

Access: 8.3 miles up Needle Creek Trail (FS 504) from Animas River drainage and 8 miles up Vallecito Creek Trail (FS 529)

Stock tips: Limited campsites and grazing for stock users

Though Johnson Creek has a makeshift log bridge crossing as you begin the trail after leaving the meadow at its junction with Vallecito Creek, high spring waters frequently wash it away. The crossing can be very precarious in high water. Take all precautions to ensure your safety. Side streams which enter Johnson Creek can also be challenging during run-off. Ascending Johnson Creek Trail to Columbine Pass is a good climb. You must travel switchbacks for 4 miles through timber, and only after reaching timberline will you find nice campsites.

About a mile below the summit of Columbine Pass, the trail levels out, and Columbine Lake, which offers possible high alpine camping, can be seen to the right. The weather can be very severe at this altitude with no tree protection. The fragile meadows are easily damaged. The steep climb beyond the lake to Columbine Pass at 12,680' goes quickly if you remember to look over your shoulder at the deep canyon through which you have traveled and back toward the beautiful Vallecito drainage. Pikas and golden eagles may be at the summit to greet you. Remember that summer thunderstorms are frequent in July and August, so plan on crossing the summit before noon.

Johnson Creek is named after Miles T. Johnson, a civilian who accompanied the McCauley military expedition of 1877. Johnson and two other men are credited with unlocking the mining operations in the Needle Mountains.


ROCK CREEK TRAIL
FOREST SERVICE TRAIL 655

Length:                 7.5 miles
Trailhead elevation:    10,100'
Ending elevation:       12,200' at Continental Divide
Difficulty:             More difficult
Cautions:               High Elevation thunderstorms
                        Stream crossings

Access: 14 miles up Vallecito Creek Trail (FS 529)

Stock tips: This trail is used by stock groups en route to high lakes or crossing from the Vallecito drainage to the Pine drainage. Limited campsites and grazing exist.

An initial steep climb greets you as you start up Rock Creek. You will reach meadows after a couple of miles which offer camping at the upper end. The trail follows Rock Creek which must be crossed just before mile 4 where a side trail breaks away south and ascends to Rock Lake at 11,840'.

The main trail continues beyond Rock Creek, which flows from Rock Lake. After passing under a towering cliff, the trail climbs a series of switchbacks, then turns north to end at the Continental Divide Trail at mile 7.5. Flint Creek Trail (FS 527) coming up from the Pine River drainage meets Rock Creek Trail before the climb to the Continental Divide. High alpine camping and fishing is possible, though summer storms can be severe.

LOS PIÑOS (PINE) RIVER TRAIL
FOREST SERVICE TRAIL 523

| | |
|---|---|
| Length: | 22 miles |
| Trailhead elevation: | 7,900' |
| Ending elevation: | 10,600' at Weminuche Pass |
| Difficulty: | Moderate |
| Cautions: | Heavy use by day hikers and stock groups |
| | First 3 miles cross private property |
| | Numerous stream crossings |

Access: Drive east from Durango on Florida Road (C.R. 240) or north on C.R. 501 from Bayfield to Vallecito Lake. Continue along west shore for 5 miles to a junction with FDR 602. Turn left and drive 4 miles to the Pine River Campground. The trailhead is located at the end of the road.

Stock tips: This trail, because of its gentle elevation gain is a favorite of stock users. It offers a variety of camping opportunities and grazing in open valleys.

Los Piños River Trail begins on private property, the U.S. Forest Service having gained a right-of-way for access to the wilderness. The ranch owner has been very gracious to hikers and stock users, and it is important that all users respect private property rights while traversing the first 3 miles. This section of the trail is flat, passing through stands of Ponderosa pine and Douglas fir. The first stream crossing, Indian Creek, occurs within a mile and can be difficult in the spring.

Fishing is not allowed until you enter the wilderness at mile 3. As the valley opens up, meadows extend along the trail and by the river. At mile 6 you will find a well constructed bridge crossing Lake Creek, which empties water from Emerald and Moon Lakes into the Los Piños River. Emerald Lake is named after Emerald Patrick who started the first fish hatchery in Southwestern Colorado around 1884, then sold it to the state.

Lake Creek Trail (FS 528) turns left just past the bridge, while the Los Piños River Trail continues along by the river. Numerous impacted campsites exist around the Pine/Lake Creek junction. Wilderness regulations require all campsites be located at least 100 feet from water.

After crossing Lake Creek, the canyon narrows, and a section of steep trail follows. The valley opens up again in a mile and a half, and good campsites will begin to be available in the meadows. This area is known as Willow Park. The trail then moves through aspen groves where numerous chew marks on the trees tell of hungry porcupines and elk during the winter.

Another steep section just before Flint Creek switchbacks over rocky ledges, and at mile 12, Flint Creek must be waded. Flint Creek Trail (FS 527) branches left through the meadow before the creek crossing. Limited campsites can be found in this area.

The Los Piños River Trail begins climbing through aspen forests, and soon passes above elaborately constructed beaver ponds. The route then enters another large open valley. Sierra Vandera Trail (FS 524) branches to the right and crosses the Pine River at mile 14. There are several social trails in this area as a result of heavy usage along and across the river. Don't be confused because the Pine River remains to the east of the trail the entire length as you ascend it to Weminuche Pass.

A mile after crossing South Canyon Creek the trail passes the historic Granite Peak Guard Station at mile 16. The log cabin itself is not visible from the trail, but the old rail fence alerts you to this Forest Service outpost constructed in 1915 and used for forest management during the early days of the San Juan

National Forest. It is still used by Forest Service trail crews and wilderness rangers, as well as volunteer groups who spend time helping maintain wilderness trails.

Approximately a half mile beyond the guard station you will pass the Divide Lakes and Granite Lake Trailheads (FS 539) accessed on the east side of the Los Piños River. The Pine River Trail passes through conifer trees before climbing out into open meadows again. Snowslide Canyon Trail (FS 653) splits from the Los Piños River Trail at mile 18, heading to the east. The Los Piños River Trail gains slight elevation before passing the junction of Rincon La Osa Trail (FS 525), which turns to the west. It then climbs gently into the open meadows of Weminuche Pass and the Continental Divide. The trail traverses through this gorgeous alpine valley for 2 miles until it connects with the Weminuche Creek Trail (FS 523) coming from the east side of the Continental Divide.

Other trails take off from this one before it junctions with the Weminuche Creek Trail, including the Continental Divide Trail (FS 813) which follows Rincon La Vaca, and the Highline Trail (FS 564) which turns north to access the Rio Grande Pyramid and The Window. Campsites are abundant in the alpine meadows.This gentle pass was heavily used by Ute Indians who hunted the area during summer months.

The Raber Lohr and Fuchs Ditches, which transport water from Rincon La Vaca Creek and the upper Pine River to the eastern side of the Continental Divide also span the valley. These ditches, constructed in 1935, long before the Weminuche Wilderness was designated in 1975, were grandfathered in as an acceptable use by the 1964 Wilderness Act. They transport water from Rincon La Vaca Creek and the North Fork of the Pine River to the Rio Grande River drainage on the eastern slope of the Continental Divide.

LAKE CREEK TRAIL
FOREST SERVICE TRAIL 528

| | |
|---|---|
| Length: | 9 miles |
| Trailhead elevation: | 8,400' |
| Ending elevation: | 11,600' at Moon Lake |
| Difficulty: | More difficult |
| Cautions: | Camping restrictions around lakes |
| | Steep climb from Emerald to Moon |
| | Difficult stream crossings |
| | Heavy summer use |

Access: Six miles up Pine River Trail (FS 523), past Lake Creek Bridge, branching left up Lake Creek.

Stock tips: Stock travel occurs on this trail, but camping is not possible in the closure area near Emerald Lake. Limited camping is available 1/2 mile north of Emerald Lake.

Because Emerald Lake is the third largest natural lake in Colorado and because of its natural beauty, it is heavily used by wilderness travelers. The lake is over a mile long, and actually consists of two lakes, with Big Emerald feeding into Little Emerald. Special fishing regulations are in effect for these waters. Note regulations posted at the Los Piños River Trailhead, and obtain Colorado Division of Wildlife brochures for information. Also check fishing information in this book.

The trail departs up Lake Creek at mile 6.5 from the Los Piños River Trail, beginning a steep ascent above the roaring creek. It levels out at mile 2 where Hell Creek branches south. The trail begins another steep climb up and over a wide snowslide path. Notice the trees that have been swept down the hillside, across the trail and then up the adjacent slope.

The trail now enters a thick stand of conifers, then climbs within a half mile to the camping area, your signal that you are nearing the lakes. Signs are posted before Little Emerald Lake, beyond which camping is not allowed. Campsites can be found above and below the trail at these signs. Camping or grazing stock within 1/2 mile north of Emerald Lake is also prohibited. A posted sign designates the restricted area.

The trail continues above Little and Big Emerald Lakes, following the rolling terrain of the shoreline, and after 2 miles travels beyond the lakes into open meadows. Lake Creek will have to be forded at this point, and can be quite swift during run-off.

At approximately mile 7 you will again cross Lake Creek and begin a steep uphill climb that contours around the side of a large basin and finally levels at the huge waterfall which is immediately below Moon Lake. You will have to cross the outlet from Moon Lake before reaching its shore at mile 9. This high alpine lake is above timberline and is frequently frozen until July. Little camping is available in its vicinity because the shoreline is boggy.

FLINT CREEK TRAIL
FOREST SERVICE TRAIL 527

Length:                    7 miles
Trailhead elevation:       9,200'
Ending elevation:          11,600' at Flint Lake
Difficulty:                More difficult
Cautions:                  Alpine thunderstorms
                           Stream crossings

Access: 12 miles up Pine River Trail (FS 523), immediately prior to crossing Flint Creek.

Stock tips: Stock travel is frequent on this trail as groups traverse from the Pine River drainage to the Vallecito River drainage. No camping, grazing or stock are allowed between FS525 and FS527 to the shore of Flint Lake, or within 200 feet of the west shoreline.

Flint Creek Trail begins in a meadow, but soon embarks on a gentle climb beside Flint Creek. After a mile of hiking you will see the prominent Pope's Nose across the creek. Limited campsites exist along the stream in this lower area. Wilderness regulations require all campsites to be 100 feet from water. Do not expect to stop at Barebottom Park, which is marked on the map. This rocky hillside has no room for campsites because of its bumpy terrain. One can puzzle the origin of the name as they continue for another mile where several good campsites will be available.

The trail crosses several side streams as it rapidly gains elevation. After mile 4 you must cross Flint Creek, which can require cautious wading. The trail now continues on the north side of the stream through spruce/fir stands until it reaches Flint Lake at mile 7. Rincon La Osa Trail (FS 525) turns north immediately before Flint Lake, carrying you over the Continental Divide to the Ute Lakes area. If you continue west past Flint Lake you will connect with Rock Creek Trail (FS 655), which originates in the Vallecito Basin drainage.

DIVIDE LAKES TRAIL
FOREST SERVICE TRAIL 539

| | |
|---|---|
| Length: | 1.8 miles |
| Trailhead elevation: | 9,900' at Pine River |
| Ending elevation: | 10,000' at junction |
| Difficulty: | Moderate |
| Cautions: | Heavy backpacking and stock travel |
| | Difficult Pine River crossing |

Access: 16 miles up the Pine River Trail (FS 523), across the Pine River. Markers indicate the junction with the Weminuche Trail from Poison Park Trailhead a half-mile past the Guard Station.

Stock tips: Many stock groups travel this trail coming in from the Poison Park area along the Weminuche Trail.

This trail might be considered an extension of the Weminuche Trail originating above Williams Creek Reservoir. After crossing the Pine River, Divide Lakes Trail climbs gently into a conifer stand. Within a half mile you will reach the small lakes. Limited camping is available here. The trail continues past the lakes and connects with the Weminuche Trail at mile 1.8. Divide Lakes Trail is heavily used, despite its short length.


GRANITE LAKE TRAIL

| | |
|---|---|
| Length: | 1 mile |
| Trailhead elevation: | 9,900' at Pine River crossing |
| Ending elevation: | 10,400' at lake |
| Difficulty; | Difficult |
| Cautions: | Rocky shoreline |
| | No camping available |

Access: 16 miles up the Pine River Trail (FS 523) east of the Pine River. The trail turns north and heads upriver as it climbs to Granite Lake.

Stock tips: Not recommended for stock.

Granite Lake, nestled in between steep slopes, offers no camping. Climbing the trail to see the lake can be a nice day trip. Granite Peak nearby is only 10,700' elevation, slightly higher than the lake's elevation. This rounded peak lends its name to the U.S. Forest Service Guard Station below on the Pine Creek Trail.

SNOWSLIDE CANYON
FOREST SERVICE TRAIL 653

| Length: | 4 miles |
|---|---|
| Elevation gain: | 10,200' at trailhead |
| Ending Elevation: | 11,900' at Continental Divide |
| Difficulty | Difficult |
| Cautions: | Some steep sections |
| | Trail may be indistinct in places |

Access: 18 miles up Pine River Trail (FS 523), across the Pine River to the east.

Stock tips: Stock travel on this trail is possible.

After crossing the Pine River and traveling approximately one mile along the trail, you enter Snowslide Canyon. You must cross Snowslide Creek as it flows into the Pine River. A gentle climb will bring you out of the mouth of the canyon as the trail skirts the north side of the creek through aspen trees. Note the many snowslide paths in the first mile or so of the trail.

After about 2 miles of climbing in a spruce/fir forest the trail breaks into open meadows and approaches the Continental Divide at the head of the canyon. Post markers help you stay on the trail as you ascend the last 2 miles to the Continental Divide Trail. These high alpine meadows offer camping sites, but they are fragile and have a very short growing season.

RINCON LA OSA TRAIL
FOREST SERVICE TRAIL 525

| | |
|---|---|
| Length: | 6 miles |
| Trailhead elevation: | 10,100' |
| Ending elevation: | 12,200' at Continental Divide |
| Difficulty: | Difficult |
| Cautions: | Boggy areas |
| | Stream crossings |
| | Alpine thunderstorms |

Access: 19 miles up the Pine River Trail(FS 523) and north along La Osa Creek.

Stock tips: The lower portion of this trail passes through a beautiful valley. Permittee stock camps are found in this area.

"La Osa" means the bear in Spanish, and one can imagine this as the summer home of grizzlies who used to roam the Weminuche Wilderness. The basin gets its name from a fight which supposedly occurred between a Spanish sheepherder and an old mother grizzly. The last grizzlies that wandered in the Weminuche Wilderness probably roamed this area.

You must cross La Osa Creek shortly after leaving the trailhead. Thereafter you will be traveling along its northern shore. The trail climbs out of the Pine River Valley through dense forests in an area of springs and bogs that have necessitated much trail work by the Forest Service. There are many lengthy walkways constructed to help preserve the trail. You enter the wide meadow at about mile 2. The meandering La Osa stream provides vital riparian habitat along its banks.

The trail will skirt away from the stream near a small lake at approximately mile 4 and begin a brisk climb through forest cover. There is an old trail that ascends through the valley, but this has been abandoned by the Forest Service because of severe erosion. A new trail now travels along the edge of the valley through the trees. You will break out of the woods and be above timberline in the final mile. The trail skirts high above the valley across windswept peaks before joining the Continental Divide Trail. This area can be very confusing because of the number of social trails created. Follow rock cairns and post markers to help locate your junction.

Good camping can be found in the valley before you begin the climb to the Continental Divide. Wilderness regulations require all campsites be 100' from water.

# 14

# Pagosa Ranger District Trail Descriptions

The area of the Weminuche that lies on the south slope of the San Juan Mountains between Weminuche Creek and Wolf Creek Pass receives moderate use during the summer, with the exception of a few very popular destinations. It is highly attractive to hunters, so the trailheads are filled to capacity during the fall rifle seasons. The area contains the headwaters of the Piedra and West Fork San Juan Rivers. Pagosa Peak, Saddle Mountain and the Window--a passage through a sheer, vertical wall--are landmarks that are visible for great distances.

Within this area we are seeing increased use, and some areas are showing the effects of this use. Even with increasing numbers of visitors, the Weminuche Wilderness can retain its quality if those who visit will use techniques designed to minimize the impacts of their activities.

As Wilderness Program Coordinator on the Pagosa District, I am charged with maintaining "an enduring resource of wilderness" for present and future generations. Management of wilderness can be a challenging task. People are passionate about wilderness. Wilderness is many things to many people, but designated wilderness was not intended to be everything to everyone. My personal definition of wilderness is based upon my experiences there and my values. It is similar, but not identical to that expressed in the Wilderness Act of 1964. In my work it is important for me to measure my personal values against those values defined within the Wilderness Act of 1964, the legislation that designates the Weminuche Wilderness and U.S. Forest Service management direction. Those values that do not "fit" must be set aside--not lost, not forgotten, but set aside when I am making decisions regarding designated wilderness.

Phyllis Decker
Wilderness Program Coordinator
Pagosa Springs Ranger District
P.O. Box 301
Pagosa Springs, Colorado 81147
Phone: 970 264-2268
FAX: 970 264-1538

WEMINUCHE (POISON PARK) TRAIL
FOREST SERVICE TRAIL 592

LENGTH:                     11 miles
Trailhead elevation:        9,100'
Ending elevation:           10,200' at junction with Pine River Trail
Difficulty:                 Moderate
Cautions:                   Rough stream crossings
                            Heavy stock use
                            Limited camping

Access: Drive U.S. 160 for 3 miles west of Pagosa Springs. Turn north on Piedra Road (FDR 631). Drive 22 miles to Williams Lake Road (FDR 640). Just past Williams Reservoir turn left on FDR 644. Drive 3 miles to the trailhead.

Stock Tips: Stock grazing is restricted in the park at the junction of Weminuche and East Fork Trails.

The trail begins outside Wilderness boundaries with a drop into the Weminuche Valley. It skirts private property, and at mile 2 intersects Falls Creek and Hossick Creek Trails (FS 585). Only after passing Hossick Creek Trail do you enter the Weminuche Wilderness. The trail up to this point is a well-improved off-road route. Respect private property that is adjacent to the wilderness in this area by staying on the trail.

Weminuche Trail travels a short distance west before heading north again, crossing Hossick Creek. This creek can be a difficult crossing during runoff. The trail now enters a large meadow and begins to climb into a canyon. The hiking trail splits from the old stockway at about mile 4.

Weminuche Trail continues through an open area known as Elk Park and then reaches the roaring East Fork (FS 659) of the Weminuche River at about mile 7. East Fork Trail cuts right from the Weminuche Trail after crossing the river. Be prepared for a difficult crossing at this point since there is no bridge. Though there is good camping in this area, horse grazing is prohibited in the park because of impacts to the meadows. Wilderness regulations require all campsites to be at least 100 feet from water.

The trail continues its gentle ascent and at about mile 8 reaches the Divide Lakes Trail (FS 539) which turns left. Weminuche Creek Trail continues to the right, beginning to climb again after crossing Weminuche Creek. It passes close to Granite Lake, with a half mile side trail that goes to the lake. Continuing on the main trail, you  begin your descent into the Pine River Valley, passing across the meadows of Snowslide Canyon and its trail (FS 653) before reaching your junction with the Pine River Trail at mile 11. You will have to wade Snowslide Creek as well as the Pine River to reach the intersection.

## EAST FORK OF WEMINUCHE TRAIL
## FOREST SERVICE TRAIL 659

| | |
|---|---|
| Length: | 6 miles |
| Trailhead elevation: | 9,500' |
| Ending elevation: | 11,100' |
| Difficulty: | Most difficult |
| Cautions: | Trail becomes indistinct at about mile 5 |
| | Severe elevation gain in spots |

Access: 7 miles up the Weminuche Trail (FS 592)

Stock Tips: Steep, rough, rocky and narrow. Not recommended for inexperienced riders/stock.

After crossing the East Fork of Weminuche Creek the East Fork Trail turns east, following the stream. A fairly steep ascent must be negotiated before the trail levels off in meadows. The trail crosses East Fork twice, then follow its path through a rugged canyon to high country located below Hossick Mountain. It enters a large meadow in a cul-de-sac formed by towering mountains that encircle it. Avalanche chutes are obvious in this high country.

East Fork Trail accesses rugged country that testifies to the pristine nature of the Weminuche Wilderness. Camping in the meadows is possible.

HOSSICK CREEK TRAIL
FOREST SERVICE TRAIL 585

| | |
|---|---|
| Length: | 7.5 miles |
| Trailhead elevation: | 8,400' |
| Ending elevation: | 11,200' at Squaw Pass |
| Difficulty: | More difficult |
| Cautions: | Stream crossings |
| | Severe elevation gain in spots |
| | High altitude thunderstorms |

Access: Two miles up the Weminuche Trail (FDR 592).

Stock Tips: Not recommended for inexperienced riders/stock.

This trail can be a challenge in some sections to the experienced back country traveler. The trail follows Hossick Creek gorge through a dense forest. It levels out into a basin used as a stock camp at approximately mile 5 near the head of Hossick Creek. Cimarrona Peak, at 12,538' towers to the right. Camping is available in the basin, and if your destination is Hossick Lake, you might want to stop here to camp, then day hike to the lake.

After leaving the basin, Hossick Creek Trail begins to climb severely again, soon meeting Hossick Lake Trail (FS 602) which turns left. If you continue to the right on Hossick Creek Trail you will travel above timberline at 12,000' to the Cimarrona Creek drainage. The Cimarrona Creek Trail junction (FS 586) is met at mile 6.5 just at timberline. You can then follow the Cimarrona Creek Trail up to another divide before dropping down to Squaw Pass at 11,200'. Camping opportunities in this high country are limited.

HOSSICK LAKE TRAIL
FOREST SERVICE TRAIL 602

| | |
|---|---|
| Length: | .6 mile |
| Trailhead elevation: | 11,800' at junction |
| Ending elevation: | 11,900' at lake |
| Difficulty: | Difficult |
| Cautions: | Alpine thunderstorms |
| | Limited camping and not recommended because |
| | of lightning |

Access: 5.5 miles up Hossick Creek Trail (FS 585).

Taking a left off Hossick Creek Trail, you follow a path through rugged country to drop to the shores of Hossick Lake. The area offers a spectacular view, but don't expect easy camping on the lake's shore. No flat spots are available. Wilderness regulations require all campsites be 100 feet from water.

CIMARRONA TRAIL
FOREST SERVICE TRAIL 586

| | |
|---|---|
| Length: | 8 miles |
| Trailhead elevation: | 8,400' |
| Ending elevation: | 11,200' at Squaw Pass |
| Difficulty: | More difficult |
| Cautions: | Limited camping |
| | High elevation storms |
| | Steep ascents |
| | Limited water sources |

Access: Drive 3 miles west of Pagosa Springs on U.S. 160. Turn north on Piedra Road (FSR 631), and drive 22 miles to Williams Reservoir Road (FDR 640). Drive 4 miles to Cimarrona Creek Campground. The trailhead is left of the road near the campground entrance.

Stock Tips: Limited feed and water restrict camping.

Cimarrona Creek Trail travels 4 miles through heavy forests. At about mile 2 it begins to switchback into the high country and gains significant elevation in the next 4 miles. You are traveling through volcanic rock country where rock formations can be very interesting.

The trail levels out near a waterfall, where limited camping is possible. The trail meets Hossick Creek Trail Junction at about mile 6.5, crosses a ridge, then descends to Squaw Pass at 11,200'.

WILLIAMS CREEK TRAIL
FOREST SERVICE TRAIL 587

| | |
|---|---|
| Length: | 12 miles |
| Trailhead elevation: | 8,400' |
| Ending elevation: | 11,900' Continental Divide |
| Cautions: | Stream crossings |
| | High altitude storms |
| Difficulty: | Moderate to mile 4.5, then difficult |

Access: Drive west from Pagosa Springs on U.S. 160 for 3 miles. Turn left on the Piedra Road (FDR 631) and drive 22 miles to Williams Lake Road(FDR 640). Follow to end and Williams Creek Trailhead.

Stock Tips: Drop-off below trail necessitates careful passing.

Williams Creek Trail climbs along a hillside into a dense spruce/fir forest. Because the trail skirts along the hill, passing horse packers can be challenging. After a couple of miles the trail levels out and moves through open meadows. The Indian Creek Trail (FS 588) cuts right at mile 3. Stream crossings are minor until you cross Williams Creek at about mile 4.

After the stream crossing, Williams Creek Trail travels through meadows again. Campsites are available until the canyon narrows at approximately mile 6. From this point you will have to climb a couple of steep benches before reaching a junction at mile 8.5 where the Williams Lake Trail (FS 664) cuts right and Williams Creek Trail jogs left under high ridges to begin its steep climb to the Continental Divide. Both routes are about 3 miles in length. Good camping can be found below the junction. Upon reaching the Continental Divide Trail by way of Williams Lake, you can look below to Trout Lake on one side and Williams Lake on the other.

WILLIAMS LAKE TRAIL
FOREST SERVICE TRAIL 664

| | |
|---|---|
| Length: | 3.5 miles |
| Trailhead elevation: | 10,700' |
| Ending elevation: | 11,700' at lake |
| Difficulty: | Most difficult |
| Cautions: | Lake is at timberline, so fires are inappropriate |
| | High alpine thunderstorms |
| | Boggy, fragile riparian area around lake |
| | |
| Access: | 8.5 miles up Williams Creek Trail (FS 587). |
| | |
| Stock Tips: | Grazing for livestock is nonexistent at the lake. Camping with stock is possible 1/2 mile before reaching Williams Lake. |

This trail gains elevation quickly as it ascends a rugged slope, crossing several streambeds, and climbs in 3 miles to the high Williams Lake, located at 11,700' elevation. The trail passes a waterfall on the left side before the rocky route climbs out into a boggy alpine meadow beside the lake. Fires are not recommended above timberline, and previous campers seeking firewood have destroyed old gnarly alpine trees near the lake. Camping opportunities for the hardy exist, but wilderness regulations require that campsites be at least 100 feet from water.

Williams Lake lies in a basin below the Continental Divide. Continuing beyond the lake, one reaches the Continental Divide in another half mile, where views into Trout Lake and the upper reaches of Trout Creek and Red Lakes Trail are available.

INDIAN CREEK TRAIL
FOREST SERVICE TRAIL 588

| | |
|---|---|
| Length: | 8.5 miles |
| Trailhead elevation: | 9,000' at junction |
| Ending elevation: | 11,500' at Continental Divide |
| Difficulty: | More difficult |
| Cautions: | Stream crossings |
| | Steep switchbacks |

Access: 3 miles up Williams Creek Trail (FS 587)

Indian Creek Trail divides to the right approximately 3 miles up Williams Creek Trail. Williams Creek must be crossed, and this can be a challenge during spring run-off. The trail climbs through volcanic rock country. After another 2 miles, you must cross Indian Creek, only to cross back over shortly thereafter. The trail will then level out into Palisade Meadows at mile 3, a favorite camping area.

Upon entering the meadows, the trail divides, with the left fork, Palisade Meadows Cut-off (FS 651), climbing out through timber to the Continental Divide Trail in 3 miles. The switchbacks on the upper Palisade Meadows Cut-off are fairly steep and difficult to travel.

The main Indian Creek Trail goes south of the creek at Palisade Meadows and climbs east to cross the Middle Fork of the Piedra River at approximately mile 7. A large park where camping is possible extends along the Middle Fork of the Piedra River before the crossing. To continue on your route you must climb out of the river valley, traveling some rather steep switchbacks for a couple of miles to reach the Continental Divide Trail. Be prepared to follow cairns and post markers when the trail becomes unclear in the meadows near the Continental Divide.

MIDDLE FORK TRAIL
FOREST SERVICE TRAIL 589

Length:                  11 miles
Trailhead elevation:     8,400'
Ending elevation:        12,100' at Continental Divide
Difficulty:              Most difficult
Cautions:                Stream crossings
                         High alpine storms
                         Limited camping opportunities

Access: Travel on U.S. 160 west from Pagosa Springs 3 miles, and turn north on the Piedra Road (FDR 631). Travel 17.8 miles to FDR 636 (Toner Road). Turn right and drive approximately 6 miles to the end of the road at Middle Fork Trailhead.

Stock Tips: Rough, steep trail.

The trail begins with a crossing of Middle Fork Creek, difficult during spring run-off and flash flooding. It then climbs steeply up Lean Creek Canyon. There is limited camping on this steep route that leads to Palomino Mountain and the Continental Divide. The trail passes under Sugarloaf Mountain at about mile 5, descends slightly and then sustains an elevation above 12,000' for the remainder of the trip. Window Lake at 6 miles and Monument Lake at 8 miles can be accessed from the trail. Limited campsites are available near these lakes. Contouring through high peaks, the trail offers little retreat from high alpine storms. It is a challenging, difficult route.

ANDERSON TRAIL
FOREST SERVICE TRAIL 579

Length:                  8 miles
Trailhead elevation:     9,200'
Ending elevation:        11,200' at Fourmile Lake
Difficulty:              Moderate
Cautions:                Limited campsites

Access: Turn north in Pagosa Springs on North 5th Street to Lewis Street which becomes Fourmile Road. After 9 miles, turn right on FDR 645 and continue for 5 miles to the trailhead.

Stock Tips:     Stock travel to Fourmile Lake via Anderson Trail
                is the recommended route.

Anderson Trail travels left as you leave the joint trailhead of Anderson and Fourmile Stock Trails. This is a relatively easy trail that ascends gently through somewhat steep terrain, traversing under the base of Pagosa Peak to the west. There is limited camping along the first 5 miles of the trail which reaches Fourmile Lake at mile 7. As you follow Anderson Trail across the stream at the mouth of the lake, it turns south for a mile to a junction with Fourmile Stock Trail (FS 569). The northern end of Fourmile Stock Trail accesses Turkey Creek Lake.

FOUR MILE STOCK TRAIL
FOREST SERVICE TRAIL 569

Length:                 8.5 miles
Trailhead elevation:    9,200' at trailhead
Ending elevation:       11,200' at Turkey Creek Lake
Difficulty:             Difficult
Cautions:               A few sections are rocky and very rough.
                        Stream crossings

Access: Follow the description given for Anderson Trail.

Stock Tips: This trail is not recommended for horse use between the trailhead and the junction at mile 6. Use Anderson Trail instead.

Fourmile Stock Trail follows an old stockway, and you will see the yellow signs still posted on trees along the way. The trail initially descends through dense trees to the valley floor, then begins a gentle climb out. At about mile 3, the trail crosses a stream flowing from a waterfall which cascades from a 300' cliff. It then begins a steep climb through volcanic rocks, passing another major waterfall on Fourmile Creek in about a half mile. Three crossings of the creek are required within a mile. These crossings can be difficult. At mile 5 the trail meets Anderson Trail (FS 579). Anderson Trail follows the north side of the stream to Fourmile Lake, and the Fourmile Stock Trail continues to Turkey Creek Lake.

TURKEY CREEK TRAIL
FOREST SERVICE TRAIL 580

| | |
|---|---|
| Length: | 20 miles |
| Trailhead elevation: | 8,200' |
| Ending elevation: | 12, 200' at saddle above East Fork of Piedra |
| Difficulty: | Easy to wilderness boundary, then most difficult |
| Cautions: | Fenced area near trailhead is grazed. Please close gates. Trail is indistinct in some areas. Route finding may be necessary. Stream Crossings Heavy stock traffic |

Access: Travel 7 miles east of Pagosa Springs to Jackson Mountain Road (FDR 037). Turn left and travel 5 miles to the end of the road.

Stock Tips: Limited stock sites between wilderness boundary and upper meadows.

The first 4 miles of Turkey Creek Trail are not in wilderness. This section offers gentle hiking and frequent campsites. Cattle grazing occurs along the first few miles of the trail. Please close gates when the fence is up.

Turkey Creek Trail begins with a half-mile descent along a well maintained route, then crosses a ditch by way of a plank bridge or the ford downstream. After crossing the ditch, the trail turns right and follows an old road for the next couple of miles through lush meadows and aspen forests. At about mile 4 you enter the Weminuche Wilderness and shortly thereafter cross Turkey Creek. This is one of several crossings that can be difficult. A large heavily impacted camp is found just across the creek.

The canyon now closes in and the trail begins to gain elevation. The creek crashes through rocks below, and interesting rock formations as well as water falls can be seen across the way. There are limited campsites to be found along this section until about mile 8 where the trail crosses the creek again in a marshy flat section. It continues climbing to reach a junction with Fourmile Stock Trail at approximately mile 11. Fourmile Stock Trail (FS 569) cuts back to Turkey Creek Lake. The lake, which is barely visible through the trees, offers a few campsites.

Turkey Creek Trail forks to the right, climbing up the mountainside along switchbacks that pass through a spruce/fir forest for slightly more than a mile. The trail then climbs above timberline into alpine meadows through which you travel for the next three miles. These meadows drop steeply to valleys below. They are dotted with lakes and the heads of several creek drainages.

Turkey Creek Trail skirts up and down across several passes and around basins, losing and gaining elevation. You may often lose sight of the trail because of the lush grasses in the meadows. Watch for trail posts to help keep you on track. The trail contours around sharp rugged mountains, some of which are over 13,000 feet, before reaching the final saddle at mile 15.

It now descends into the East Fork of the Piedra River. You must travel from above tree line at over 12,200' elevation down into the fir forests and the East Fork of the Piedra at mile 17.5. When you enter the East Fork Valley, be certain to look closely for post markers that mark the trail across the valley floor and into the trees on the opposite side. The trail climbs along the north edge of the valley for a couple of miles before it reaches the Continental Divide Trail just above the Piedra Gauging Station.

Camping along the East Fork of the Piedra is good. You may see sheep in this area during the mid-summer months since there is a grazing allotment in these alpine meadows.


WEST FORK TRAIL
FOREST SERVICE TRAIL 561

| Length: | 13 miles |
|---|---|
| Trailhead elevation: | 8,100' |
| Ending elevation: | 11,700' at Continental Divide |
| Difficulty: | More difficult |
| Cautions: | Heavy day traffic to springs |
| | Trail begins on private property |
| | No campfires allowed at springs |
| | Camp only in designated sites between Beaver |
| | Creek Trail junction and upper West Fork crossing. |
| | Steep switchbacks on upper trail |

Access: Drive 15 miles east of Pagosa Springs on U.S. 160. Turn north on West Fork Road (FDR 648). Drive past West Fork Campground and across the creek to the end of the road in 3 miles.

Stock Tips: Camping with stock not allowed between Beaver Creek Trail junction and upper West Fork crossing. Rough, rocky sections.

West Fork Trail traverses through private property for the first mile, and care must be taken to remain on the route. The trail passes through spruce/fir forests, crossing Burro Creek via a bridge in 1.5 miles. It gently ascends through the forest to a bridge crossing over West Fork Creek at mile 3. Beaver Creek is crossed shortly thereafter by bridge.

At approximately mile 4.5, after a fairly steep climb out of West Fork Creek basin you reach a junction with Beaver Creek Trail, which branches to the right. The trail stays high above the creek, and in another half mile reaches the vicinity of the hot springs. This area is heavily impacted by campsites and social trails because of heavy use of the springs. Fires are not permitted in this area because of the scarcity of downfall and impacts of campfires. Camp only in designated sites. Wilderness regulations require all campsites be 100 feet from water unless designated.

The canyon widens in the area of the springs. Then the trail begins climbing heavily forested slopes after crossing West Fork Creek. Shortly beyond the stream crossing are a series of very steep switchbacks that ascend high above West Fork Creek. This can be a difficult climb if you are not in condition or acclimated to the high altitude. The trail will once again descend to West Fork.

At approximately mile 8 the trail crosses the creek through very boggy meadows. The trail can be difficult to find as you leave the river, but if you follow along the right side of the creek, you will pick it up again. This meadow area offers camping if you choose to stop before ascending to the Continental Divide. Remember to observe the 100 foot restriction when camping near the stream.

The trail now contours around a mountainside toward the East Fork of the Piedra, its valley visible through the trees. West Fork Trail levels out before its junction with the Continental Divide Trail, and high mountain campsites are available in this area. You will see part of an old water diversion system and the Piedra Gauging Station as the trail turns north. It intersects the Continental Divide Trail at mile 13. As you continue north for a mile on the Continental Divide Trail you will intersect Turkey Creek Trail (FS 580) which drops into the

East Fork of the Piedra Valley. West Fork Trail and Turkey Creek Trail were formerly known as the Rainbow Trail, and old trail markers designating the Rainbow Trail can still be found in places. Campsites are available along the East Fork drainage.

BEAVER MEADOWS TRAIL
FOREST SERVICE TRAIL 560

| | |
|---|---|
| Length: | 9 miles |
| Trailhead elevation: | 9,000' |
| Ending elevation: | 12,000' at Continental Divide |
| Difficulty: | More difficult |
| Cautions: | Slide area near Beaver Meadows |

Access: 4.5 miles up the West Fork Trail (FS 561).

Stock Tips: Difficult stock travel across slide area.

This trail begins 4.5 miles up the West Fork Trail, branching to the right approximately a mile beyond the Beaver Creek crossing. The trail ascends very steep switchbacks between West Fork Canyon and Beaver Creek. At mile 5 the trail crosses Beaver Creek and enters Beaver Meadows where camping is possible.

Continuing beyond the meadow, the trail climbs to timberline at approximately mile 8 and the Continental Divide Trail in another mile. Post markers indicate the trail as it traverses the alpine meadows. The upper reaches of Beaver Creek Trail offer difficult travel, and camping is limited.

# 15

# Divide Ranger District Trail Descriptions

The Divide District encompasses the portion of the Weminuche Wilderness that is found in the Rio Grande National Forest. It extends from Wolf Creek Pass north to Stony Pass. Its western boundary is the Contintal Divide. The Continental Divide Trail which enters the Weminuche Wilderness near Beartown is under the supervision of this district.

Trails in the eastern section of the Weminuche Wilderness begin at a higher elevation, making many of them gentler in their access to the Continental Divide. Numerous lakes and streams are found along the trails, and the beautiful open valleys and high alpine meadows contrast significantly to the other two districts.

Numerous stock users utilize the trails of the Divide District, particularly during hunting season. Perhaps because of its remoteness, this portion of the wilderness receives less traffic and use. There are many opportunities for point to point and loop traveling along the trails.

Jody Fairchild
Wilderness Program Coordinator
Divide Ranger District
13308 West Highway 160
Del Norte, Colorado 81132
Phone: 719-657-6403

ARCHULETA LAKE TRAIL
FOREST SERVICE TRAIL 839

Length:                7 miles
Trailhead elevation:   9,300'
Ending elevation:      11,800' at Archuleta Lake
Difficulty:            Difficult
Cautions:              Heavy day use at the reservoir
                       Heavy stock travel
                       200 foot camping restriction near Archuleta Lake

Access: Follow U.S. 160, 10.5 miles west of South Fork. Turn right on the Big Meadows Road (FDR 430). Travel 1.5 miles to the reservoir. The trail begins by the boat launch at the reservoir, following by its shore for approximately a mile before heading up the creek. Driving east from Pagosa Springs, the Big Meadows Road is 7.5 miles east of Wolf Creek Pass.

Stock tips : Though the trail is moderate and offers easy access for horses, wilderness regulations require they be restrained 300 feet from the lake's shoreline.

Archuleta Lake Trail offers gentle hiking for the first 4 miles as it follows the South Fork of the Rio Grande, which empties into Big Meadows Reservoir. As the canyon closes in, the trail becomes steeper. The trail crosses Archuleta Creek at about mile 4, continuing on the north side of the creek through open meadows. An old trail no longer maintained and in bad shape, the South Fork Trail, goes to the left at this point, connecting with a short trail that ends at Spruce Lakes.

Fingers of Aspen stands extend up the slopes on the north side of Archuleta Creek Trail, while Mt. Hope towers above. Spruce-fir stands close in at mile 6 as the trail begins its final steep ascent to Archuleta Lake. The area surrounding the lake itself has been heavily used by hikers and stock users. This has necessitated regulations that prohibit camping within 200 feet of the lake. Additionally, the shoreline can be quite boggy. Camping is possible below the stream immediately prior to the lake's outlet.

HOPE CREEK TRAIL
FOREST SERVICE TRAIL 837

| | |
|---|---|
| Length: | 6 miles |
| Trailhead Elevation: | 9,500' at trailhead |
| Ending Elevation | 12,000' at Highline Trail |
| Difficulty: | More difficult |
| Cautions: | High alpine thunderstorms |
| | Sheep grazing allotment |

Access: Follow the route described to Archuleta Creek Trail, but continue past Big Meadows Reservoir for about 3 miles to the trailhead marker at a bend in the road. The trail skirts the north side of Hope Creek. If you reach Shaw Lake you've gone too far. Parking along the road is limited.

Stock tips: Stock travel on this trail is possible.

Hope Creek Trail is used by both stock users and day hikers. It goes from spruce/aspen areas along the creek to high alpine meadows at the base of Sawtooth Mountain. The first 3 miles up to the Weminuche Wilderness boundary follow a gentle incline on the north side of the stream. The trail then climbs more steeply, alternately passing through meadows and spruce stands. The last half mile of the trail is above timberline. There are a couple of stream crossings which can be difficult in the spring. Camping is possible in the meadows near the stream crossings, but wilderness regulations require all campsites be 100 feet from water.

Hope Creek Trail provides access to the Highline Trail (FS 822) which skirts south along the alpine ridge to intercept the Continental Divide Trail (FS 813). The Continental Divide Trail has curled around Archuleta Lake from Wolf Creek Pass to begin its lengthy passage through the Weminuche Wilderness to the Silverton area and beyond. Winds and severe weather can be a challenge as you crest the summit. Camping opportunities are limited, as is water above timberline.

KITTY CREEK TRAIL 837
FOREST SERVICE TRAIL 837

| | |
|---|---|
| Length: | 5 miles |
| Trailhead elevation: | 9,500' |
| Ending elevation: | 12,000' at Highline Trail |
| Difficulty: | More difficult |
| Cautions: | Steep and susceptible to wind fall trees |
| | Sheep grazing allotment |
| | High alpine storms |

Access: Follow the directions given for Archuleta Creek Trail, but continue past Big Meadows Reservoir 3.5 miles to Shaw Lake. Park at the southern end of the lake and follow along its shore to the trailhead, crossing the road to ascend the trail which follows along the creek.

Stock tips: This trail is accessible to stock travel.

This trail climbs out of the basin of Shaw Lake and begins a steep ascent to a junction with the Highline Trail (FS 822). Almost two-thirds of Kitty Creek Trail is outside the wilderness, and it is used as a sheep access for alpine pastures.

The trail climbs to Table Mountain after leaving Kitty Creek at approximately mile 3. Because of its proximity to Hope (FS 837), Archuleta (FS 839), Highline (FS 822), and Hunters Lake Trails, it offers opportunity for loops and point to point trips that are not too long. Keep in mind, however, that all these trails climb above timberline, and severe weather can be encountered, whatever the season. Additionally, campsites can be difficult to find, and access to water in high alpine country is limited.

HUNTERS LAKE / HIGHLINE TRAIL
FOREST SERVICE TRAIL 822

| | |
|---|---|
| Length: | 10 miles |
| Trailhead elevation: | 10,500' at Hunters Lake |
| Ending elevation: | 12,400' at Divide |
| Difficulty: | Moderate to difficult |
| Cautions: | High elevation storms |
| | Heavy stock travel in lake region |
| | Limited camping and water sources above timberline |

Access: Follow the access for Archuleta Creek Trail, but continue past Big Meadows Reservoir on developed FDR 430 until it deadends after approximately 10 miles at the Highline Trailhead. Hunters Lake Trailhead is approximately one-half mile before the road end near a loading ramp.

Stock tips: This trail is accessible to stock travel.

Hunters Lake Trail, a very short trail, skirts the Wilderness boundary as it winds through a boggy meadow into a spruce-fir forest and reaches the lake in less than one mile. Continuing past the lake, the trail passes through open meadows before it intersects Lake Creek Trail (FS 430) in a half mile. Most of Lake Creek Trail is not in the Wilderness. The two, after joining, begin traversing gentle switchbacks to reach Highline Trail in approximately a mile. This is a slightly shorter access to the upper section of the trail.

Highline Trailhead is accessed at the turn-around for the road. It begins a gentle climb up through the spruce-fir forest and meets the intersection of Lake Creek and Hunters Lake Trails after approximately 3 miles. Highline Trail offers gentle travel until it reaches the Stairsteps, a rough rocky protrusion on the lower reaches of Table Mountain. After ascending the stairsteps, you will have spectacular views of surrounding mountain ranges.

You must follow rock cairns across Table Mountain for the next 5 miles, winding south on an up-and-down route through alpine country toward Sawtooth Mountain. You will meet Hope Creek Trail at about mile 8 as it joins Highline, and then climb out at the Continental Divide Trail in another 2 miles. Be prepared for severe weather and summer storms. Winds can blow ferociously in this area. Also keep in mind that summer storms can be severe above timberline. Camping is almost non-existent above timberline, and finding water sources can be a challenge.

ROARING FORK TRAIL
FOREST SERVICE TRAIL 807

| | |
|---|---|
| Length: | 3 miles |
| Trailhead elevation: | 11,200' |
| Ending elevation: | 9,600' at Goose Creek |
| Difficulty: | More difficult |
| Cautions: | Cattle grazing allotment |
| | Steep ascent to trailhead |
| | Limited camping |

Access: Travel southwest of Creede on Colorado Highway 149 for 7 miles to Middle Creek Road (FDR 523). Follow road signs giving directions and distances to North Lime Creek Trailhead, approximately 12.5 miles. The trail follows an old 2-track to the wilderness boundary.

Stock tips: This trail is accessible to stock travel.

Roaring Fork Trail is used almost exclusively as an access to other trails. Before the trail reaches the wilderness it opens up into a large meadow where a grazing allotment is used in the summer. This can obscure the trail because of numerous animal paths. You will then pass through large aspen stands and begin a steep downhill route to Goose Creek. The last section of switchbacks can offer a challenging climb out after a long day of hiking. Limited camping opportunities exist.


GOOSE CREEK TRAIL
FOREST SERVICE TRAIL 827

| | |
|---|---|
| Length: | 12 miles |
| Trailhead elevation: | 9,600' |
| Ending elevation: | 11,800' at Goose Lake |
| Difficulty: | Moderate to difficult |
| Cautions: | Private property adjacent to trail |
| | Summer thunderstorms |
| | Limited camping at lakes |
| | Boggy meadows |

Access: Goose Creek Trail is accessed by way of Roaring Fork Trail (FS 807), 3 miles below its trailhead.

Stock tips: This trail is accessible to stock travel.

This trail basically travels through Goose Creek Valley. Though easy to follow, it has four creek crossings that can be hazardous during high run-off. The trail begins descending into Goose Creek Valley immediately after it leaves Roaring Forks Trail junction. Within a mile it is skirting the creek through wide open valleys. Aspen forests cover the adjacent hillsides. The trail crosses Fisher Creek after 1.5 miles. It then follows a gradual ascent for another 5 miles to a junction where Sawtooh Trail continues for 3.5 miles toward Sawtooth Mountain and the Continental Divide Trail (FS 813) while the main branch follows Goose Creek through spruce-fir forests and the adjacent wet meadows. Camping is abundant along the lower portions of Goose Creek Trail.

The ascent is gradual for 8 miles as the trail parallels Goose Creek. Anticipate steep switchbacks as the trail climbs to upper treeless slopes and the saddle between Little Goose Lake and Goose Lake. No camping is available around the little lake, which is above timberline. In another half mile the trail begins a descent to Goose Lake. Camping is limited here, and better sites can be found down Ivy Creek to the north of the lake. Goose Creek Trail ends at its junction with the Fisher Creek Trail (FS 826).

IVY CREEK TRAIL
FOREST SERVICE TRAIL 805

| | |
|---|---|
| Length: | 9.9 miles |
| Trailhead elevation: | 9,200' |
| Ending elevation: | 11,800' at Goose Lake |
| Difficulty: | Moderate to difficult |
| Cautions: | Sheep grazing allotment |
| | Severe summer thunderstorms |
| | Stream crossings |

Access: Travel southwest of Creede on Colorado 149 for 7 miles to Middle Creek Road (FDR 523). Follow FDR 523 for 10.5 miles to Ivy Creek Campground. The trailhead is at the east end of the campground.

Stock tips: This trail is accessible to stock travel.

Ivy Creek Trail climbs away from the campground at a moderate grade. After approximately a mile it crosses Ivy Creek which can be a challenge during run-off, and continues a gradual climb through open parks adjacent to the creek. Within 2 miles the trail leaves the creek bottom and ascends through spruce/fir stands before returning to the creek. Again the trail crosses the creek, also difficult, and meanders along the edge of an open park adjacent to the stream. Then it begins a series of switchbacks to ascend to a ridge. The switchbacks have recently been reworked, but the rock scree can be treacherous in wet weather. At the open park on the dividing ridge, the trail grade flattens out, and the route passes through a series of parks and scattered timber for the remaining distance to Goose Lake.

Camping exists in numerous places along Ivy Creek, but old impacted sites in the vicinity of Goose Lake are often less than the required 100 feet from water. It would be better to camp below on Ivy Creek where good sites can be found, then day hike a short distance to the lake.

FERN CREEK TRAIL
FOREST SERVICE TRAIL 815

| | |
|---|---|
| Length: | 15 miles |
| Trailhead elevation: | 9000' |
| Ending elevation: | 11,200' at Little Ruby, 10,000' at junction with Squaw Creek Trail |
| Difficulty: | More difficult |
| Cautions: | First 4 miles are non-wilderness and open to motorized and mountain bike travel |

Access: Travel southwest from Creede on Colorado Highway149 for 16 miles to Fern Creek Road (FDR 522). Follow this for one mile to the Fern Creek Trailhead.

Stock tips: This trail is accessible to stock travel.

Fern Creek Trail follows an old stock driveway and is used primarily for access to the Ruby Lake area. The trail begins with a steep 3-mile climb to Little Ruby Lake at 11,200' elevation. Just beyond and to the south of the trail is Fuchs Reservoir. A short connecting trail turns south and skirts Fuchs Reservoir to the larger Ruby Lake. After passing the lakes, the trail connects with and travels for approximately a mile with Texas Creek Trail (FS 816), which goes to Red Lakes. The trails climb through a small stand of spruce before heading gradually downhill to Texas Creek, which must be crossed and can be a challenge, depending on run-off conditions. The climb out of Texas Creek is not difficult.

Camping can be found in the meadows that are in this area. Though old mining cabin sites still exist on the north shore of Ruby Lake they are protected by the 1979 Archeological Resources Act and should not be disturbed.

After leaving the flat, Texas Creek Trail turns south, and Fern Creek Trail turns west, making a winding descent through spruce into Little Squaw Creek drainage. The trail crosses Little Squaw Creek, then skirts along its south side for approximately a mile. It then turns steeply uphill toward Chief Mountain. Once out of the timber, the trail climbs through grassy parks for another mile. The trail is not well defined in the meadow area, so watch for old stock driveway signs on trees and trail post markers.

Fern Creek Trail then heads north from the meadow and connects with Squaw Creek Trail (FS 814). This is an extremely steep 2-mile descent. Camping is very limited in this area. You will reach Thirty Mile Campground and the southern end of the Rio Grande Reservoir after 2 miles of travel along Squaw Creek Trail.

TEXAS CREEK TRAIL
FOREST SERVICE TRAIL 816

| | |
|---|---|
| Length: | 12.9 miles |
| Trailhead elevation: | 9,100' |
| Ending elevation: | 12,200' at Continental Divide |
| Difficulty: | More difficult |
| Cautions: | Severe elevation gain in spots |

Access: Follow Fern Creek Trail (FS 815) 5 miles to Ruby Lake. Texas Creek Trail begins just beyond the lakes.

Stock tips: This trail is accessible to stock travel.

Texas Creek Trail begins at mile 5 on the Fern Creek Trail (FS 815) in the Ruby Lakes area. The trail passes north of Ruby Lake. It parallels Fern Creek Trail and crosses Texas Creek in approximately a mile. Texas Creek Trail then branches south to follow the creek. Because of the open terrain, excellent campsites can be found in this area, but marshy areas do exist. Wilderness regulations require that all campsites be 100 feet from water.

The trail skirts close to the creek, then crosses to the east side of Texas Creek into high alpine grasslands. Then it traverses the grassy slopes and crosses the creek again, proceeding toward Red Lakes in a southeasterly direction. Chief Mountain is visible to the right. Continuing across the high meadows, look for trail markers and posts to keep you on route. After passing Red Lakes, Texas

Creek Trail descends into Trout Lake basin before climbing up to its junction with the Continental Divide Trail (FS 813).

RED LAKES TRAIL
FOREST SERVICE TRAIL 889

| | |
|---|---|
| Length: | 4.3 miles |
| Trailhead elevation: | 11,200' |
| Ending elevation: | 12,200' at lakes |
| Difficulty: | More difficult |
| Cautions: | Steep sections |

Access: Follow Fern Creek Trail for five miles to Ruby Lake. Then follow the trail as it skirts to the left of Ruby Lake and Fuchs Reservoir.

Stock tips: This trail is accessible to stock travel.

The Red Lakes Trail is one of two trails that provide access from Big Ruby Lake to Red Lakes, and beyond to the Continental Divide by way of Texas Creek Trail (FS 816). The trail follows the lake's northeasterly shoreline, then makes a steep ascent away from Ruby Lake and outside the wilderness. Once out of the trees and into the meadows, the trail offers a view of Ruby Lakes and the Continental Divide. The trail then climbs through alpine meadows and circles in a southeasterly direction around the lakes. Red Lakes Trail ends at its junction with Texas Creek Trail immediately beyond Red Lakes.

SQUAW CREEK TRAIL
FOREST SERVICE TRAIL 814

| | |
|---|---|
| Length: | 9.9 miles |
| Trailhead elevation: | 9,400' |
| Ending elevation: | 11,200' at Squaw Pass |
| Difficulty: | Difficult |
| Cautions: | Heavy day hiking and horse travel |
| | Steep ascent to Continental Divide |

Access: Travel southwest of Creede on Colorado 149 for 20 miles to the Rio Grande Reservoir Road (FDR 520). Then drive 10 miles to Thirty Mile Campground. The trail is signed on the West Campground Loop Road.

Stock tips: Horses and stock users must unload at special areas located 1/4 mile south of 30-Mile Campground. Travel to the Divide is steep.

Squaw Creek Trail primarily parallels Squaw Creek from Thirty Mile Campground to the Continental Divide at Squaw Pass. The trail meanders up Squaw Creek drainage at a gradual grade, after a short climb away from the campground. Camping opportunities are numerous along the trail. Wilderness regulations require that all campsites be 100 feet from water.

After crossing Squaw Creek shortly beyond the trailhead by way of a bridge, the trail wanders through grassy meadows adjacent to the creek. At about mile 2, Fern Creek Trail (FS 815) will fork to the left and south, while Squaw Creek Trail stays with the stream continuing a gentle ascent.

The trail forks at approximately mile 5, with a cut-off crossing the stream to Squaw Lake, and the main trail continuing along Squaw Creek. Post markers may be followed if the trail becomes indistinct in the meadows. It may become boggy in places. The final half mile of the trail to Squaw Pass is somewhat rocky and steeper than the previous section. The trail is well defined and easy to follow for its entire length.

## SQUAW LAKE TRAIL
## FOREST SERVICE TRAIL 890

| | |
|---|---|
| Length: | 4 miles |
| Trailhead elevation: | 10,400' |
| Ending elevation: | 12,400' at Continental Divide |
| Difficulty | Most difficult |
| Cautions: | Summer alpine storms |

Access: Squaw Lake Trail begins 5.5 miles up Squaw Creek Trail.

Stock tips: Stock users must unload at special areas located 1/4 mile south of Thirty Mile Campground. Steep ascent to the Continental Divide.

Squaw Lake Trail begins roughly 5.5 miles up Squaw Creek Trail (FS 814).

The trail turns southwest, crosses Squaw Creek by way of a bridge, then begins a steady climb through mixed old growth spruce/fir timber. The lower segment of this trail was reconstructed recently. Switchbacks were created to reduce the severity of the 1,500 foot elevation gain from the trailhead to Squaw Lake. An earthen dam was built to raise Squaw Lake in 1938. The trail circles north of the lake after reaching it, then climbs steeply to intersect the Continental Divide Trail (FS 813). Camping opportunities are limited.

A loop is possible if one travels south on the Continental Divide Trail (FS 813) to its junction with Squaw Creek Trail, which can then be descended back to the trailhead at Rio Grande Reservoir.

WEMINUCHE CREEK TRAIL
FOREST SERVICE TRAIL 523

| | |
|---|---|
| Length: | 6 miles |
| Trailhead elevation: | 9,400' |
| Ending elevation: | 10,600' at Continental Divide |
| Difficulty: | Moderate |
| Cautions: | Heavy day hiking and horse use |
| | Difficult stream crossings during run-off |

Access: Travel southwest of Creede on Colorado highway 149 for 20 miles to the Rio Grande Reservoir Road (FDR 520), then approximately 10 miles to Thirty Mile Campground. Park in day use parking, and follow markers to trailhead.

Stock tips: Stock users must use unloading areas located 1/4 mile south of Thirty Mile Campground.

For its first 1.5 miles, Weminuche Trail skirts along the side of Rio Grande Reservoir. The old wagon route which crossed Stony Pass to Silverton ran along the bottom of the canyon before it was flooded in 1905 by the reservoir. The trail is rather narrow and can be challenging when passing stock users, since the slope falls away precipitously to the reservoir below. Courtesy must be shown by everyone for other users. The trail turns up Weminuche Creek, where a bridge allows safe crossing.

Weminuche Creek Trail then climbs through a narrow canyon for a short distance before leveling out to a gradual ascent in open meadows. The trail follows along and above the stream to Weminuche Pass. Another crossing of Weminuche Creek occurs at about mile 4, followed in another half mile by Highline Creek. Both can be challenging during run-off.

At mile 5 the trail reaches Weminuche Pass and the headweaters of the Los Piños River. The open meadow which extends to the upper junction with the Los Piños River Trail (FS 523) and the Continental Divide Trail (FS 813) offers camping, as do areas around Highline Creek. The Raber Lohr Ditch constructed in 1935 is also located in this valley.

John A. McMurtrie, chief engineer of the Denver & Rio Grande Railroad in 1879, recommended the rail route to Durango and Silverton be contructed up the Rio Grande valley from South Fork. Durango's line was proposed to cross Weminuche Pass and follow the Pine River into the western valleys of the San Juan Forest and Durango. Silverton's access would have been by way of the Rio Grande River headwaters and over Cunningham Pass. Though the proposed route would have been shorter and more easily constructed, McMurtrie's recommendations were ignored. Fortunate for us today, since the Weminuche and Pine River Valleys would have been developed and heavily used. We would not have this beautiful wilderness because of that development.

Highline Trail (FS 564) branches north shortly after the Highline stream crossing and climbs beneath the Window and the Pyramid. The large open meadow extends for a mile or more before the descent along the Los Piños Trail on the western side of the Continental Divide.

HIGHLINE TRAIL UNDER THE RIO GRANDE PYRAMID
FOREST SERVICE TRAIL 564

| Length: | 4 miles |
|---|---|
| Trailhead elevation: | 10,600' |
| Ending elevation: | 12,400' at junction with Continental Divide |
| Difficulty: | More difficult |
| Cautions: | Steep ascent |
| | Alpine thunderstorms |

Access: This trail turns right 5 miles up Weminuche Trail.

Stock tips: This trail is accessible to stock travel.

Highline Trail cuts right shortly after Highline Creek and climbs through spruce-fir trees into high alpine country below The Window (La Ventanna) and the Rio Grande Pyramid. The Pyramid is 13,821' elevation and The Window is 12,857' elevation. Legends from Spanish gold mining days plus their outstanding location on a high mountain ridge give them prominence in Weminuche Wilderness history. Both landmarks also have significance in Ute Indian history. The trail cuts immediately below them to intersect Rincon La Vaca and the Continental Divide Trail. Severity of the climb makes this a challenging hike for anyone. Nor is the trail maintained. Camping opportunities are limited.

UTE CREEK, EAST UTE, UTE LAKE, TWIN LAKES TRAIL NETWORK
UTE CREEK TRAIL - FOREST SERVICE TRAIL 819
EAST UTE CREEK TRAIL - FOREST SERVICE TRAIL 824
UTE LAKE TRAIL - FOREST SERVICE TRAIL 905

| | |
|---|---|
| Length: | 12 miles |
| Trailhead elevation: | 9,600' |
| Ending Elevation: | 12,400' at Continental Divide |
| Difficulty: | Difficult |
| Cautions: | Heavy day hiking, backpacking and horse travel |
| | Camping restrictions near lakes |
| | Stream crossings |

Access: Travel southwest of Creede on Colorado Highway 149 for 20 miles. Turn on Rio Grande Reservoir Road (FDR 520) and travel approximately 16 miles to Ute Creek Trailhead. Park in a large open meadow. The Rio Grande River must be crossed to reach the trail. The river can be very dangerous during spring run-off.

Stock tips: Narrow trail with steep drop-off in spots.

Ute Creek Trail begins with a difficult crossing of the Rio Grande River. Early summer crossings of the river at the trailhead should not be attempted. Beyond the river, the trail skirts the reservoir for a distance, then climbs at a gentle grade along the east slope of Ute Creek. Because the slope below the trail drops severely, passing horse parties can be challenging.

Approximately 2 miles from the trailhead, the trail is carved into a short 1/4 mile segment of cliffs. Then it parallels Ute Creek for about a mile through open meadows.

The trail then turns away from the creek and starts a series of switchbacks up to Black Lake. As it ascends through a conifer forest, it crosses several streams. Black Lake is reached just past mile 6. Hereafter, the trail breaks out into a large open meadow where the confluence of East, West and Middle Ute Creeks occurs, forming the large Ute Creek which flows into Rio Grande Reservoir.

Ute Creek Trail (FS 819) continues up Ute Creek, while the old La Garita Stock Driveway, now known as West Ute Creek Trail (FS 825) goes right along that drainage about one-fourth mile south of Black Lake. The main segment of Ute Creek Trail splits along the other fingers of Ute Creek, and you must determine which you choose to hike.

East Ute Creek Trail branches left in another half mile, shortly after crossing West Ute Creek. It travels south, ascending along the East Ute Creek branch to the Continental Divide Trail in 4 miles at 12,200' elevation. The Rio Grande Pyramid and The Window are visible to the left as you hike this trail. Both landmarks have played a significant role in Native American and Spanish history. They were used as trail markers by Spanish miners who entered the area, and a legend of buried Spanish gold near them still exists. The miners were said to have been driven from the area after hiding their gold from attacking Utes.

The main Ute Creek Trail continues up Middle Ute Creek and divides again at mile 10. Ute Lake Trail (FS 825) branches left or south to overlook Ute Lake and then climbs to the Continental Divide Trail 3 miles from the junction, reaching an elevation of 12,400'. A steep descent to the lake is possible via another trail finger.

If you remain on Ute Creek Trail, you will reach another split in approximately 1.5 miles, with the left finger accessing Twin Lakes before doubling back to the Continental Divide Trail at 12,400'. The right fork takes you to the Continental Divide Trail overlooking Middle Ute Lake at 12,000'. All of these trails are clearly defined and easy to follow.

Camping opportunities in the meadows are numerous once you pass Black Lake. Campsites are limited in the vicinity of these lakes and specifically around the large Ute Lake where only a couple of sites are possible on its rocky shore.

WEST UTE CREEK TRAIL (LA GARITA STOCK DRIVEWAY)
FOREST SERVICE TRAIL 819

Length:                        5 miles
Trailhead elevation:           10,800' at junction
Ending elevation:              11,800' at Continental Divide
Difficulty:                    Moderate
Cautions:                      Stream crossings
                               Campsites prohibited within 300' of shore

Access: 7 miles up Ute Creek Trail, 1/4 mile past Black Lake, turn right through open meadow and willows.

Stock tips: Animals cannot be picketed, hobbled or grazed within 200' of the lake.

This trail is easy to hike as it passes through open grassy parks and meadows along West Ute Creek. West Ute Lake Trail climbs gently through a valley along West Ute Creek for approximately 4 miles. It crosses the creek, then begins a steep ascent through old-growth spruce/fir trees. This section of the trail was reconstructed recently. As the trail emerges from the timber, it joins the Continental Divide Trail (FS 813) and continues south to skirt the east side of West Ute Lake. Camping is available in timber below the lake. Wilderness regulations prohibit camping within 200' of this lake. Nor can animals be picketed or hobbled within 200' of the lake.

CONTINENTAL DIVIDE TRAIL

The Continental Divide Trail twists and winds for approximately 85 miles, according to Forest Service estimates, in and out of the Weminuche Wilderness from Stony Pass northeast of Silverton to Wolf Creek Pass near Pagosa Springs. There are 32 trails that ascend to the Continental Divide Trail on the three ranger districts which manage the Weminuche Wilderness, so opportunities to hike along portions of it are numerous. If you choose to explore the entire length, you will have one of the most glorious experiences available.

But don't expect an easy stroll. The trail covers rugged country, with elevations ranging from 10,600 feet to over 12,000 feet. The majority of the trail is above timberline, crossing alpine grasslands, snaking up steep, rocky, talus slopes, and weaving through willow fields, wet bogs and rock slides.

Vast panoramic views are available, with each peak rivaling the next for beauty, and distant mountain ranges lining up to be counted and photographed. You will not experience an area where more solitude can be had since few people travel the Divide Trail through the Weminuche in its entirety. Sections are used for point to point trips, as you ascend to it by one trail and then descend another.

Weather is a major challenge on the Divide Trail. Late snow will hang around in certain areas until mid-July, and if the snow has melted by July, you can expect high mountain thunderstorms that dump hail, sleet and snow to hang around thereafter. Hypothermia can be a serious threat during severe weather above timberline.

High ridges are no place to be when lightning is playing with the high peaks. There are certain rules of thumb which can be followed if a thunderstorm approaches. First, get off the ridge line. You may have to descend several hundred feet to feel safe. If caught, seek out a low, treeless section and squat on the ground.

Most of the camping along the trail is above timberline, necessitating good equipment, because the wind can howl and blow with all its fury. Temperature swings can be significant, going below freezing at night and soaring into the high 70's during the day.

Carrying adequate food for an 8 to 10 day trip can be another challenge if you are traveling on foot. You can descend to Creede en route to restock. In some areas you may also have to descend to streams or lakes to restock water since it may not be available along the trail. This can take time and energy. Additionally, you will be traveling at an elevation that can be trying for the most physically fit person after several days. Shortness of breath, lethargy, sleep loss and disorientation can all occur when you remain at a high altitude for any length of time. Altitude sickness is not to be ignored. The best treatment is to descend to lower elevations.

You may experience some difficulty in route finding as well since many social trails have been created by sheep trailing in certain areas. The weather plays havoc with trail marker posts and rock cairns set up along the way. Additionally, because it is so inaccessible and not as heavily traveled as other trails in the Weminuche Wilderness, the Divide Trail does not receive as much attention. Sections remain unmarked.

Vehicle access to a point of origin on the Divide Trail is easily gained either at Stony Pass near Silverton or Wolf Creek Pass near Pagosa Springs. Because there are well-written books devoted exclusively to travel on the Continental Divide Trail, I will give only brief information. Check the 1997 publication *Colorado's Continental Divide Trail* by Tom Lorang Jones and John Fielder for up-to-date information and directions for route-finding and access at different points. Though the U. S. Forest Service is responsible for managing the land through which the trail passes, in 1995 the Continental Divide Trail Alliance, a non-profit organization, was established to help protect, maintain, and manage the Continental Divide Trail under the leadership of Bruce and Paula Ward of Pine, Colorado. Through this organization's efforts portions of the trail are being improved each year, and improvements are expected along the Weminuche portion within the next few years.

Approximate distances, by Forest Service estimates, can be tracked as follows, beginning at Stony Pass:

Stony Pass to Nebo Pass - 11 miles
Nebo Pass to Weminuche Pass - 17 miles
Weminuche Pass to Squaw Pass -15 miles
Squaw Pass to Piedra Pass - 21 miles
Piedra Pass to Wolf Creek Pass - 19 miles

The Jones/Fielder guide gives a slightly higher mileage count, and creates a different series of trail segments. Detailed descriptions clarify where cairns or markers may be located in confusing areas, as well as the numerous parallel trails which can be confusing. Since I have only hiked the Continental Divide Trail in segments, I suggest you follow their descriptions. If traveling short sections on point to point trips, the Trails Illustrated Map is adequate for guidance. Jones' book is worth the investment if you plan to spend any time on the Continental Divide Trail.

# Endnotes

1. Donald L. Baars, *The American Alps* (University of New Mexico Press, 1992). Rob Blair, ed. , *The Western San Juan Mountains: Their Geology, Ecology, and Human History,* (University Press of Colorado, 1996). These books have been used for sources of information throughout this chapter.

2. Rob Blair, Personal interview, December, 1997.

3. Peter Lipman, "Chasing the Volcano," *Earth,* ( December, 1997).

4. Rob Blair, ed. *The Western San Juan Mountains: Their Geology, Ecology, and Human History,* (University Press of Colorado, 1996).

5. Phil Duke, Cultural Resources Report, The Grenadier Archeological Project: 1990 Season, Fort Lewis College, Durango, Colorado.

6. Gary Matlock, personal Interview, December, 1997.

7. Matlock interview.

8. James Jefferson, et al.,*The Southern Utes, A Tribal History,* (University of Utah, 1972).

9. Phil Duke report.

10. *The Southern Utes, A Tribal History.*

11. *Forest History - Volume I (1905-1971),* San Juan & Montezuma Forests, Colorado. Forest records summarize early Spanish activities and have been used for information in this chapter.

12. Allen Nossaman, *Many More Mountains, Volume 1: Silverton's Roots,* (Sundance Books, 1989).*Volume 2: Ruts into Silverton,* (Sundance Books,1993).

13.  Robert S. Rosenberg, *A History of South central Colorado prepared expressly for the Rio Grande National Forest*, (1976). Early history of travel in the San Juan Mountains comes from this source as well as San Juan National Forest history records.

14.  Rosenberg.

15.  Cathy E. Kindquist, *Stony Pass: The Tumbling and Impetuous Trail*, (San Juan County Book Company, Silverton, 1987).

16.  Kindquist.

17.  Nossaman.

18.  John M. Motter, *Pagosa Country: The First Fifty Years*, (publisher unknown).

19.  Duane Smith, *Durango Diary*, (The Herald Press, 1996) and *Rocky Mountain Boom Town: A History of Durango Colorado*, (University of Colorado Press, 1980).

20.  Louis Newell, *Field Assessment of the Rico-Rockwood Wagon Road* (A Cultural Resources Report for the San Juan National Forest, 1985).

21.  Joanne Tankersley and Mary Schroeder, *Ribs of Silver, Hearts of Gold*, (Creede Historical Society, 1992).

22.  Coert Dubois, "Report on the Proposed San Juan Forest Reserve, Colorado," (1903).

23.  Phil Duke Report.

24.  San Juan National Forest Ranger Biff Stranksy recalls accompanying his father with sheep herds into this country when he was a boy. Interview, November, 1997.

25.    Information on current cattle and sheep grazing is taken from an interview with San Juan National Forest range specialists Ron Klatt and Brad Morrison, November, 1997.

26.    Information about early tourism comes from the *San Juan Forest Service History, Vol. 1, 1905-1971.*

27.    John Sanders, "The Return of the Elk," unpublished article, Durango, Colorado.

28.    Rosenberg.

29.    Interview, San Juan National Forest Fish Specialist Dave Gerhardt, November 1997.

30.    *Forest History Vol. 1*, 1905-1971.

31.    Information on water projects in the Weminuche Wilderness comes from the Colorado Division of Water Resources, Feb., 1998.

32.    Information about early forests comes from *Forest History - Volume I, 1905-1971,* San Juan & Montezuma National Forests and *A History of Southwestern Colorado, prepared for the Rio Grande National Forest* by Robert G. Rosenberg, 1976.

33.    *A History of the Rio Grande,* Cultural Resource Inventory, (1983).

34.    Len Shoemaker, "National Forests," *Colorado Magazine,* (Vol. 21, #5, Sept. 1944).

35.    Rosenberg.

36.    Information about wilderness designation comes from the Environmental Impact Statement and Weminuche Wilderness Proposal of 1971, as well as other materials in the forest archives.

37.    Roderick Frazier Nash, *Wilderness and the American Mind*, 3rd ed. rev. (Yale University press, 1982).

38.    Henry David Thoreau, *Journal, 1852-1853, Vol. 5: The Writings of Henry David Thoreau*, (Princeton University Press, 1997).

39.    Statistics come from the 1994 Congressional Report on wilderness areas.

40.    San Juan/Rio Grande Wilderness Direction Document, 1997, and San Juan/Rio Grande Wilderness Management Direction, 1998.

41.    Gary Snyder, *A Place in Space: Ethics, Aesthetics, and Watersheds*, (Counterpoint, Washington, D.C., 1995).

42.    *Forest History, Vol. I*, (1905-1971).

43.    I have used the following books as sources of information about life zones and ecosystems: Audrey Benedict, *A Sierra Club Naturalist's Guide to the Southern Rockies*, (Sierra Club Books, 1991); Robert L. Hoover & Dale L. Wills, eds., *Managing Forested Lands for Wildlife*,( Colorado Division of Wildlife, 1987); Janine M. Benyus., *The Field Guide to Wildlife Habitats of the Western United States*, (Simon & Schuster Inc., 1989).

44.    Ann Zwinger's book *Land Above the Trees: A Guide to American Alpine Tundra*, ( Harper & Row, 1972), which I have used as a resource, gives in-depth descriptions of this mysterious and beautiful alpine world.

45.    Sources of information include CDOW's publication *Managing Forested Lands for Wildlife* and personal interview with fisheries biologist Dave Gerhardt with the San Juan National Forest.

46.    Colorado Division of Wildlife's "Rules for Observing Wildlife."

47. The excellent handbook, *Lions, Ferrets & Bears* by David M. Armstrong and published by the Colorado Division of Wildlife and the University of Colorado Museum has supplied much information for this section.

48. Colorado Division of Wildlife 1997 Annual Report.

49. "Wildlife in Danger: The status of Colorado's threatened and endangered fish, amphibians, birds, and mammals," prepared by the Colorado Division of Wildlife, 1989.

50. David Petersen, *Ghost Grizzlies: Does the Great Bear Still Haunt Colorado?* (Henry Holt and Company, New York, 1995).

51. Aldo Leopold, "The Land Ethic", *A Sand County Almanac,* (Ballantine Books, 1966).

52. This book and U.S. Forest Service publications have been used for "Leave No Trace" information.

53. Gerhardt.

54. CDOW recommendations.

55. CDOW recommendations.

56. "Backcountry Horse Use," Leave No Trace Outdoor Skills & Ethics developed by the National Outdoor Leadership School, 1993, and "Horse Sense: Packing Lightly on your National Forests," U. S. Forest Service, 1993.

57. "The Ethical Hunter," National Shooting Sports Foundation, 555 Danbury Road, Wilton, Ct. 06897.

58. Don Graydon, ed. *Mountaineering: The Freedom of the Hills,,* 5th ed., (The Mountaineers of Seattle, 1992).

59.     Information about climbing and safety in the Weminuche Wilderness
        comes from Walt Walker, Director of Outdoor Pursuits, Fort Lewis
        College, Durango, Colorado, March 1998. Walt has worked with the
        La Plata County Search and Rescue Team for years, assisting in the
        rescue of numerous people.

60.     A book that describes many routes in the Weminuche is
        *The San Juan Mountains, A Climbing and Hiking Guide* by
        Robert F. Rosebrough, (Cordillera Press, Inc., 1988).

61.     Much information about outfitting and packing in the
        Weminuche Wilderness came from Tom Van Soelen, owner of
        San Juan Outfitting, Durango, Colorado, interviewed in March , 1998.

62.     Colorado Outfitters Association, 1997 Directory.

63.     Interview with Randy Houtz, Trail Maintenance Supervisor,
        San Juan National Forest, February, 1998.

64.     Trail Construction and Maintenance Notebook, U.S. Forest
        Service Trail Notebook 4E42A25, October, 1996.

65.     Allen Nossaman's books *Many More Mountains, Volumes 1, 2 and 3*,
        have provided many of the historical facts included in the trail
        descriptions. Information also comes from personal interview with
        Mr. Nossaman in April, 1998. This meticulous historian continues to
        record the history of Silverton in wonderful detail and is a
        delightful storyteller.

# Bibliography of Sources and Suggested Reading

Armstrong, David. *Lions, Ferrets and Bears*. Colorado Division of Wildlife and the University of Colorado Museum, 1993.

*A Proposal for the Weminuche Wilderness*, prepared by the Rio Grande and San Juan National Forests, U.S. Department of Agriculture Forest Service, August 2, 1971.

Baars, Donald L. *The American Alps*: *The San Juan Mountains of Southwest Colorado*. Albuquerque: University of New Mexico Press, 1992.

Baars, Donald L. *Red Rock Country: A Geologic History of the Colorado Plateau*. New York: Doubleday / Natural History Press, 1972.

Benedict, Audrey DeLella. *A Sierra Club Naturalist's Guide to The Southern Rockies*. San Francisco: Sierra Club Books, 1991.

Benyus, Janine M. *The Field Guide to Wildlife Habitats of the Western United States*. New York: Simon & Schuster Inc., 1989.

Blair, Rob, ed. *The Western San Juan Mountains: Their Geology, Ecology, and Human History*. Fort Lewis College Foundation: University Press of Colorado, 1996.

Brown, Robert L. *Ghost Towns of the Colorado Rockies*. Caldwell, Idaho: Caxton Printers, Ltd. 1969.

Burgess, Charles D., et al. "Wilderness Information of the World-Wide-Web: Characteristics of the Sample and their Information Needs," Aldo Leopold Wilderness Research Institute, Missoula, Montana, 1997.

Colorado Division of Water Resources files, Durango, Colorado, February, 1998.

Colorado Division of Wildlife 1997 Annual Report.

Colorado Outfitters Association, 1997 Directory.

Dubois, Coert. "Report on the Proposed San Juan Forest Reserve, Colorado," 1903.

Duke, Phil. *Cultural Resources Report, The Grenadier Archeological Project: 1990 Season*. Dept. of Anthropology, Fort Lewis College, Durango, Co.

Eberhart, Perry. *Guide to the Colorado Ghost Towns and Mining Camps*. 4th ed. Chicago: Sage Books, 1969.

*Environmental Impact Statement and Weminuche Wilderness Proposal. 1971*, in the San Juan National Forest archives.

Gebhardt, Dennis. *A Backpacking Guide to the Weminuche Wilderness*, Durango: Basin Reproduction, 1976.

Gorte, Ross W. "Wilderness: Overview and Statistics." *A Congressional Research Service Report for Congress prepared by the Environment and Natural Resources Policy Division, December 2, 1994*.

Graydon, Don, ed. *Mountaineering: The Freedom of the Hills*, 5th ed. The Mountaineers of Seattle, 1992.

Guennel, A.K. *Guide to Colorado Wildflowers, Volume 2: Mountains*. Westcliffe Publishers, 1995.

Hampton, Bruce and David Cole. *Soft Paths: How to Enjoy Wilderness Without Losing It*. Stackpole Books, 1988.

Helmuth, Ed and Gloria Helmuth. *The Passes of Colorado: An Encyclopedia of Watershed Divides*. Boulder: Pruett Publishing, 1994.

Hendee, John C., et al, eds. *Wilderness Management*, 2nd ed. rev. Golden: North American Press, 1990.

Hoover, Robert L. and Dale L. Wills, eds. *Managing Forested Lands for Wildlife*. Denver: Colorado Division of Wildlife, 1987.

Jones, Tom Lorang and John Fielder. *Colorado's Continental Divide Trail, The Official Guide*. Englewood, Colorado: Westcliffe Publishers, 1997.

Jefferson, James, et al. *The Southern Utes: A Tribal History*. Ignacio, Colorado: Southern Ute Tribe, 1972.

Kindquist, Cathy E. *Stony Pass: The Tumbling and Impetuous Trail*. Silverton, Colorado: San Juan County Book Company, 1987.

Leopold, Aldo. "The Land Ethic." *A Sand County Almanac*. New York: Ballantine Books, 1966.

Lipman, Peter. "Chasing the Volcano." *Earth*, December, 1997.

Litz, Brian and Lenore Anderson. *Wilderness Ways*. Denver: Colorado Outward Bound School, 1993.

Motter, John M. *Pagosa Country: The First Fifty Years* (no date or publisher provided).

Myers, Steven J. *Notes from the San Juans: Thoughts About Fly Fishing and Home*. New York: Lyons & Burford, 1992.

Nash, Roderick Frazier. *Wilderness and the American Mind*, 3rd. ed. rev. New Haven: Yale University Press, 1982.

Nossaman, Allen. *Many More Mountains, Volume I: Silverton's Roots*. Denver: Sundance Publications 1989.

Nossaman, Allen. *Many More Mountains, Volume II: Ruts into Silverton*. Denver: Sundance Publications, 1993.

Nossaman, Allen. *Many More Mountains, Volume III: Rails into Silverton*. Denver: Sundance Publications, 1998.

Petersen, David. *Ghost Grizzlies*. New York: Henry Holt & Co., 1995.

Rennicke, Jeff. *Colorado Wildlife*, Number Six of Colorado Geographic Series. Falcon Press, 1990.

Rosebrough, Robert F. *The San Juan Mountains: A Climbing and Hiking Guide*. Evergreen: Cordillera Press, 1988.

Rosenberg, Robert S. *A History of Southcentral Colorado prepared expressly for the Rio Grande National Forest,* 1976.

Sander, John. "The Return of the Elk," an unpublished article in San Juan National Forest archives.

*San Juan and Montezuma National Forest History, Vol. 1, 1905-1971.*

Shoemaker, Len. "National Forests." *Colorado Magazine,* (Vol. 21, #5, September, 1944).

Smith, Duane. *Durango Diary.* Durango: The Durango Herald Press, 1996.

Smith, Duane. *Rocky Mountain Boomtown: A History of Durango, Colorado.* Boulder: University of Colorado Press, 1980.

Snyder, Gary. "Politics of Ethnopoetics," *A Place in Space: Ethics, Aesthetics, and Watersheds.* Washington, D.C.: Counterpoint, 1995.

"The Ethical Hunter," National Shooting Sports Foundation, 555 Danbury Rd., Wilton, Ct. 06897.

Thoreau, Henry David. *Journal, 1852-1853, Vol. 5: The Writings of Henry David Thoreau.* Boston: Princeton University Press, 1997.

Watkins, T.H. and Patricia Byrnes, eds. *The World of Wilderness: Essays on the Power and Purpose of Wild Country.* Niwot, Colorado: Roberts Rinehart Publishers, 1995.

*Weminuche Wilderness Primer.* Pagosa Chapter, San Juan National Forest Association. Durango: Print Master, 1992.

*Wilderness Management Direction, Initial Environmental Assessment for the Amendment to the Land and Resource Management Plans,* San Juan-Rio Grande National Forests, 1997.

*Wilderness Management Direction, Decision Notice and Final Environmental Assessment Amending the Land and Resource Management Plans, San Juan and Rio Grande Forests,* August 3, 1998.

Whitney, Stephen. *Western Forests*. New York: Alfred A. Knopf, 1990.

*Wilderness Management Philosophy in the Rocky Mountain Region*, USDA, Forest Service, Rocky Mountain Region, 1989.

"Wildlife in Danger: The status of Colorado's threatened or endangered fish, amphibians, birds, and mammals," Colorado Division of Wildlife pamphlet.

Zwinger, Ann H. and Beatrice E. Willard. *Land Above the Trees: A Guide to American Alpine Tundra*. New York: Harper & Row, 1972.

Zwinger, Ann H. *Beyond the Aspen Grove*. New York: Random House, 1970.

PERSONAL INTERVIEWS

Blair, Robert, Professor of Geology, Fort Lewis College, Durango, Colorado, December, 1997.

Gerhardt, Dave, San Juan National Forest fish specialist, November, 1997.

Houtz, Randy,. Trail specialist, San Juan National Forest, February, 1998.

Klatt, Ron, Range specialist, San Juan National Forest, November, 1997.

Matlock, Gary, Retired archeologist, San Juan National Forest, December, 1997.

Morrison, Brad, Range Specialist, San Juan National Forest, December, 1997.

Smith, Duane, Professor of History, Fort Lewis College, Durango, Colorado, August, 1997.

Stransky, Biff, Wilderness ranger, San Juan National Forest, August, 1997.

Upchurch, Jim, Wilderness manager, San Juan/Rio Grande National Forests, April, 1997.

VanSoelen, Tom, Owner, San Juan Outfitting, Durango, Colorado, March, 1998.

Walker, Walt, Director of Outdoor Pursuits, Fort Lewis College, Durango, Colorado, March, 1998.

# Sources and Meanings of Place Names
## in and around the Weminuche Wilderness*

Bayfield - named for an early settler, W. A. Bay

Cimmaron - Spanish for wild or unruly

Colorado - Spanish for red color

Creede - named after an early settler, N. C. Creede

Cumbres - Spanish for summit

Del Norte - Spanish for "of the north"

Dolores - Spanish for sorrow or pain

Durango - named for the mining town of Durango in Mexico

Emerald Lake - possibly named after Emerald Patrick, an early Silverton resident and brother of Flint Patrick

Endlich Mesa - named for one of the surveyors on the Hayden expedition

Fisher Mountain - named after John Fisher, a prospector who made the first gold discovery in 1892 on this mountain

Flint Fork - named by prospectors because of hardness of the rock in the watershed or possibly after Flint Patrick, an early Silverton resident

Florida - Spanish for flowers

Fort Lewis - name of a Colonel Lewis who was killed by Indians near Pagosa Springs

Goose Creek - originally called Hot Springs Creek by Hayden in 1877, but later changed to Goose Creek because of the many wild geese found there in early days

Grizzly Peak - named by Hayden expedition after an incident with a bear

Hermosa - Spanish for beautiful

Highland Mary - possibly named after Robert Bruce's poem

Hinsdale - named for George A. Hinsdale, an early settler

Howardsville - named for George W. Howard who was with the Baker party

Huerfano - Spanish for an orphan

Ignacio - Spanish for St. Ignacius

Johnson Creek - named after Miles T. Johnson who accompanied the McCauley survey expedition

Jumper Creek - named by prospectors because of claim jumping along its shores in the 1890's

Kennedy Mountain - named after William Kennedy, an early prospector who died in the Needle Mountains. Kennedy was buried at Ten Mile Creek.

La Garita - Spanish for a sentry box

La Plata - Spanish for silver

La Posta - Spanish for the post office or stopping place

La Ventanna - Spanish for the window

Las Animas - Spanish for river of lost souls (Rio de las Animas Perdidas)

Leopard Creek - named by early miners because of the mottled appearance of the watershed

McCauley Peak - named after Lt. C.A.H. McCauley, who led a survey expedition in 1869 to find a crossing over the Continental Divide and a site for a military installation in the San Juan Basin

Manitou - Ute for the Creator

Mount Valois - named after Lt. Gus Valois who accompanied the McCauley mapping expedition

Pagosa - Ute for healing waters

Palomino Mountain - named for the granite colored like a palomino horse

Piedra River - Spanish for rock, river of the standing rock (Chimney Rock)

Rio de Los Piños - Spanish for river of pines

Rincon La Osa - Spanish for cave of the bear, named after a fight between a Spanish sheepherder and an old mother grizzly bear in 1904

Rio Grande del Norte - Spanish for the large river of the north

Runlet Peak - named for an early prospector in the Cave Basin area

San Juan - Spanish for St. John

San Luis - St. Louis

San Miguel - Spanish for St. Michael

Sheep Mountain - known for large herds of bighorn sheep that grazed here

Silverton - "silver town"

Stony Pass - named by early travelers into Silverton who ascended this rocky pass

Ten Mile Creek - a stage stop that was ten miles from from Silverton

Tierra Amarilla - yellow earth

Toner Mountain - named for early homesteader, John Toner

Treasure Mountain - named after lost treasure supposedly left by French miners in area of Summitville

Tres Piedras -Spanish for three rocks

Trimble Springs - named for W. C. Trimble, a Durango settler and prospector

Trout Creek - named for the fine fishing that existed here

Ute Creek - named after the indigenous people whose summer travel routes followed the various forks of the creek

Utahs or Utes - Ute for the people

Vallecito - Spanish for little valley

Weminuche Pass - named after one band of the Ute people, the Weeminuche

Windom Peak - named after the U.S. Secretary of the Treasury, William Windom

* Information taken from forest records and other sources, including *Pioneers of the San Juan Country* , Volumes I, II, III, and IV, Sarah Platt Decker Chapter, (The Out West Printing and Stationery Company, Colorado Springs, Colorado, 1942), Allen Nossaman's Volumes 2 and 3 of *Many More Mountains*, (Sundance Books, 1993 and 1998) and the *Weminuche Wilderness Primer* published by the Pagosa Chapter of the San Juan Mountains Association, Pagosa Springs, Colorado, 1992.

# Addresses For More Information

San Juan National Forest Supervisor's Office
Bureau of Land Management
15 Burnett Court, Durango, Colorado 81301
970-247-4874

Columbine Ranger District
367 S. Pearl, Box 439, Bayfield, Colorado 81122
970-882-2512

Pagosa Ranger District
2nd and Pagosa Street, Box 310, Pagosa Springs, Colorado 81147
970-264-2268

Divide Ranger District
13308 W. Hwy 160, Del Norte, Colorado 81144
719-657-3321

Colorado Division of Wildlife
151 E. 16th St., Durango, Colorado 81301
970-247-0855

San Juan Mountains Association
P.O. Box 2261, Durango, Colorado 81302
970-385-1210

# Appendix A

## Complete Text of the Wilderness Act

Public Law 88-577 (16 U.S. C. 1131-1136)
88th Congress, Second Session
September 3, 1964

AN ACT

To establish a National Wilderness Preservation System for the permanent good of the whole people, and for other purposes.

Be it enacted by the Senate and House of Representatives of the United States of America in Congress assembled.

SHORT TITLE

SECTION 1. This Act may be cited as the "Wilderness Act."

WILDERNESS SYSTEM ESTABLISHED STATEMENT OF POLICY

SECTION 2. (a) In order to assure that an increasing population, accompanied by expanding settlement and growing mechanization, does not occupy and modify all areas within the United States and its possessions, leaving no lands designated for preservation and protection in their natural condition, it is hereby declared to be the policy of the Congress to secure for the American people of present and future generations the benefits of an enduring resource of wilderness. For this purpose there is hereby established a National Wilderness Preservation System to be composed of federally owned areas designated by the Congress as "wilderness areas," and these shall be administered for the use and enjoyment of the American people in such manner as will leave them unimpaired for future use and enjoyment as wilderness, and so as to provide for the protection of these areas, the preservation of their wilderness character, and for the gathering and dissemination of information regarding their use and enjoyment as wilderness; and no Federal lands shall be designated as "wilderness areas" except as provided for in this Act or by a subsequent Act.

(b) The inclusion of an area in the National Wilderness Preservation System notwithstanding, the area shall continue to be managed by the Department and agency having jurisdiction thereover immediately before its inclusion in the National Wilderness Preservation System unless otherwise provided by Act of Congress. No appropriation shall be available for payment of expenses or salaries for the administration of the National Wilderness Preservation System as a separate unit nor shall any appropriations be available for additional personnel stated as being required solely for the purpose of managing or administering areas solely because they are included within the National Wilderness Preservation System.

DEFINITION OF WILDERNESS

(c) A wilderness, in contrast with those areas where man and his works dominate the landscape, is hereby recognized as an area where the earth and its community of life are untrammeled by man, where man himself is a visitor who does not remain. An area of wilderness is further defined to mean in this Act an area of undeveloped Federal land retaining its primeval character and influence, without permanent improvements or human habitation, which is protected and managed so as to preserve its natural conditions and which (1) generally appears to have been affected primarily by the forces of nature, with the imprint of man's work substantially unnoticeable; (2) has outstanding opportunities for solitude or a primitive and unconfined type of recreation; (3) has at least five thousand acres of land or is of sufficient size as to make practicable its preservation and use in an unimpaired condition; and (4) may also contain ecological, geological, or other features of scientific, educational, scenic, or historical value.

NATIONAL WILDERNESS PRESERVATION SYSTEM -
EXTENT OF SYSTEM

SECTION 3. (a) All areas within the national forests classified at least 30 days before the effective date of this Act by the Secretary of Agriculture or the Chief of the Forest Service as "wilderness," "wild," or "canoe" are hereby designated as wilderness areas. The Secretary of Agriculture shall -

(1) Within one year after the effective date of this Act, file a map and legal description of each wilderness area with the Interior and Insular Affairs Committees of the United States Senate and the House of Representatives, and such descriptions shall have the same force and effect as if included in this Act: Provided, however, that correction of clerical and typographical errors in such legal descriptions and maps may be made.

(2) Maintain, available to the public, records pertaining to said wilderness areas, including maps and legal descriptions, copies of regulations governing them, copies of public notices of, and reports submitted to Congress regarding pending additions, eliminations, or modifications. Maps, legal descriptions, and regulations pertaining to wilderness areas within their respective jurisdictions also shall be available to the public in the offices of regional foresters, national forest supervisors, and forest rangers.

Classification. (b) The Secretary of Agriculture shall, within ten years after the enactment of this Act, review, as to its suitability or nonsuitability for preservation as wilderness, each area in the national forests classified on the effective date of this Act by the Secretary of Agriculture or the Chief of the Forest Service as "primitive" and report his findings to the President.

Presidential recommendation to Congress. The President shall advise the United States Senate and House of Representatives of his recommendations with respect to the designation as "wilderness" or other reclassification of each area on which review has been completed, together with maps and a definition of boundaries. Such advice shall be given with respect to not less than one-third of all the areas now classified as "primitive" within three years after the enactment of this Act, and the remaining areas within ten years after the enactment of this Act.

Congressional approval. Each recommendation of the President for designation as "wilderness" shall become effective only if so provided by an Act of Congress. Areas classified as "primitive" on the effective date of this Act shall continue to be administered under the rules and regulations affecting such areas on the effective date of this Act until Congress has determined otherwise. Any such area may be increased in size by the President at the time he submits his recommendations to the Congress by not more than five thousand acres with no more than one thousand two hundred acres in any one compact unit; if it is proposed to increase the size of any such area by more than five thousand acres or by more than one thousand two hundred and eighty acres in any one compact unit the increase in size shall not become effective until acted upon by Congress. Nothing herein contained shall limit the President in proposing, as part of his recommendations to Congress, the alteration of existing boundaries of primitive areas or recommending the addition of any contiguous area of national forest lands predominantly of wilderness value. Notwithstanding any other provisions of this Act, the Secretary of Agriculture may complete his review and delete such areas as may be necessary, but not to exceed seven thousand acres, from the southern tip of the Gore Range-Eagles Nest Primitive Area, Colorado, if the Secretary determines that such action is in the public interest.

Report to President. (c) Within ten years after the effective date of this Act the Secretary of the Interior shall review every roadless area of five thousand contiguous acres or more in the national parks, monuments, and other units of the national park system and every such area of, and every roadless island within, the national wildlife refuges and game ranges, under his jurisdiction on the effective date of this Act and shall report to the President his recommendation as to the suitability or nonsuitability of each such area or island for preservation as wilderness.
Presidential recommendation to Congress. The President shall advise the President of the Senate and the Speaker of the House of Representatives of his recommendation with respect to the designation as wilderness of each such area or island on which review has been completed, together with a map thereof and a definition of its boundaries. Such advice shall be given with respect to not less than one-third of the areas and islands to be reviewed under this subsection within three years after enactment of this Act, not less than two-thirds within seven years of enactment of this Act, and the remainder within ten years of enactment of this Act.

Congressional approval. A recommendation of the President for designation as wilderness shall become effective only if so provided by an Act of Congress. Nothing contained herein shall, by implication or otherwise, be construed to lessen the present statutory authority of the Secretary of the Interior with respect to the maintenance of roadless areas within units of the national park system.

Suitability. (d)(1) The Secretary of Agriculture and the Secretary of the Interior shall, prior to submitting any recommendations to the President with respect to the suitability of any area for preservation as wilderness.

Publication in Federal Register. (A) give such public notice of the proposed action as they deem appropriate, including publication in the Federal Register and in a newspaper having general circulation in the area or areas in the vicinity of the affected land;

Hearings.

(B) hold a public hearing or hearings at a location or locations convenient to the area affected. The hearings shall be announced through such means as the respective Secretaries involved deem appropriate, including notices in the Federal Register and in newspapers of general circulation in the area: Provided that if the lands involved are located in more than one State, at least one hearing shall be held in each State in which a portion of the land lies;

(C) at least thirty days before the date of a hearing advise the Governor of each State and the governing board of each county, or in Alaska the borough, in which the lands are located, and Federal departments and agencies concerned, and invite such officials and Federal agencies to submit their views on the proposed action at the hearing or by no later than thirty days following the date of the hearing.

(2) Any views submitted to the appropriate Secretary under the provisions of this subsection with respect to any area shall be included with any recommendations to the President and to Congress with respect to such area.

Proposed modification.

(e) Any modification or adjustment of boundaries of any wilderness area shall be recommended by the appropriate Secretary after public notice of such proposal and public hearing or hearings as provided in subsection (d) of this section. The proposed modification or adjustment shall then be recommended with map and description thereof to the President. The President shall advise the United States Senate and the House of Representatives of his recommendations with respect to such modification or adjustment and such recommendations shall become effective only in the same manner as provided for in subsections (b) and (c) of this section.

USE OF WILDERNESS AREAS

SECTION 4. (a) The purposes of this Act are hereby declared to be within and supplemental to the purposes for which national forests and units of the national park and wildlife refuge systems are established and administered and--

(1) Nothing in this Act shall be deemed to be in interference with the purpose for which national forests are established as set forth in the Act of June 4, 1897 (30 Stat.11), and the Multiple-Use Sustained-Yield Act of June 12, 1960 (74 Stat. 215). (2) Nothing in this Act shall modify the restrictions and provisions of the Shipstead-Nolan Act (Public Law 539, Seventy-first Congress, July 10, 1930; 46 Stat. 1020), the Thye-Blatnik Act (Public Law 733, Eightieth Congress, June 2, 1948; 62 Stat.568), and the Humphrey-Thye-Blatnik-Andresen Act (Public Law 607, Eighty-fourth   Congress, June 22, 1956; 70 Stat. 326), as applying to the Superior National Forest or the regulations of the Secretary of Agriculture.

(3) Nothing in this Act shall modify the statutory authority under which units of the national park system are created.  Further, the designation of any area of any park, monument, or other unit of the national park system as a wilderness area pursuant to this Act shall in no manner lower the standards evolved for the use and preservation of such park, monument, or other unit of the national park system in accordance with the Act of August 25, 1916, the statutory authority under which the area was created, or any other Act of Congress which might pertain to or affect such area, including, but not limited to, the Act of June 8, 1906 (34 Stat. 225; 16 U.S.C. 432 et seq.); section 3(2) of the Federal Power Act (16 U.S.C. 796 (2); and the Act of August 21,1935 (49 Stat. 666; 16 U.S.C. 461 et seq.).

(b) Except as otherwise provided in this Act, each agency administering any area designated as wilderness shall be responsible for preserving the wilderness character of the area and shall so administer such area for such other purposes for which it may have been established as also to preserve its wilderness character. Except as otherwise provided in this Act, wilderness areas shall be devoted to the public purposes of recreational, scenic, scientific, educational, conservation, and historical use.

PROHIBITION OF CERTAIN USES

(c) Except as specifically provided for in this Act, and subject to existing private rights, there shall be no commercial enterprise and no permanent road within any wilderness area designated by this Act and except as necessary to meet minimum requirements for the administration of the area for the purpose of this Act (including measures required in emergencies involving the health and safety of persons within the area), there shall be no temporary road, no use of motor vehicles, motorized equipment or motorboats, no landing of aircraft, no other form of mechanical transport, and no structure or installation within any such area.

SPECIAL PROVISIONS

(d) The following special provisions are hereby made:

(1) Within wilderness areas designated by this Act the use of aircraft or motorboats, where these uses have already become established, may be permitted to continue subject to such restrictions as the Secretary of Agriculture deems desirable. In addition, such measure may be taken as may be necessary in the control of fire, insects, and diseases, subject to such conditions as the Secretary deems desirable.

(2) Nothing in this Act shall prevent within national forest wilderness areas any activity, including prospecting, for the purpose of gathering information about mineral or other resources, if such activity is carried on in a manner compatible with the preservation of the wilderness environment. Furthermore, in accordance with such program as the Secretary of the Interior shall develop and conduct in consultation with the Secretary of Agriculture, such areas shall be surveyed on a planned, recurring basis consistent with the concept of wilderness preservation by the Geological Survey and the Bureau of Mines to determine the mineral values, if any, that may be present; and the results of such surveys shall be made available to the public and submitted to the President and Congress.

Mineral leases, claims, etc.

(3) Notwithstanding any other provisions of this Act, until midnight December 31, 1983, the United States mining laws and all laws pertaining to mineral leasing shall, to the same extent as applicable prior to the effective date of this Act, extend to those national forest lands designated by this Act as "wilderness areas"; subject, however, to such reasonable regulations governing ingress and egress as may be prescribed by the Secretary of Agriculture consistent with the use of the land for mineral location and development and exploration, drilling, and production, and use of land for transmission lines, waterlines, telephone lines, or facilities necessary in exploring, drilling, production, mining, and processing operations, including where essential the use of mechanized ground or air equipment and restoration as near as practicable of the surface of the land disturbed in performing prospecting, location, and, in oil and gas leasing, discovery work, exploration, drilling, and production, as soon as they have served their purpose. Mining locations lying within the boundaries of said wilderness areas shall be held and used solely for mining or processing operations and uses reasonably incident thereto; and hereafter, subject to valid existing rights, all patents issued under the mining laws of the United States

affecting national forest lands designated by this Act as wilderness areas shall convey title to the mineral deposits within the claim, together with the right to cut and use so much of the mature timber therefrom as may be needed in the extraction, removal, and beneficiation of the mineral deposits, if the timber is not otherwise reasonably available, and if the timber is cut under sound principles of forest management as defined by the national forest rules and regulations, but each such patent shall reserve to the United States all title in or to the surface of the lands and products thereof, and no use of the surface of the claim or the resources therefrom not reasonably required for carrying on mining or prospecting shall be allowed except as otherwise expressly provided in this Act: Provided, That, unless hereafter specifically authorized, no patent within wilderness areas designated by this Act shall issue after December 31, 1983, except for the valid claims existing on or before December 31, 1983. Mining claims located after the effective date of this Act within the boundaries of wilderness areas designated by this Act shall create no rights in excess of those rights which may be patented under the provisions of this subsection. Mineral leases, permits, and licenses covering lands within national forest wilderness areas designated by this Act shall contain such reasonable stipulations as may be prescribed by the Secretary of Agriculture for the protection of the wilderness character of the land consistent with the use of the land for the purposes for which they are leased, permitted, or licensed. Subject to valid rights then existing, effective January 1, 1984, the minerals in lands designated by this Act as wilderness areas are withdrawn from all forms of appropriation under the mining laws and from disposition under all laws pertaining to mineral leasing and all amendments thereto.

Water resources and grazing.

(4) Within wilderness areas in the national forests designated by this Act, (1) the President may, within a specific area and in accordance with such regulations as he may deem desirable, authorize prospecting for water resources, the establishment and maintenance of reservoirs, water-conservation works, power projects, transmission lines, and other facilities needed in the public interest, including the road construction and maintenance essential to development and use thereof, upon his determination that such use or uses in the specific area will better serve the interests of the United States and the people thereof than will its denial; and (2) the grazing of livestock, where established prior to the effective date of this Act, shall be permitted to continue subject to such reasonable regulations as are deemed necessary by the Secretary of Agriculture. (5) Other provisions of this Act to the contrary notwithstanding, the management of the Boundary Waters Canoe Area, formerly designated as the Superior, Little Indian

Sioux, and Caribou Roadless Areas, in the Superior National Forest, Minnesota, shall be in accordance with regulations established by the Secretary of Agriculture in accordance with the general purpose of maintaining, without unnecessary restrictions on other uses, including that of timber, the primitive character of the area, particularly in the vicinity of lakes, streams, and portages: Provided, That nothing in this Act shall preclude the continuance within the area of any already established use of motorboats.

(6) Commercial services may be performed within the wilderness areas designated by this Act to the extent necessary for activities which are proper for realizing the recreational or other wilderness purposes of the areas.

(7) Nothing in this Act shall constitute an express or implied claim or denial on the part of the Federal Government as to exemption from State water laws.

(8) Nothing in this Act shall be construed as affecting the jurisdiction or responsibilities of the several States with respect to wildlife and fish in the national forests.

STATE AND PRIVATE LANDS WITHIN WILDERNESS AREAS

SECTION 5. (a) In any case where State-owned or privately owned land is completely surrounded by national forest lands within areas designated by this Act as wilderness, such State or private owner shall be given such rights as may be necessary to assure adequate access to such State-owned or privately owned land by such State or private owner and their successors in interest, or the State-owned land or privately owned land shall be exchanged for federally owned land in the same State of approximately equal value under authorities available to the Secretary of Agriculture:

Transfers, restriction. Provided, however, That the United States shall not transfer to a State or private owner any mineral interests unless the State or private owner relinquishes or causes to be relinquished to the United States the mineral interest in the surrounded land.

(b) In any case where valid mining claims or other valid occupancies are wholly within a designated national forest wilderness area, the Secretary of Agriculture shall, by reasonable regulations consistent with the preservation of the area as wilderness, permit ingress and egress to such surrounded areas by means which have been or are being customarily enjoyed with respect to other such areas similarly situated.

Acquisition. (c) Subject to the appropriation of funds by Congress, the Secretary of Agriculture is authorized to acquire privately owned land within the perimeter of any area designated by this Act as wilderness if (1) the owner concurs in such acquisition or (2) the acquisition is specifically authorized by Congress.

## GIFTS, BEQUESTS, AND CONTRIBUTIONS

SECTION 6. (a) The Secretary of Agriculture may accept gifts or bequests of land within wilderness areas designated by this Act for preservation as wilderness. The Secretary of Agriculture may also accept gifts or bequests of land adjacent to wilderness areas designated by this Act for preservation as wilderness if he has given sixty days advance notice thereof to the President of the Senate and the Speaker of the House of Representatives. Land accepted by the Secretary of Agriculture under this section shall become part of the wilderness area involved. Regulations with regard to any such land may be in accordance with such agreements, consistent with the policy of this Act, as are made at the time of such gift, or such conditions, consistent with such policy, as may be included in, and accepted with, such bequest.

(b) The Secretary of Agriculture or the Secretary of the Interior is authorized to accept private contributions and gifts to be used to further the purposes of this Act.

## ANNUAL REPORTS

SECTION 7. At the opening of each session of Congress, the Secretaries of Agriculture and Interior shall jointly report to the President for transmission to Congress on the status of the wilderness system including a list and descriptions of the areas in the system, regulations in effect, and other pertinent information, together with any recommendations they may care to make.

Approved September 3, 1964.
Legislative History:

House Reports: No. 1538 accompanying H.R. 9070 (Committee on Interior & Insular Affairs) and No. 1829 (Committee of Conference).

Senate Report: No. 109 (Committee on Interior & Insular Affairs).

Congressional Record:

Vol. 109 (1963): April 4, 8, considered in Senate.

April 9, considered and passed Senate.
Vol. 110 (1964):    July 28, considered in House. July 30, considered and passed House, amended, in lieu of H.R. 9070.   August 20, House and Senate agreed to conference report.

# Appendix B

## Backcountry Regulations

* Maximum group size:  no more than 15 people per group, with a maximum combination of people and stock not to exceed 25 in any one group for all wilderness areas.

* Camping is not permitted within 100 feet of streams or lakes, unless exceptions are justified by terrain or specific design which protects the riparian and aquatic resources.

* Camping, except at designated sites, and restraining or grazing of recreational livestock are not permitted with 1/4 mile of: Little Emerald Lake.

* Camping and overnight use with recreational livestock, except in designated sites, and campfires and grazing of recreational livestock are not permitted within 1/2 mile of the north shore and 3/4 mile of the other shores of:  Emerald Lake.

* Camping and overnight use with recreational livestock, except in designated sites, and campfires and grazing of recreational livestock is prohibited within a defined area around:  Rainbow Hot Springs (West Fork Trail).

* Camping is not permitted within the drainage basin of: Twin Lakes (Needle Creek drainage).

* Camping, campfires, and restraining or grazing recreational livestock are not permitted within 200 feet of:  Fourmile Lake, West Ute Lake, Archuleta Lake.

* Camping, campfires, and restraining or grazing recreational livestock are not permitted within 200 feet of the west and north shores or between the lakeshore and trails #527 (Flint Creek) and #525 (La Osa) at: Flint Lake.

* No camping in or within 100 feet of areas signed as "reserved" or "assigned" to permitted commercial outfitter camps.

* Woodburning, (i.e. campfires and wood stoves) is not permitted within the following areas:  Needle Creek Drainage, Vestal Basin (drainage of Vestal Creek).

* Prohibit use or entrance with a motor vehicle, bicycle, wagon, cart, or other mechanized transport, except persons with wheelchairs as a necessary medical appliance.  No motorized equipment, such as chainsaws, is permitted.

* Prohibit pets from harassing wildlife or other people.  Pets must be under voice control or physical restraint.

* Disposal of human waste and wash water is prohibited within 100 feet of any water source.

* Cutting or damaging live trees without a permit is prohibited.

# Appendix C

# Topographic Map Index

Engineer Mountain
Electra Lake
Snowdon Peak
Mountain View Crest
Lemon Reservoir
Howardsville
Storm King Peak
Columbine Pass
Vallecito Reservoir
Pole Creek Mountain
Rio Grande Pyramid
Emerald Lake
Granite Peak
Finger Mesa
Weminuche Pass
Granite Lake
Hermit Lakes
Little Squaw Creek
Cimarrona Peak
Bristol Head
Workman Creek
Palomino Mountain
Pagosa Peak
Spar City
South River Peak
Saddle Mountain
Lake Humphreys
Mount Hope
Wolf Creek Pass

# Appendix D

## Passes and Major Watersheds In and Near The Weminuche

| Name | Elevation |
|------|-----------|
| Trimble Pass | 12,860' |
| Squaw Pass | 12,210' |
| Stony Pass | 12,588' |
| Weminuche Pass | 10,622' |
| Ute Pass | 9,944' |
| The Window | 12,857' |
| Nebo Pass | 12,460' |
| Ute Pass | 12,702' |
| Hunchback Pass | 12,493' |
| Cunningham Pass | 12,180' |
| Storm King-Silex | 12,820' |
| Knifepoint | 12,860' |
| Ruby Pass | 12,900' |
| Twin Thumbs | 13,060' |
| Columbine Pass | 12,700' |
| Trimble Pass | 12,860' |
| The Notch | 10,140' |
| Wolf Creek Pass | 10,850' |
| Coalbank Pass | 10,640' |
| Molas Pass | 10,899' |
| Engineer Pass | 12,800' |
| Cinnamon | 12,620' |
| Windy Pass | 9,940' |

Names and elevations taken from Ed Helmuth's *Passes of Colorado: An Encyclopedia of Watershed Divides,* (Pruett Publishing Company, 1994).

# Appendix E

## Bird Distribution
## In The Weminuche

| Species | Sub-Alpine | Douglas-Fir | Ponderosa Pine | Lodgepole Pine | Aspen |
|---|---|---|---|---|---|
| Bluebird, Mtn | X | X | X | X | X |
| Western | | | X | | X |
| Bunting, Indigo | | | X | X | |
| Lazuli | | X | X | X | |
| Bushtit | | | | | X |
| Chickadee, Black-capped | X | X | X | X | X |
| Mountain | X | X | X | X | X |
| Creeper, Brown | X | X | X | X | X |
| Croosbill, Red | X | X | X | X | |
| Dove, Mourning | X | X | X | X | X |
| Eagle, Golden | X | X | X | X | X |
| Falcon, Am. Peregrine | X | X | X | X | X |
| Prairie | X | X | X | X | X |
| Finch, Cassin's | X | X | X | X | X |
| Flicker, Common | X | X | X | X | X |
| Flycatcher, Least | X | X | | X | X |
| Western | X | X | X | X | X |
| Goldfinch, Am. | | X | X | | |
| Goshawk | X | X | X | X | X |
| Grosbeak, Evening | X | X | X | X | |
| Grouse, Blue | X | X | X | X | X |
| Hawk, Cooper's | | X | X | X | X |
| Red-tailed | X | X | X | X | X |
| Sharp-shinned | X | X | X | X | X |
| Hummingbird, Broad-tailed | | X | X | X | X |
| Black-chinned | | X | X | X | X |
| Rufous | X | X | X | X | X |
| Jay, Gray | X | X | X | X | X |
| Pinyon | | | X | | X |
| Steller's | X | X | X | X | X |
| Junco, Dark-eyed | X | X | X | X | X |
| Gray-headed | X | X | X | X | X |
| Kestrel, American | X | X | X | X | X |
| Kingbird, Western | | X | X | | X |
| Kinglet, Golden-crowned | X | X | X | X | X |
| Ruby-crowned | X | X | X | X | X |
| Magpie, Black-tailed | X | X | X | X | |
| Nutcracker, Clark's | X | X | X | X | |
| Nuthatch, Pygmy | X | | X | X | X |
| Red-breasted | X | X | X | X | X |
| White-breasted | X | X | X | X | X |

*continued on the next page*

# Bird Distribution
# In The Weminuche, cont'd

| Species | Sub-Alpine | Douglas-Fir | Ponderosa Pine | Lodgepole Pine | Aspen |
|---|---|---|---|---|---|
| Ovenbird | | X | X | X | X |
| Owl, Boreal | X | X | X | X | |
|    Flammulated | X | X | X | | X |
|    Great horned | X | X | X | X | X |
|    Pygmy | | X | X | X | |
|    Saw-whet | X | X | X | | X |
|    Spotted | X | X | X | X | X |
| Pewee, Western | X | X | X | X | X |
| Pidgeon, Band-tailed | X | X | X | X | X |
| Raven, Common | X | X | X | X | X |
| Redpoll, Common | X | X | X | X | X |
| Redstart, Am. | | X | X | X | X |
| Robin, Am. | X | X | X | X | X |
| Sapsucker, Williamson's | X | | X | X | X |
| Siskin, Pine | X | X | X | X | |
| Solitaire, Townsend's | X | X | X | X | X |
| Sparrow, Chipping | | X | X | X | X |
|    Lincoln's | X | X | X | X | X |
|    Song | X | X | X | X | X |
|    Vesper | X | X | X | X | X |
|    White-crowned | X | X | X | X | X |
| Swallow, Bank | | X | X | | |
|    Tree | X | X | X | | |
|    Violet-green | X | X | X | X | X |
| Swift, White-throated | X | X | X | X | X |
| Tanager, Western | X | X | X | X | X |
| Thrush, Hermit | X | X | X | X | X |
|    Swainson's | X | X | X | X | X |
| Turkey, Merriam's | X | X | X | X | X |
| Vireo, Warbling | X | X | X | X | X |
| Vulture, Turkey | X | X | X | X | X |
| Warbler, Magnolia | | X | X | | |
|    Wilson's | X | | X | X | X |
|    Yellow | | X | X | X | X |
|    Yellow-rumped | X | X | X | X | X |
| Wawing, Bohemian | X | X | X | X | X |
| Woodpecker, Downy | X | X | X | X | X |
|    Hairy | X | X | X | X | X |
|    Northern three-toed | X | X | X | X | X |
| Wren, Canyon | | X | X | | |
|    Rock | X | X | X | X | X |

Information taken from *Managing Forested Lands for Wildlife*, Colorado Division of Wildlife, 1987

# Appendix F

## Mammal Distribution In The Weminuche

| Species | Sub-Alpine | Douglas-Fir | Ponderosa Pine | Lodgepole Pine | Aspen |
|---|---|---|---|---|---|
| Badger | X | X | X | X | X |
| Bat, Big brown | | X | X | X | X |
| Silver-haired | | X | X | X | X |
| Townsend's | | X | X | | X |
| Bear, Black | X | X | X | X | X |
| Beaver | | | | | X |
| Bighorn sheep | X | | X | X | X |
| Bobcat | | X | X | X | X |
| Chipmunk, Co. | | X | X | | |
| Least | X | X | X | | X |
| Cottontail, Nuttall's | X | X | X | X | |
| Coyote | X | X | X | X | X |
| Deer, Mule | X | X | X | X | X |
| Elk (Wapiti) | X | X | X | X | X |
| Fox, Red | X | X | X | X | X |
| Goat, Mountain | X | | | | |
| Hare, Snowshoe | X | X | X | X | X |
| Jackrabbit, white-tailed | X | X | X | X | X |
| Lion, Mountain | X | X | X | X | X |
| Lynx,Canada | X | | | | |
| Marmot, Yellow-bellied | X | X | X | X | X |
| Marten, Pine | X | X | | X | |
| Moose, Shiras | X | | | | |
| Mouse, Deer | X | X | X | X | X |
| House | | X | X | X | X |
| Western Jumping | X | | X | X | X |
| Myotis, Little brown | | X | X | X | X |
| Long-legged | | X | X | | |
| Pocket Gopher, Northern | X | X | X | X | X |
| Porcupine | X | X | X | X | X |
| Shrew, Dwarf | X | X | X | X | X |
| Masked | X | X | X | X | X |
| Wandering | X | X | X | X | X |
| Skunk, Striped | X | X | X | X | X |
| Squirrel, Abert's | | | X | | |
| Golden-mantled | X | X | X | X | X |
| Red | X | X | | X | |
| Vole, Heather | X | X | | X | |
| Long-tailed | X | X | X | X | X |
| Montane | X | X | X | X | X |
| Southern redbacked | X | X | | X | X |

*continued on the next page*

# Mammal Distribution
# In The Weminuche, cont'd

| Species | Sub-Alpine | Douglas-Fir | Ponderosa Pine | Lodgepole Pine | Aspen |
|---|---|---|---|---|---|
| Weasel, Long-tailed | X | X | X | X | X |
| Short-tailed | X | X | X | X | X |
| Wolverine | X | X | X | X | X |
| Woodrat, bushy-tailed | X | X | X | X | X |

Information taken from *Managing Forested Lands for Wildlife,* Colorado Division of Wildlife, 1987

# Appendix G

## Litter Lasts This Long

| | |
|---|---|
| Cigarette Butts | 1 - 5 years |
| Aluminum Cans | 80 - 100 years |
| Orange Peels | Up to 2 years |
| Plastic Bags | 10 - 20 years |
| Glass Bottles | 1 million years |
| Tin Cans | 50 years |
| Wool Socks | 1 - 5  years |
| Plastic Bottles | Indefinitely |

**If you pack it in...pack it out !**

# Appendix H

## San Juan Mountains Association
## Its History and Programs

The mission statement of the San Juan Mountains Association (SJMA) explains why this dedicated organization has been so successful. The statement says, "The San Juan Mountains Association is a non-profit, volunteer organization which promotes and provides education, conservation and interpretation of natural and cultural resources on public lands of Southwestern Colorado. Our goal is to instill in the public a land ethic--a sense of pride and stewardship toward our public lands." Working in partnership with the U.S. Forest Service, SJMA is guided by an appointed board of local citizens who respond to the needs of visitors and users of public lands with timely programs and publications.

SJMA, since its formation in 1988, has followed its mission and created numerous offerings that involve and educate people living near the San Juan/Rio Grande National Forests, as well as visitors who come to Southwestern Colorado year-round. As a non-partisan, non-advocacy entity, SJMA's membership includes representatives from every forest user group--hikers, hunters, stock users, backpackers, fishermen, bikers and residents young and old who share the belief that public lands are a valuable and timeless resource.

SJMA's involvement with public education continues to grow. It recognizes the needs of citizens which the U.S. Forest Service is unable to answer either because of funding or limited staff and jumps to the task of responding. Today its programs include its premier Wilderness Information Specialist Program (WIS), begun in 1989, which brings volunteers from around the country to walk the trails and share Leave-No-Trace information with Weminuche Wilderness travelers. SJMA began the "Ghost Riders" program in 1995. Stock travelers now ride the wilderness trails sharing ideas about Leave-No-Trace animal travel. Ghost Riders also includes Junior Ghost Riders who learn the art of teaching wilderness skills to others. Summer field seminars utilize the expertise of local botanists, historians, geologists and other scholars who share their knowledge with visitors. Forest Works and the Youth Corp connect local youth to U.S. Forest Service professionals through study and work programs. Other programs include the Wilderness Ranger Workshop that trains wilderness rangers from throughout the West and the Chimney Rock Interpretive Program.

Each fall SJMA sponsors the Share the Trails Team Triathlon for horse travelers, mountain bikers and hikers. Teams composed of the three user groups "compete" on the same trail, thus instilling the ethic of sharing the trails and respecting each other. Over 50 teams now enter the event.

SJMA has published numerous books, newspaper supplements, brochures and other educational materials. For further information on its programs, membership or tax-deductible program underwriting opportunities, contact the San Juan Mountains Association at P.O. Box 2261, Durango, Colorado, 81302 or by phone at 970-385-1210.

# Appendix I

## San Juan Mountains Association
## Membership Application Form

As a member, you will be entitled to members only discounts at area businesses as well as the following annual benefits:
Annual Dues:

> Oak        $10
> Quarterly Newsletter
> 10% discount on items sold by SJMA
>
> Pine       $25
> Quarterly Newsletter
> 10% discount on items sold by SJMA
> Special SJMA gift
>
> Aspen      $50
> Quarterly Newsletter
> 10% discount on items sold by SJMA
> 10% discount on Field Seminars for
>     members and family
> Special SJMA gift
>
> Spruce      $100
> Quarterly Newsletter
> 10% discount on items sold by SJMA
> 10% discount on Field Seminars
> Special SJMA gift
> Two Field Seminars passes
>
> Snow Cap    $500
> Same as Spruce above
> including six Field Seminars passes.

Make check payable to SJMA or charge to: Visa _____ Mastercard _____

Account Number _____ Exp. Date_____

Return to: SJMA, Post Office Box 2261, Durango, Colorado 81302-2261

# Appendix J

## Chronology of Wilderness Development

1872 - Yellowstone becomes the world's first national park.

1890 - Yosemite Valley was set aside as a national wilderness preserve

1891 - The first national forest reserve was established.

1897 - Congress creates the National Forest System.

1916 - Congress creates the National Park System.

1917 - Landscape Architect Frank Waugh surveys recreational potential in national forests and finds they have "direct human value" as opposed to economic value only.

1919 - Forest Planner Arthur Carhart recommends Trapper Lake in Colorado's White River National Forest not be developed for summer homes.

1924 - Ecologist Aldo Leopold convinces USFS to set aside 574,000 acres on the Gila National Forest in New Mexico as a national wilderness recreation preserve.

1926 - USFS Chief William Greeley requires an inventory of all de facto wilderness on the National Forests.

1929 - USFS issues the L-20 Regulations to establish "primitive" areas in national forests.

1930 - Congress designates over 1 million acres in northern Minnesota as the Superior Primitive area.

1935 - The Wilderness Society is begun by Bob Marshall.

1939 - USFS regulations direct review and reclassification of primitive areas as "Wilderness," "wild," or "roadless" depending on size.

1950 - Conservationists prevent damming the Colorado River in Dinosaur National Monument, saving a large wilderness area from flooding.

1956 - The first draft of the Wilderness Act is written by Howard Zahniser.

1964 - President Lyndon Johnson signs the Wilderness Act on September 3.

1968 - Wild and Scenic Rivers Act protects rivers with outstanding wild, scenic, and recreational values.

1971 - USFS began a Roadless Area Review and Evaluation (RARE) of national forest lands to assess wilderness suitability.

1974 - Weminuche Wilderness Area established
1976 - Federal Land Policy and Management Act is passed mandating BLM to inventory and study all of its roadless lands and make recommendations for wilderness.
1978 - Congress passed the Endangered American Wilderness Act, and designated significant wilderness areas in the West.
1979 - A more extensive RARE study was completed (RARE II) of 62 million acres, giving Congress impetus to designate wilderness on a state-by-state basis in the 1980's.
1980 - Alaska National Interest Lands Conservation Act which more than tripled the size of the wilderness system was passed. 56.5 million acres were designated in Alaska.
1991 - The California Desert Act was passed by U.S. House of Representatives, but failed in the Senate. The bill is presently under consideration.
1993 - The Colorado Wilderness Act was passed, creating additional wilderness acres in Colorado.

Source: The Wilderness Society, *"Keeping It Wild: A Citizen Guide to Wilderness Management,"* 1992.

*Personal Notes*

*Personal Notes*

*Personal Notes*

*Personal Notes*

For additional copies of this book,
send completed order form to:

The Durango Herald Small Press Co.
Post Office Box 719
Durango, Colorado 81302

or phone

800-530-8318, extension 273

Sorry, No C.O.D. available

---------------------------------------------------------------------------------

Please send _____ copies of B. J. Boucher's *Walking in Wildness* at $17.95, plus
$4.00 for shipping and handling for each book. Colorado residents please add 7%
sales tax. Canadian orders require a postal money order in U.S. funds. Please
allow 4 to 6 weeks for delivery.

Check/Money order for $_____ is enclosed.
(Make payable to The Durango Herald Small Press Co.)

Please charge my     Visa     Mastercard

Card # _____ Expires_____

Signature _____

Name _____

Company _____

Address _____

City/State/ZipCode _____